Fundamentals of Software-Defined Networking

The **Fundamentals of Software-Defined Networking: Towards Intelligent and Flexible Networks** is a comprehensive, beginner-friendly guide to Software-Defined Networking (SDN), specifically designed for educators, trainers, and professionals transitioning into modern networking. It offers a structured, standards-based approach that starts with fundamental networking concepts and builds up to advanced SDN architectures. Focusing on accessibility and practical application, it emphasizes open-source tools and real-world labs that can be implemented in low-resource environments. It covers key SDN technologies, including OpenFlow, SD-WAN, SD-LAN, NFV, LISP, and orchestration with Ansible while integrating Python-based automation and RESTful APIs.

Key Features

- Progressive, beginner-friendly structure ideal for academic and training settings.
- Hands-on labs using open-source tools such as ONOS, Ryu, Open vSwitch, and Python, plus real-world case studies and projects.
- Vendor-neutral content with no reliance on proprietary technologies.
- Supplementary materials, including scripts and emulator images, are available online: http://github.com/sadiqui-ali/SDN_resources.

This book is beneficial for instructors, students, and IT professionals seeking a practical and comprehensive introduction to SDN. Moreover, it is particularly suited for training environments where cost-effective, standards-based learning is essential.

Fundamentals of Software-Defined Networking

Towards Intelligent and Flexible Networks

Ali Sadiqui and
Moulay Rachid Filali

CRC Press is an imprint of the
Taylor & Francis Group, an **informa** business

Designed cover image: Ali Sadiqui and Moulay Rachid Filali

First edition published 2026
by CRC Press
2385 NW Executive Center Drive, Suite 320, Boca Raton FL 33431

and by CRC Press
4 Park Square, Milton Park, Abingdon, Oxon, OX14 4RN

CRC Press is an imprint of Taylor & Francis Group, LLC

ISBN: 9781041154297 (hbk)
ISBN: 9781041154280 (pbk)
ISBN: 9781003679394 (ebk)

DOI: 10.1201/9781003679394

Typeset in Palatino
by codeMantra

Access the Support Material: www.github.com/sadiqui-ali/SDN_resources

Contents

Acknowledgments

Review committee:

- Mr. **Abdechafik** Elghattas: Engineering trainer and Cisco certification manager at OFPPT.
- Mr. **Raouf Hassan**: Engineering trainer and Cisco certification manager at OFPPT.

Preface

The writing of this book represents a special effort to provide a comprehensive and standardized perspective on Software-Defined Networking (SDN) technology. It differs from existing works in several respects, addressing the specific needs of computer networking educators, often overlooked in current publications.

First of all, although there is a great deal of documentation on SDN technology, the novice reader can quickly feel lost due to the scarcity of a single work dealing exhaustively with the subject. Indeed, the majority of available resources start with intermediate or even advanced notions, often forcing the reader to go back to assimilate basic concepts not covered, or focus on a particular product. This fragmented approach makes learning difficult for newcomers to the field.

In this book, we have made accessibility a priority. It offers a progressive treatment of concepts, starting with network fundamentals, then guiding the reader through the essential principles of SDN, while maintaining a strictly standards-based approach. This approach not only facilitates the assimilation of technical notions, but also ensures that the reader can understand how these concepts are implemented in market products, without being restricted to a specific commercial framework.

As a result, this book is particularly aimed at trainers and teachers seeking to train qualified people in the field of SDN. The outline has been carefully crafted to make learning as fluid as possible, progressing from simple notions to more complex concepts.

The Labs included in this book have been designed to be pragmatic, taking into account the hardware and software constraints present in educational environments, whether in the classroom or on student workstations. The aim is to provide trainers with comprehensive teaching tools, enabling learners to master both the theories and Lab-based applications of this technology.

As such, this book is intended as a comprehensive, accessible guide for anyone wishing to learn or improve their skills in the world of SDN, while remaining rooted in both the adherence to standards and the industrial realities of the market.

We wish you an excellent read and a rewarding exploration of SDN technology.

Author Biographies

Ali Sadiqui is an accomplished instructor and researcher, holding a Ph.D. in Computer Science and currently teaching at the Specialized Institute of Applied Technologies in Meknes. Specializing in computer networks, cloud computing, and cybersecurity, he is the author of several internationally recognized books and scientific publications.

With a career at OFPPT, Dr. Sadiqui has extensive experience in higher education. He teaches courses on computer architecture, preparation for Cisco certifications, database management, and programming in various languages such as Python, Java, and C. Before his academic career, he worked as an IT Service Manager.

Dr. Sadiqui is a prolific innovator. His doctoral dissertation introduced a pioneering system for automatic Arabic speech recognition. He is also the inventor of a patented multilayer internet filtering system, which combines a secure cloud architecture with a simplified interface.

Beyond teaching, he actively contributes to the OFPPT ecosystem as a member of committees for pedagogical validation, digitalization, and the design of final examinations. His commitment to supervising student projects has enabled many of his students to receive awards in national competitions. Engaged in the community, he has also promoted scientific research within several associations to introduce children to programming and robotics.

Mr. Moulay Rachid Filali is the Certification Manager at the Specialized Institute of Applied Technologies (ISTA) in Meknes, part of the OFPPT network. In this role, he oversees a strategic portfolio of professional certifications in the field of information technology. His mission is to equip future professionals with robust technical skills aligned with international standards.

A recognized expert in network and systems environments, Mr. Filali leads the training and preparation of students for several major industry certifications. He provides comprehensive support for Cisco certification tracks, including both CCNA and CCNP, focusing on advanced skills in network installation, configuration, and administration. He also oversees the Microsoft Certified Professional (MCP) certification, ensuring trainees master Microsoft technologies and their operational ecosystems. In the field of cybersecurity, he prepares candidates for the Fortinet–FortiGate certification, which emphasizes the management of next-generation firewalls. Additionally, he ensures thorough preparation for Linux certification, essential for careers in system administration, cloud computing, and DevOps.

Thanks to his expertise and rigorous teaching approach, Mr. Filali plays a key role in developing learners' competencies, contributing significantly to their successful integration into the fast-evolving technology sector.

Instructions for Lab Activities

The following instructions must be followed by trainers to ensure proper execution of Labs and optimize trainee learning.

1. Trainee Level Check

Before starting the hands-on exercises, it is essential to ensure that trainees possess a sufficient level of competence in network addressing and routing, as this foundational knowledge is critical for fully understanding and engaging with the lab activities. Participants are expected to have prerequisite skills, including a general understanding of IP networks, VLANs, routing, and VPNs at a CCNA-equivalent level, as well as some basic exposure to scripting, particularly in Python.

2. Minimum Workstation Configuration

The Labs have been developed and tested on machines with the following technical characteristics:

- Processor: Intel Core I5 (6th generation)
- RAM: 16 GB
- Operating system: Windows 10 (latest update)

It is the trainer's responsibility to ensure that classroom workstations meet or exceed these minimum configurations. This ensures that trainees will be able to carry out their Labs without encountering any performance-related problems.

3. Presentation of the Emulator to Be Used

Part of the first session should be devoted to presenting the network emulator (such as GNS3 or equivalent). The trainer should explain how it works as well as the instructions for its proper use. This introduction will enable trainees to familiarize themselves with the tool and use it effectively during the Lab sessions.

4. Access to Images Used in the Book

All the system images used in this book are available under a free license or are intended for educational or trial use (limited time only). Trainers can download these images directly from the corresponding official websites.

5. Hardware and Software Preparation

To optimize the time allocated to Labs, the trainer should prepare the network equipment images and the necessary software in advance. This includes the equipment image files, the scripts to be used, and a number of guides and resources available at the following link: https://github.com/sadiqui-ali/SDN_resources.

6. Possibility of Case Studies or Projects

The trainer has the possibility to combine the skills acquired by the trainees through several Labs in order to design a case study or research project. This approach can promote a better understanding of concepts by applying them to concrete scenarios.

These instructions aim to ensure that the Labs are carried out under optimum conditions, thus promoting smooth, relevant learning for the trainees.

1

Network Fundamentals and Technological Developments

In this chapter, we'll look at the crucial transformations that have taken place in the field of networking. First, we'll explore the limits of traditional network architectures, whose rigidity and complexity hinder adaptability and innovation. Next, we'll introduce the concept of software-defined networking (SDN), a revolutionary approach that promises to overcome these challenges.

We'll look at the significant benefits of SDN, including its flexibility, scalability, and operational efficiency. The chapter will also detail the main components that make up SDN, as well as the different network models based on this technology. We'll take a closer look at SDN orchestration through the North and South application programming interfaces (APIs), the pillars of this orchestration.

In addition, we'll provide an overview of the main SDN controllers and discuss the architecture and protocols used in a multi-controller SDN network. To illustrate these concepts concretely, we will conclude with examples of how SDN architecture is used in various practical contexts, demonstrating its impact and transformative potential in the world of networking.

This chapter covers the following topics:

1. Introduction
2. Traditional network architecture
3. Limits of traditional network architectures
4. SDN network overview
5. Advantages of an SDN network
6. Main SDN components
7. API north and south: The pillars of SDN orchestration
8. SDN network models
9. Example of an SDN architecture
10. Main SDN controllers: An overview
11. SDN multi-controller network
12. Chapter conclusion

1.1 Introduction

Since their inception, computer networks have played a central role in technological progress. They have enabled communication and collaboration on an unprecedented scale. The advent of the Internet marked a decisive turning point in the modern era of networked

DOI: 10.1201/9781003679394-1

communications, triggering a gradual transformation of networks towards more sophisticated, interconnected structures. However, despite this considerable progress, traditional network architectures have shown their limitations. In the face of exploding data volumes and growing demand for connectivity, they are struggling to meet today's needs.

To address these challenges, IT networks needed to be rethought, and more flexible and scalable architectures had to be developed to adapt to the demands of a constantly changing world.

1.2 Traditional Network Architectures

Traditional network equipment was often designed for specific tasks, making it difficult to update or adapt to new requirements. Their architectural design hampers business agility and the ability to quickly adapt to evolving user and application needs.

In these architectures, network equipment such as routers and switches integrates the control plane and the data plane in a coupled fashion. The function of each plane can be described as follows:

- **Control plane:** This plane is responsible for route management and routing decisions. Protocols typically used in this plane include RIP, OSPF, EIGRP, **border gateway protocol** (BGP), and IGMP, among others.
- **Data plane:** This plane is responsible for routing data packets according to decisions made by the control plane. Protocols and elements associated with this plane include ARP, MPLS, Ethernet, and IP, among others.

In traditional network architectures, decision-making and traffic routing functions are closely tied to the hardware and software specific to these devices, limiting network flexibility and scalability (Figure 1.1).

1.3 Limits of Traditional Network Architectures

This approach has several disadvantages, which we can summarize as follows:

- **Rigidity:** Network configuration changes often require manual intervention on each piece of equipment, which can be tedious and error-prone.
- **Limited scalability:** Adding new equipment or new functions can be complex and costly, as it often involves upgrading or replacing existing hardware.
- **Difficulty of automation:** Traditional network management is often manual and reactive, making it difficult to automate tasks and adapt quickly to change.
- **Poor visibility:** It is difficult to get a global view of the network and understand the causes of performance or security problems.

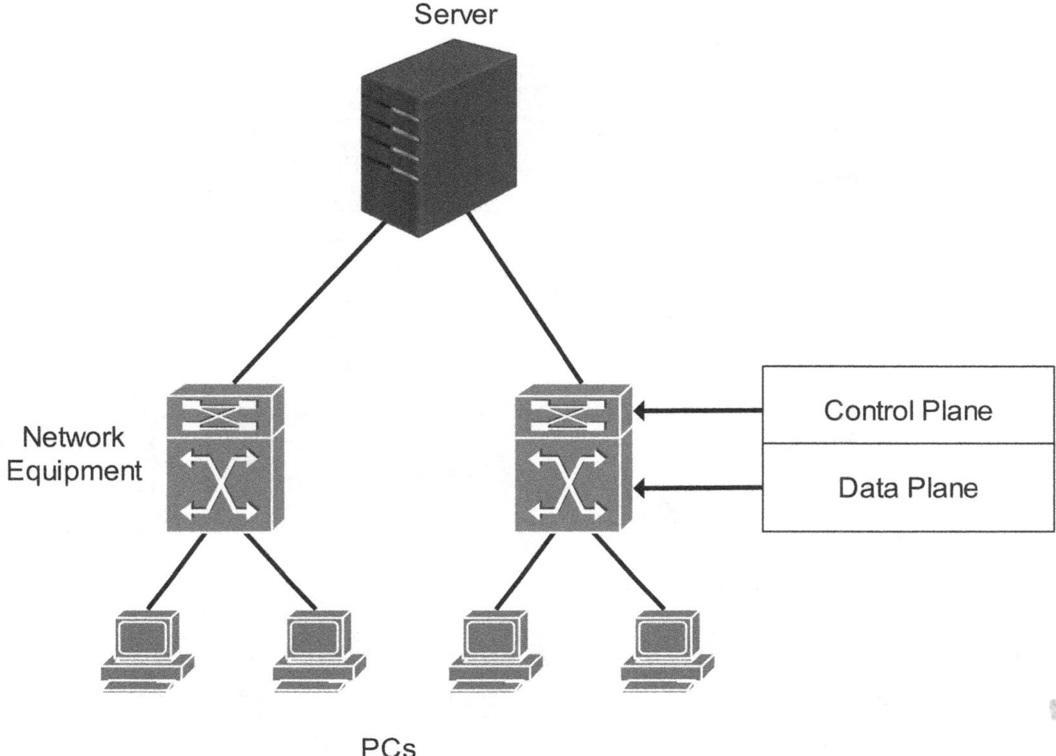

FIGURE 1.1
Traditional network architecture.

Modern network architectures, such as SDN, enable the separation of control and data planes. The control plane is centralized in a software controller, while the data plane is distributed across network devices.

1.4 SDN Network Overview

SDN marks a significant advance in network design and management. Unlike traditional methods, which require each piece of equipment to be configured individually, SDN favors centralized management. This technology is distinguished by separating the control and application planes from the data plane, thereby shifting management from the hardware layer to higher-level software layers. This not only allows for more precise control of network traffic but also enhances efficiency through the integration of advanced network management and analytics applications (Figure 1.2).

Table 1.1 highlights the fundamental differences between traditional network architectures and those based on SDN, looking at key aspects such as infrastructure, management, abstraction, automation, and visibility.

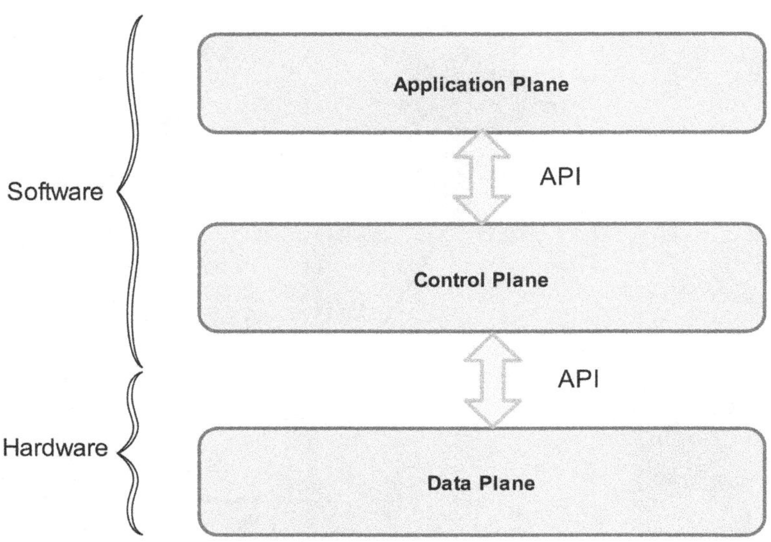

FIGURE 1.2
The three functional planes in an SDN network.

TABLE 1.1
Fundamental Differences between Traditional and SDN-Based Network Architectures

	Traditional Network	SDN Network
Network infrastructure	Consisting of hardware equipment such as switches and routers.	Can be based on hardware or on fully virtualized components.
Easy management	Requires manual configuration of each device independently.	Centralize administrative management, configuration, and deployment of resources within a unified control plan.
Abstraction	Integration of control and data transfer functions on the same physical device.	Separates the network management process from data transfer via software solutions.
Automation	Fixed and invariable, with limited capacity for automated adjustments or programming.	Highly programmable and adaptable to meet changing network needs and facilitate maintenance.
Visibility	Separate configuration and management for each device, reducing transparency across the entire network.	Unified management and configuration via a centralized interface, improving network-wide visibility.

1.5 Advantages of an SDN Network

The following is a list of the significant advantages offered by an SDN network:

- **Centralized management:** SDN offers centralized network management, enabling a consistent overview and administration across the entire network.
- **Flexibility and adaptability:** Thanks to its software-based nature, SDN can adapt quickly to changes, meeting the evolving requirements of businesses and users alike.

- **Process automation:** Repetitive tasks and network configuration can be automated, reducing human error and maximizing efficiency.
- **Cost reduction:** By reducing reliance on proprietary hardware and automating management, operational costs (CAPEX and OPEX) can be significantly lowered.
- **Better resource utilization:** SDN enables resources to be allocated dynamically according to need, optimizing network capacity and performance.
- **Enhanced security:** Centralization and increased visibility make it easier to identify and respond to threats, providing a better security posture.
- **Integration with other technologies:** SDN can be easily integrated with other technologies and solutions, such as Network Functions Virtualization, for even more comprehensive and flexible network management.
- **Rapid deployment:** Modifications, updates, or new feature deployments can be carried out quickly without the need for lengthy manual intervention.

1.6 Main SDN Components

SDN architecture is based on several key components that interact to provide flexibility and control. These components form the foundation on which SDN networks are built and managed (Figure 1.3).

- **The application plane:** SDN applications fit into this layer, where they communicate with the SDN controller to request network services or set policies. These applications give managers the ability to flexibly and automatically define network behaviors according to operational requirements.

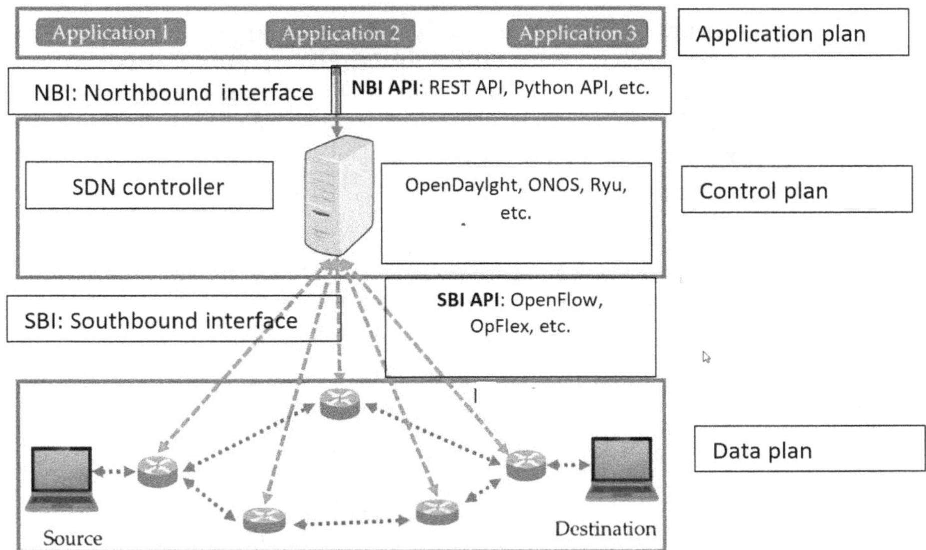

FIGURE 1.3
Main SDN components.

- **The control plane:** The SDN controller resides at the heart of this layer, acting as the brain of the SDN architecture and acting as the link between the application plane and the data plane. It centralizes decision-making and directs traffic according to predefined policies, playing the crucial role of network orchestrator.
- **The data plane:** Within this layer, also known as the transfer or hardware plane, the network infrastructure is made up of programmable devices such as switches and routers. These hardware elements execute instructions received from the SDN controller, enabling fine, reactive control over the flow of data through the network.

1.7 API North and South: The Pillars of SDN Orchestration

Communication between SDN components is facilitated by well-defined APIs, which act as communication bridges between the different layers of the architecture.

- **Northbound interface APIs:** These allow SDN applications to communicate their requirements and policies to the SDN controller, enabling them to request network services or define specific network behaviors. Northbound interfaces are essential so that operators can inject management rules and policies into the controller dynamically and flexibly, adapting the network to business and technical requirements.
- **Southbound interface APIs:** These provide a communication channel between the controller and transfer plane elements, such as switches and routers. These southbound interfaces allow the controller to transmit control decisions to hardware or virtual devices, orchestrating data flow across the network. Instructions can be transmitted for configuration, performance management, monitoring, and reacting to network events in real time.

These two sets of APIs work together to ensure harmonious coordination between applications, controller, and network infrastructure, forming the communicative backbone that supports the entire SDN architecture. In addition, the EST/OUEST (E/W Interface) APIs, which facilitate communication between different SDN controllers, will be covered in the section dedicated to multi-controller SDN networks.

Specific details concerning APIs will be covered in Chapter 2.

1.8 SDN Network Models

- SDN networks have several key models and architectures that have been developed to improve network flexibility, management, and performance (Table 1.2). Here are the most common models:
- **Centralized controller model:** This is the classic SDN model, where a centralized controller makes all decisions concerning packet routing in the network. The controller has a global view of the network, enabling it to efficiently manage traffic and policies.

TABLE 1.2

Evaluation of SDN Models: Features, Interfaces, and Limitations

SDN Model	Centralized Controller Model	Programming-Based Model	Overlay and Underlay Networks Model	Hybrid SDN Model
Functionality	Centralized controller model	Programming-based model	Overlay and Underlay Networks model	Hybrid SDN model
Interfaces	Open and standardized (OpenFlow).	Direct APIs.	Virtual for Overlay, physical for Underlay.	Hybrids (physical and virtual)
Benefits	Interoperability, flexibility, centralized control.	Granular control, high customizability.	Flexibility, isolation, scalability.	Gradual migration, preserving existing investments.
Disadvantages	Single point of failure, potential complexity.	Requires advanced programming skills.	Dependence on an underlying high-performance physical network.	Can become complex to manage with mixed network elements.

- **Hybrid model:** This model combines SDN elements with traditional network technologies. This allows network administrators to gradually integrate SDN without requiring a complete overhaul of the existing infrastructure.
- **Programming-based model:** In this model, an application, which can be centralized or distributed, interacts directly with network devices via APIs. This approach enables network devices to be controlled and configured individually, offering fine granularity in network management. Applications can reside on a centralized controller or even be embedded directly on network devices, enabling specific tasks such as security, performance management, and dynamic load balancing.
- **Intent-based networking:** This model, a subset of programming-based SDN, employs a high-level approach where administrators specify desired outcomes (intents), and the system automatically configures the network to meet these requirements. This simplifies network management and reduces configuration errors.
- **Overlay and underlay networks:** SDN networks can be implemented as overlay networks that are virtually built on top of physical networks (Underlay). This makes it possible to create separate logical networks for different needs without modifying the underlying physical infrastructure.

1.9 An Example of SDN Architecture in Action

SDN architecture has revolutionized the way networks are designed, managed, and optimized. Here are some of the key use cases for which SDN has been deployed, along with examples of the companies associated with each use case:

- **SD-LAN (Software-Defined Local Area Network):**
  - Apply the SDN concept to LANs.
  - Provides better management and segmentation of traffic within a campus or company.

- **SD-WAN (Software-Defined Wide Area Network):**
  - An SDN approach applied to WANs.
  - Offers simplified management, better bandwidth utilization, and optimized connectivity between branch offices, datacenters, and the cloud.
- **SDN for Data Center (Data Center SDN):**
  - Designed to optimize data center operations.
  - Improves datacenter agility, flexibility, and efficiency.
- **SD-Access (Software-Defined Access):**
  - Provides automation, simplification, and segmentation for unified access to wired and wireless networks.
  - Cisco is one of the main players promoting this approach.
  - SDN allows for dynamic traffic segmentation, isolating certain parts of the network for security or compliance reasons.
- **SDN for mobile networks:**
  - Optimizes and manages mobile networks, particularly with the adoption of 5G.
  - Enables flexible, dynamic orchestration of network resources to meet the varied needs of mobile applications.
- **SD-Storage (Software-Defined Storage):**
  - Abstracts and consolidates resources from various physical devices into unified storage pools.
  - Centralized management via policies that can automatically allocate resources, apply service levels, and manage redundancies.
  - Makes it easy to add or reduce storage resources as needed.

These different incarnations of SDN have been developed to meet the specific needs of different environments and deployment scenarios. The heart of SDN is the separation of the control plane from the data plane, enabling centralized, programmable management of network resources.

1.10 Main SDN Controllers: An Overview

The following is a list of the most commonly used SDN controllers, each accompanied by a brief description.

- **ONOS (Open Network Operating System):** ONOS is an open source SDN controller designed to deliver high availability, high performance, and maximum scalability. It is particularly well-suited to telecoms networks and service providers.
- **Ryu:** Ryu is an open source SDN controller written in Python, designed to be simple and easy to use. It supports a wide range of protocols and is often used for research and development applications.

- **Floodlight:** Floodlight is an open-source, Java-based SDN controller designed for performance and flexibility. It is widely used in production environments and research laboratories.
- **OpenDaylight:** OpenDaylight is an open-source SDN platform that provides significant flexibility and modularity, supporting a wide range of programmable network requirements. It is supported by a large community and a consortium of leading technology companies.
- **POX:** POX is a lightweight, easy-to-use SDN controller, particularly suitable for educational purposes and rapid prototyping. Written in Python, it offers great flexibility for developers looking to experiment with SDN concepts.
- **NOX:** NOX was one of the first SDN controllers, providing a robust and stable platform for the development of programmable networks. Although less widely used today, it laid the foundations for many modern controllers.
- **Cisco Application Policy Infrastructure Controller (APIC):** This is the central component of the Cisco Application Centric Infrastructure solution. It enables centralized management of application-based network policies, providing in-depth network visibility and control. APIC facilitates the automation and orchestration of network configurations while integrating advanced security tools and multi-cloud capabilities.
- **Cisco Digital Network Architecture (DNA):** A complete solution for enterprise network management, offering simplified, centralized management via the Cisco DNA Center. It integrates automation, security, and analytics capabilities to optimize network performance and resilience. DNA Center enables intuitive configuration and management of network devices, with real-time monitoring and troubleshooting capabilities. In addition, it supports integration with Cisco SD-WAN solutions, enabling consistent management of enterprise networks.

1.11 SDN Multi-Controller Network

1.11.1 Advantages of a Multi-Controller Network

An SDN network can contain multiple SDN controllers for a number of reasons, including resilience, scalability, and optimized resource management. Here's a detailed explanation of these reasons.

- **Resilience and high availability:** By using multiple controllers, the network can ensure continuity of service even in the event of failure of one of the controllers. This ensures uninterrupted network management and control.
- **Scalability:** As the network grows, a single controller can become a bottleneck. Multiple controllers enable load balancing, ensuring better performance and more efficient resource management.
- **Decentralization:** In large, geographically distributed networks, it's more efficient to have local controllers manage network segments close to them, thus reducing latency and optimizing performance.

- **Specialized management:** Different controllers can be used for specific tasks or to manage different types of traffic, improving the network's flexibility and adaptability to different conditions and requirements.

1.11.2 Architecture of a Multi-Controller SDN Network

Here are the different architectures for integrating multiple SDN controllers in a network:

- **Hierarchical architecture:** In this configuration, a main controller manages several subordinate controllers. The main controller coordinates global decisions, while subordinate controllers manage specific segments of the network (Figure 1.4).
- **Flat (distributed) architecture:** All controllers operate at the same level, collaborating and sharing information to make decisions. All controllers collaborate equally and can respond to requests from any network element. This approach requires a consensus protocol to avoid conflicts and ensure a consistent view of the network (Figure 1.5).
- **Network partitioning:** The network is divided into segments or zones, each managed by a dedicated controller. Each controller responds only to requests from elements in its own zone. Controllers communicate with each other for coordination, but do not directly manage elements in other zones (Figure 1.6).

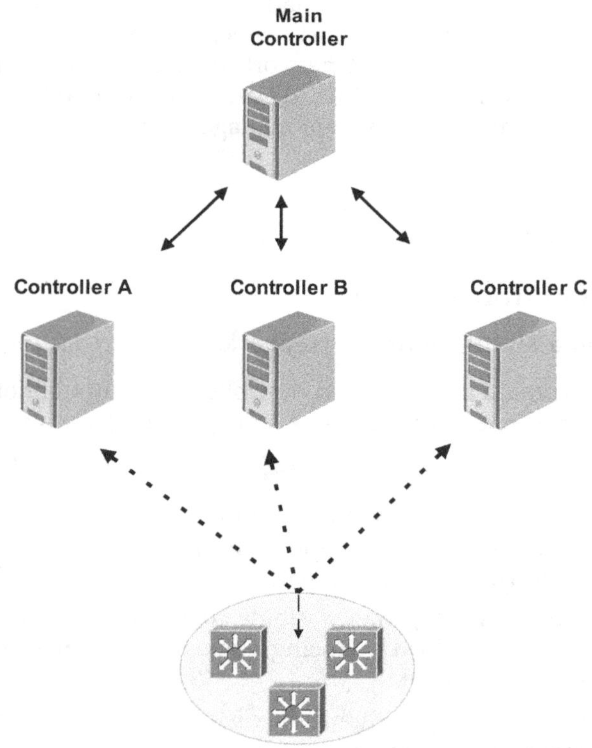

FIGURE 1.4
Hierarchical architecture.

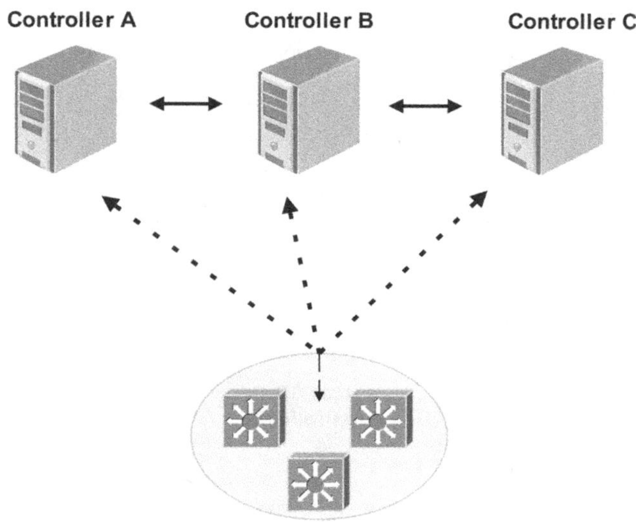

FIGURE 1.5
Flat architecture.

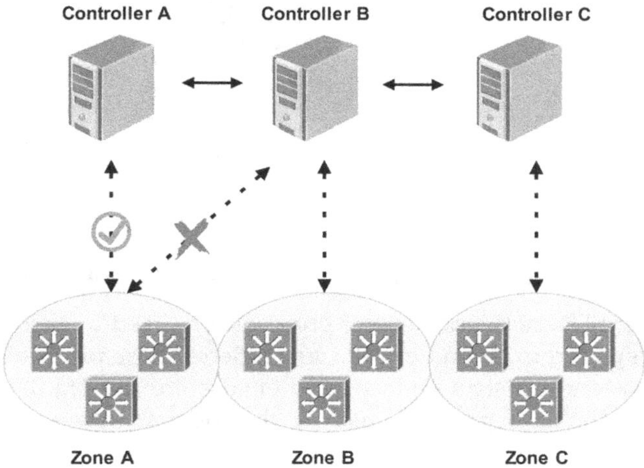

FIGURE 1.6
Network partitioning.

- **Active-active redundancy:** In this architecture, controllers work in parallel and collaboratively to create an abstraction of a "virtual SDN". This virtual SDN represents all physical controllers, ensuring unified, resilient network management. The virtual SDN distributes the load between active controllers to avoid overloads and optimize performance. In the event of a controller failure, the other controllers can immediately take over the responsibilities of the failing controller (Figure 1.7).

Understanding the differences between these architectures is crucial to designing efficient SDN networks tailored to specific needs. The choice between these architectures will depend on requirements in terms of resilience, performance, and network management complexity.

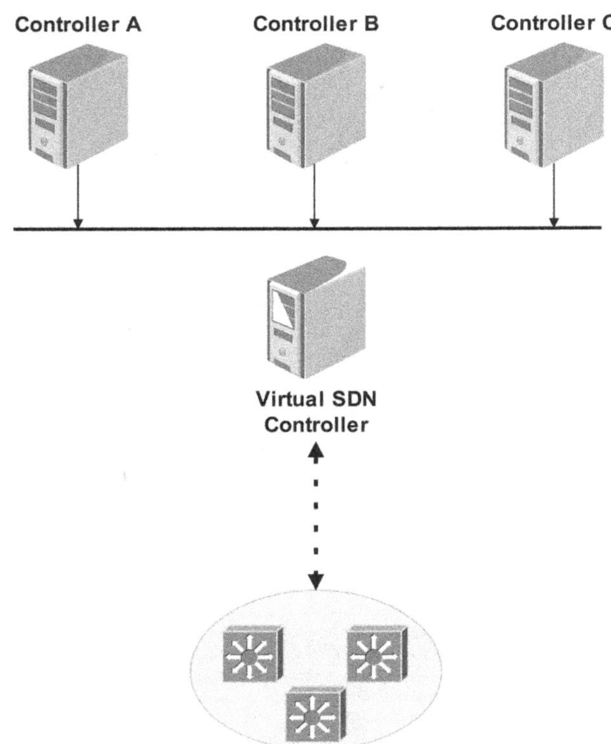

FIGURE 1.7
Active-active redundancy.

1.11.3 Protocols Used between Controllers in a Multi-Controller SDN Network

In a multi-controller SDN network, several protocols are used to ensure communication, coordination, and synchronization between controllers. These protocols help to maintain network state consistency, distribute load, and ensure effective fault tolerance. Here's a detailed overview of the main protocols used, including how they work, their advantages, and limitations.

- **East/west interface (E/W interface):** Defined by standards such as those from the Open Networking Foundation, the E/W Interface enables communication between SDN controllers.

  It facilitates the exchange of information on policies, network status, and events.
  - Advantages:
    - Enables communication between controllers from different suppliers.
    - Can be adapted to support different types of messages and interactions.
  - Limits:
- May lack maturity and universal support.
- Requires rigorous management to ensure consistency.

- **Raft:** This is a consensus protocol that ensures consistency between multiple SDN controllers by distributing the load fairly. It uses an elected *leader* to manage log operations and state replication.
  - Advantages:
    - Easier to understand and implement than other consensus protocols.
    - Ensures continuity of operations even if some controllers fail.
    - Ensures that all controllers have a consistent view of network status.
  - Limits:
    - May introduce delays in the event of frequent re-election of the leader.
    - Less effective in very large environments with many controllers.
- **Paxos:** Used to synchronize state between SDN controllers. It works by proposing values, accepting proposals, and reaching an agreement on these values.
  - Advantages:
    - Able to handle a wide range of network failures.
    - Can be adapted to operate in large-scale environments.
  - Limits:
    - More complex to implement and understand than Raft.
    - Can introduce high latency in highly dynamic environments.
- **BGP:** This is a routing protocol that enables controllers to share routing information with each other. Mainly used in partitioned architectures, it ensures the exchange of routes and communication between different network zones.
  - Advantages:
    - Widely used and well supported by many devices.
    - Enables communication between controllers from different suppliers.
  - Limits:
    - Requires precise configuration and can be complex to manage.
    - May take time to converge after network changes.
- **Path computation element communication protocol:** Used for communication between path computation elements and SDN controllers. It is used to coordinate end-to-end path computation in the network.
  - Advantages:
    - Find optimized paths for specific network requirements.
    - Supports a wide variety of path calculation scenarios.
  - Limits:
    - Can be complex to implement and maintain.
    - Depends on the efficiency and availability of the path calculation elements.
- **RESTful APIs:** Controllers can use RESTful APIs to exchange information and coordinate decisions between themselves. These APIs enable flexible, standardized communication.

- Advantages:
  - REST APIs are simple to implement and use.
  - Based on web standards, they are widely supported.
- Limits:
  - Less efficient for real-time communications than specific protocols.
  - Requires robust security measures to protect communications.

1.12 Chapter Conclusion

To conclude this chapter, we have seen how traditional network architectures are gradually being replaced by more flexible and adaptive solutions, such as SDN networks. The latter offer considerable advantages in terms of management, performance, and scalability, thus better meeting today's requirements for enterprises and digital services. SDN's core components and diverse models pave the way for continuous network innovation, enabling unprecedented customization and management of network resources. Using the example of an SDN architecture, we have illustrated the tangible impact of this technology on network simplification and optimization. This chapter lays the foundations for understanding the major technological developments that are redefining modern network infrastructure.

Lab 1: Exploring Centralized Wi-Fi Control with Cisco WLC

Objectives

- Understand and configure a WLC wireless controller in a simulated network environment using Cisco Packet Tracer.

Case Study

This case study examines the understanding and configuration of a wireless controller (WLC). It explores the fundamentals of Wi-Fi network management using a WLC, focusing on centralized configuration of access points and optimization of wireless network performance. The idea of this study is also to explore SDN architecture, since the Wi-Fi controller, although a special case, represents an example of an SDN network with centralized management.

Software to Use

- **Packet Tracer**

Network Topology

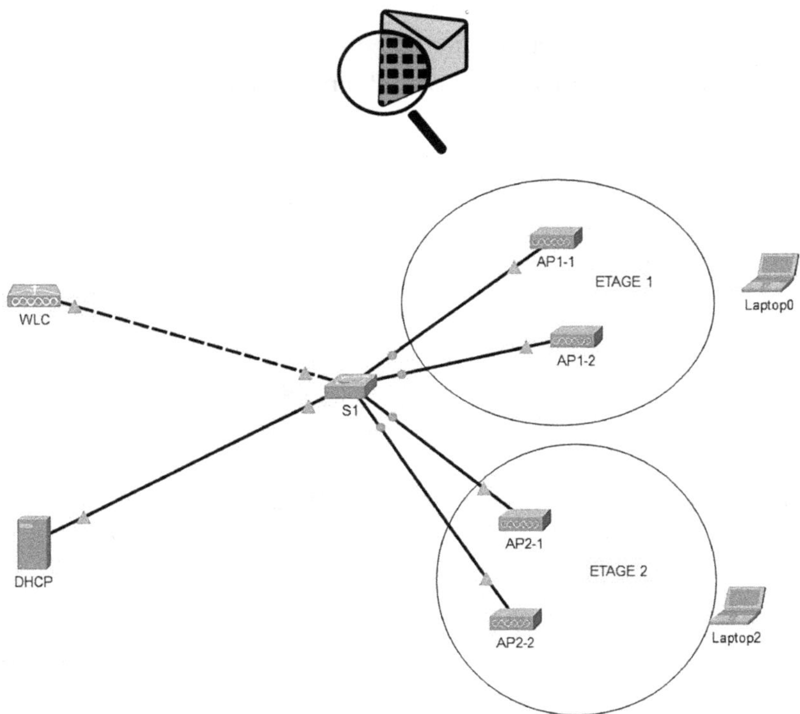

IP Address Table

Device	Interface	IP Address/Subnet Mask	Default Gateway
WLC	Management	192.168.0.10/24	–
DHCP	NIC	192.168.0.2/24	–

Part A: Establish Basic Device Configuration

1. Create the network topology.
2. Assign IP addresses to device interfaces based on the addressing table.
3. Ping the WLC and the DHCP server to ensure connectivity.

Part B: Set Up the DHCP Server Configuration

1. Configure the DHCP server scope as follows:

Scope Name	Server Pool
Start address	192.168.0.50
End address	192.168.0.100
Gateway	192.168.0.1
DNS	8.8.8.8
WLC address	192.168.0.10

2. Save settings and activate the service.
3. Verify that the access points have a DHCP configuration.

4. Verify that all access points are properly displayed in the WLC controller.

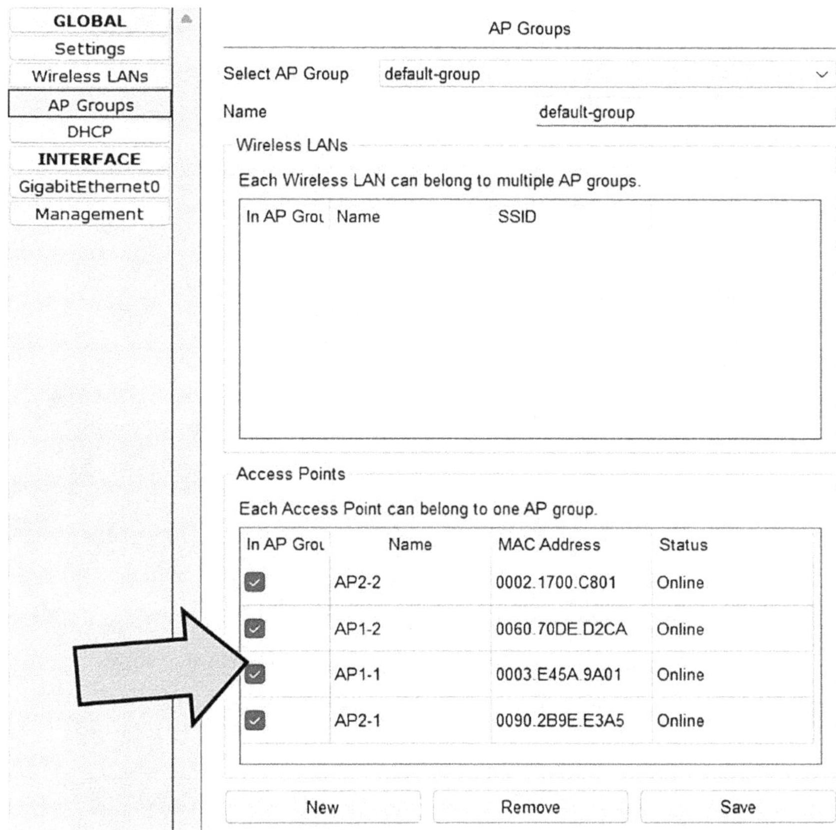

Part C: Set Up WLAN Configurations on the WLC Controller

1. On the controller, create two access point groups as follows:

Access Point Group	Access Point List
Floor1	AP1-1
Floor1	AP1-2
Floor2	AP2-1
Floor2	AP2-2

2. On the controller, create two separate WLANs with the following settings:

WLAN	SSID	Authentication
Floor1	FLOOR1	WPA-PSK: 12345678
Floor2	FLOOR2	WPA-PSK: 12345678

3. Link each WLAN with its group

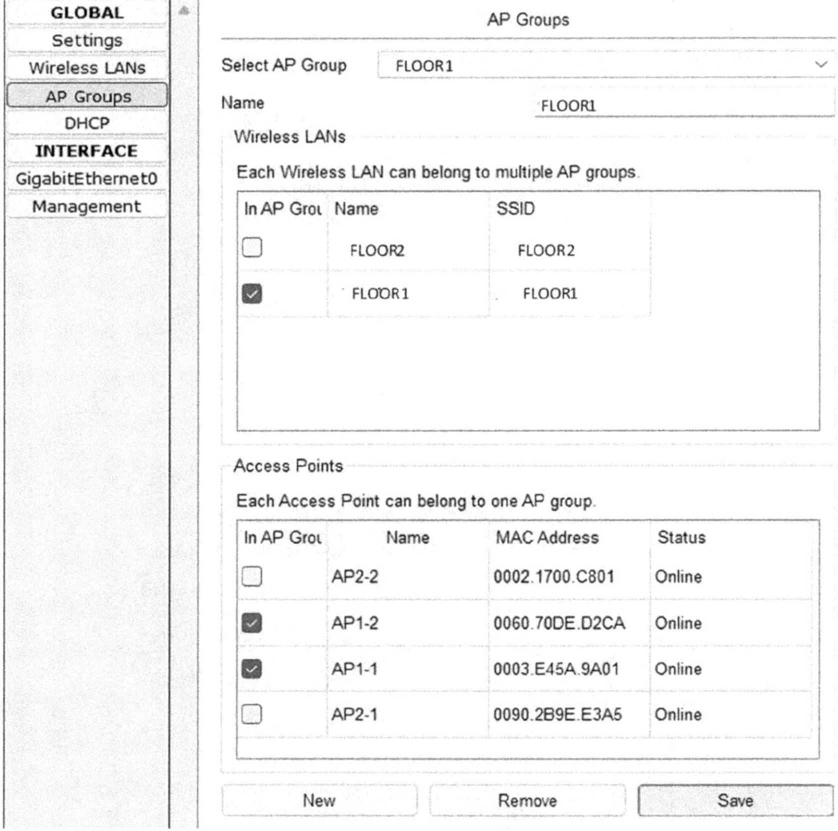

4. Use the laptops to verify the network connectivity.
5. Repeat the test, this time configuring the WLC controller via the web interface.

Lab 2: Deploying and Managing SDN Controllers with Cisco Packet Tracer

Objectives

- Understand and configure an SDN controller in a simulated network environment with Cisco Packet Tracer.

Case Study

This case study explores the application of SDN technology in IT networks to optimize and centralize device management. It highlights the benefits of a centralized approach to simplifying configuration, improving network agility, and enhancing overall control of network resources.

Software to Use

- **Packet Tracer**

Network Topology

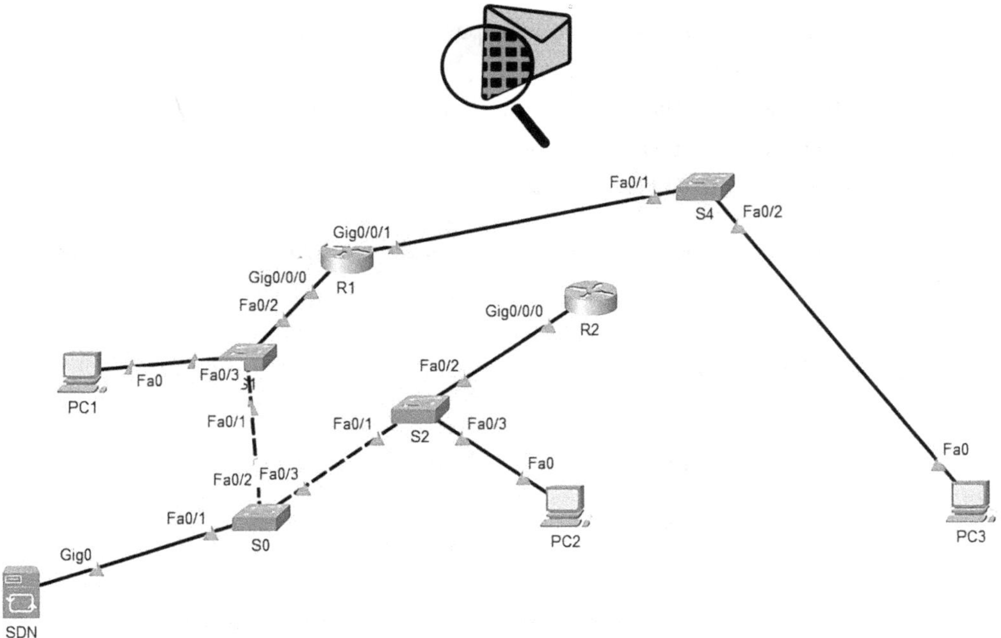

IP Address Table

Device	Interface	IP Address/Subnet Mask	Default Gateway
R1	G0/0/0	192.168.0.1/24	–
R1	G0/0/1	192.168.1.1/24	–
R2	G0/0/0	192.168.0.2/24	–
S1	VLAN1	192.168.0.3/24	
S2	VLAN1	192.168.0.4/24	
S0	VLAN1	192.168.0.5/24	
S4	VLAN1	192.168.1.10/24	192.168.1.1
SDN	NIC	192.168.0.10/24	192.168.0.1
PC1	NIC	192.168.0.6/24	192.168.0.1
PC2	NIC	192.168.0.7/24	192.168.0.1
PC3	NIC	192.168.1.2/24	192.168.1.1

Part A: Establish Basic Device Configuration

1. Create the network topology.
2. Assign IP addresses to device interfaces as specified in the addressing table.
3. Ping the SDN controller and all network elements and ensure connectivity among them.
4. On each network element:
   a. Create a user named "cisco" with the password "1234".
   b. Set up the domain name "cisco.com".
   c. Generate an RSA public key with a length of 1024 bits.
   d. Enable SSH access on each device.
   e. Set the password to "1234" for *enable* mode
5. From PC1, verify SSH access to each network device by executing the following command:

```
C:> ssh -l cisco [destination IP address]
```

Note: Replace [destination IP address] with the actual target IP address.

Part B: Discover the Basic Features of an SDN Controller

1. On PC1, open a web browser and access the SDN server:

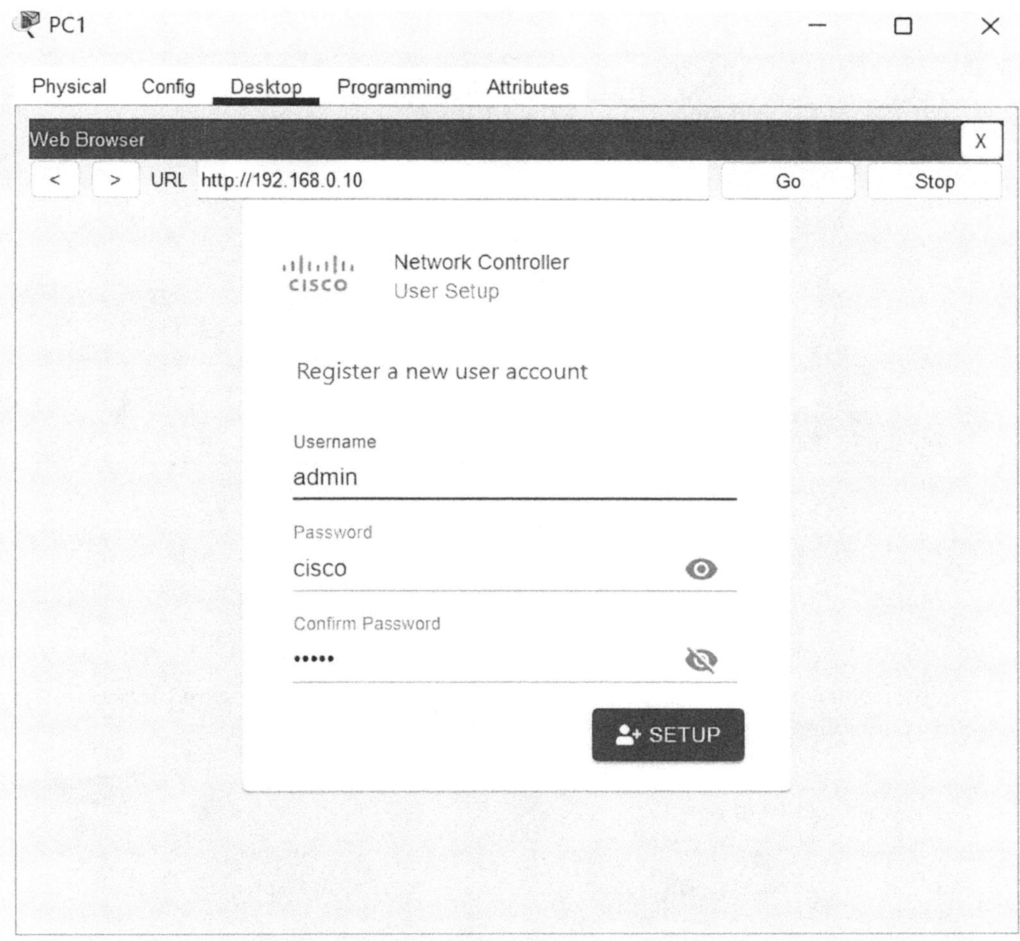

2. Create an "admin" user with the password "cisco" to access the SDN controller interface.
3. In the **"Provisioning > Credentials"** menu, create new authentication credentials:

Username	**Cisco**
Password	1234
Enable password	1234
Description	LAN password

4. On the "**Discovery**" tab, click on the "**Discovery**" button to initiate a new device discovery. Complete the window with the following information:

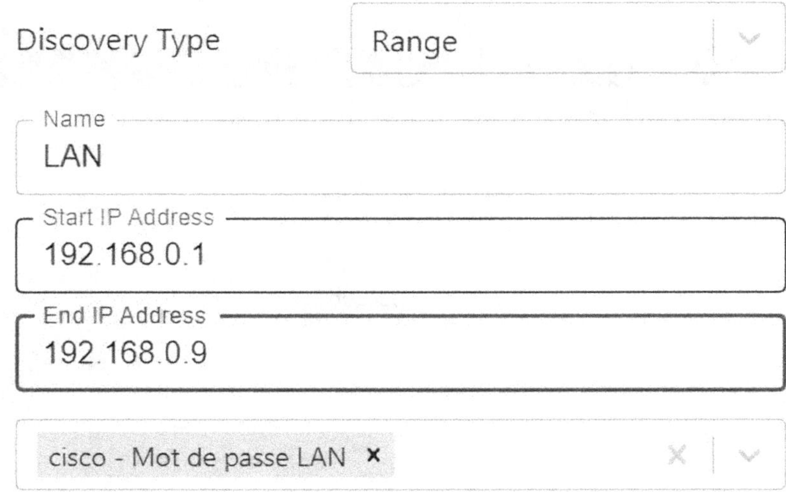

5. On the "**Network Devices**" tab, check that all network elements are present in the SDN controller list.

Network Device + DEVICE

	Hostname	Type	IP	Up Time	Last Updated	Collection Status
	R1	Router	192.168.0.1	1 hours, 13 minutes, 1 seconds	2023-11-27 23:09:11	Managed
	R2	Router	192.168.0.2	1 hours, 13 minutes, 1 seconds	2023-11-27 23:09:11	Managed
	S1	Switch	192.168.0.3	9 minutes, 52 seconds	2023-11-27 23:09:11	Managed
	S2	Switch	192.168.0.4	9 minutes, 52 seconds	2023-11-27 23:09:12	Managed
			192.168.0.10		2023-11-27 23:09:12	Unsupported
	S0	Switch	192.168.0.5	1 hours, 13 minutes, 2 seconds	2023-11-27 23:09:12	Managed
			192.168.0.9		2023-11-27 23:09:11	Unreachable

6. Click the "**DEVICE**" button to manually add switch S4. Enter its IP address, and confirm. Fill in its IP address, then confirm. Verify that the switch S4 has been added to the list.

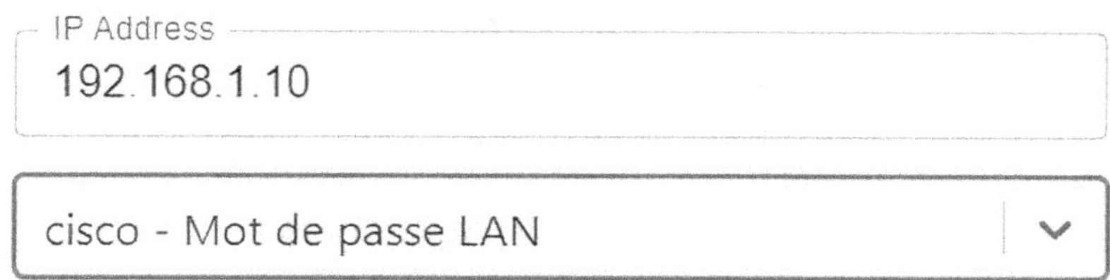

7. In the "**Assurance**" menu, navigate to the "**Topology**" tab and verify the accuracy of the displayed network topology.

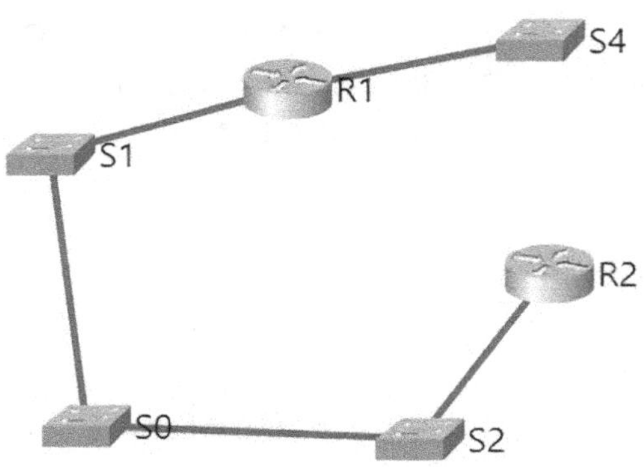

8. On the "**Assurance**" menu and "**Path Trace**" tab, visualize the communication path from PC1 to PC2 and PC3.

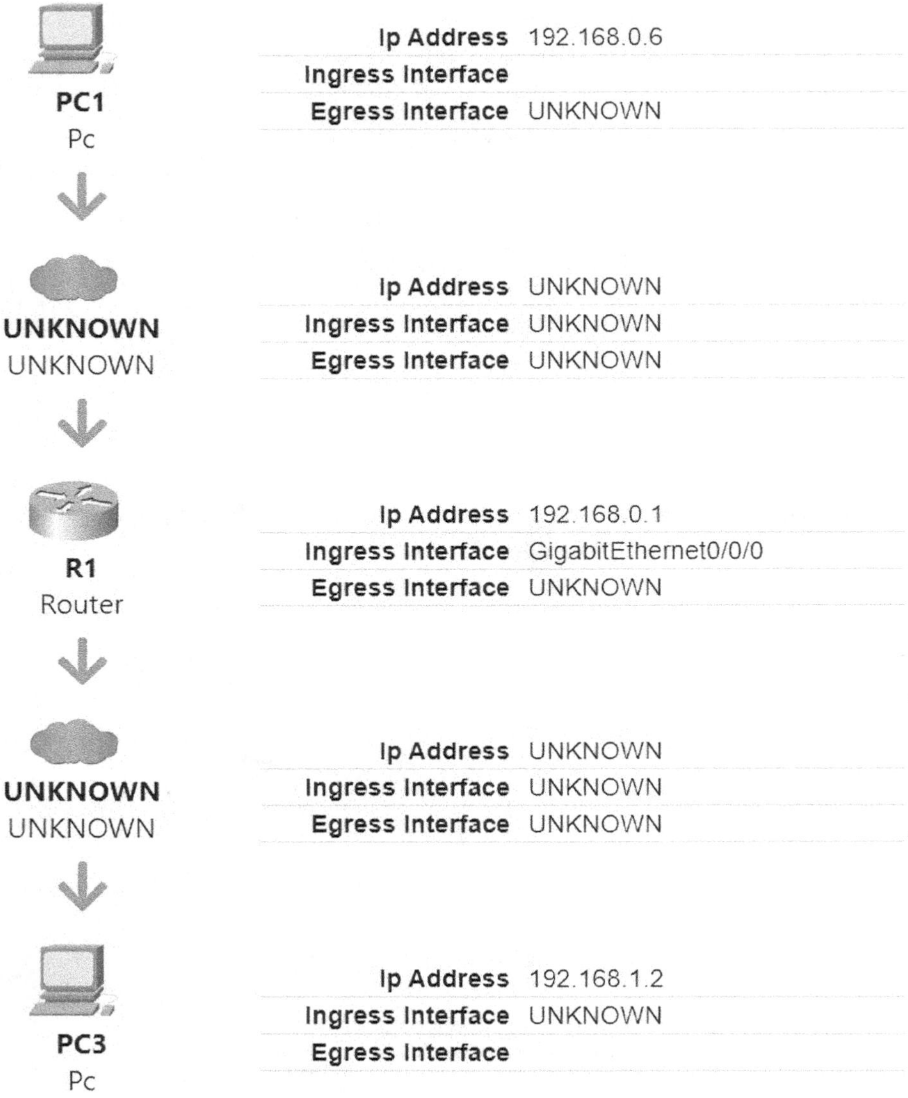

PC1
Pc

Ip Address	192.168.0.6
Ingress Interface	
Egress Interface	UNKNOWN

UNKNOWN
UNKNOWN

Ip Address	UNKNOWN
Ingress Interface	UNKNOWN
Egress Interface	UNKNOWN

R1
Router

Ip Address	192.168.0.1
Ingress Interface	GigabitEthernet0/0/0
Egress Interface	UNKNOWN

UNKNOWN
UNKNOWN

Ip Address	UNKNOWN
Ingress Interface	UNKNOWN
Egress Interface	UNKNOWN

PC3
Pc

Ip Address	192.168.1.2
Ingress Interface	UNKNOWN
Egress Interface	

Part C: Configuring Elements from an SDN Controller

1. On the "**Policy**" menu and "**Network Setting**" tab, create a network configuration as follows:

Service	**Parameters**
DNS	Domain: cisco.lan Server IP: 8.8.8.8
NTP	Server IP: 212.217.0.12
Syslog	Server IP: 192.168.1.10

   Save the above network settings.

2. Execute the **"Push Configuration"** command to deploy the configuration to all network elements.
3. Verify that the new configuration has been successfully applied to all network devices by running the sh running-config command.

2

Network Programming and Automation

This chapter dives into the technical aspects of network programmability that are essential for fully exploiting the capabilities of modern networks, especially those based on SDN. We'll start by exploring the different models of network programmability, offering various approaches to manipulating and managing network behaviors. We will then discuss the nuances between imperative and declarative programming models and analyze how each influences network design and management. This chapter also looks at application programming interfaces (APIs), which play a crucial role in enabling developers to interact efficiently with network components through programmable abstractions. Among these APIs, RESTful APIs are recognized as a standard and efficient method for interacting with networks through web interfaces, facilitating the integration of various services and applications. Finally, we'll look at how the Python language is used in network programming and SDN architectures, demonstrating its flexibility and efficiency through practical examples. This comprehensive overview aims to equip readers with the knowledge they need to navigate the ever-changing ecosystem of network programming.

This chapter covers the following topics:

1. Introduction
2. Network programming and SDN networks
3. Different network programmability models
4. Imperative or declarative programming models
5. APIs
6. Network automation via RESTful API
7. Using Python in network programming and SDN architectures
8. Chapter conclusion

2.1 Introduction

Network programming has fundamentally transformed the management, design, and implementation of network infrastructure. In the past, network configuration was often done manually, a process that was not only laborious but also error-prone. The advent of network programming has made it possible to automate these configurations, increasing agility and significantly reducing human error.

With this approach, an application—whether centralized or distributed—interacts with network devices through APIs. This approach offers the possibility of individually manipulating and configuring each network device, enabling detailed control over network management. These applications can be hosted on a centralized controller or directly

DOI: 10.1201/9781003679394-2

integrated into network devices, facilitating specific operations such as security, performance management, and dynamic load balancing.

2.2 Network Programming and SDN Networks

Network programming and SDN share a common goal: To automate and simplify the management of complex networks. Network programming provides the tools needed to determine network behavior, while SDN offers a centralized structure for executing these configurations on a large scale.

As a viable alternative to traditional SDN, network programming is particularly relevant in scenarios where purchasing an SDN controller is too costly or unsuitable for the network scale. It also proves crucial when complex tasks need to be performed simultaneously on multiple network elements, enabling efficient management and orchestration on a large scale.

Through network access libraries integrated into programming languages, the functionality of an SDN controller can be simulated in an ad hoc manner, providing automation and centralized control. While this approach differs from pure SDN, it does achieve flexibility and operational efficiency, capturing some of the benefits of SDN without requiring its complete architecture (Figure 2.1).

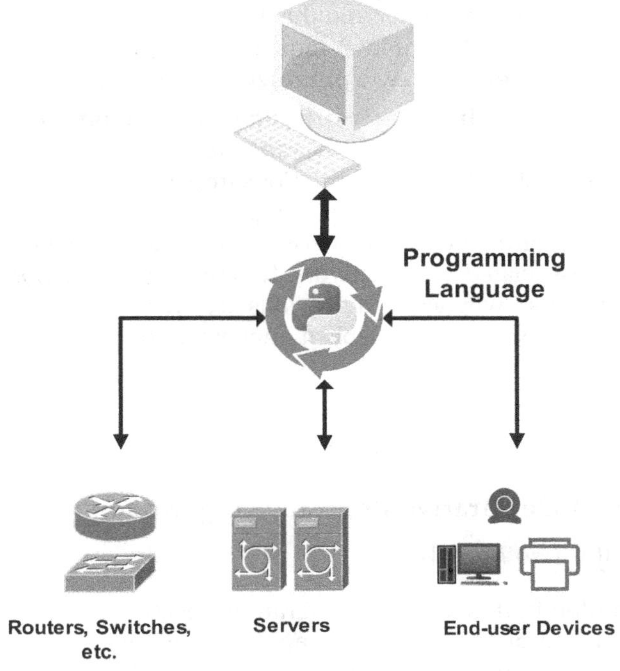

FIGURE 2.1
Network device interaction via programming.

In short, network programming, in synergy with SDN, creates unprecedented flexibility, making networks more adaptive, scalable, and easy to manage.

2.3 Different Network Programmability Models

There are a variety of network programmability models, each tailored to the specific needs of its users. For example, the technologies used to simplify the management of servers in a data center are different from those designed to improve the management of a traffic signal network in a city. These diverse solutions illustrate the model's flexibility in adapting to different contexts and requirements. There are several network programmability models:

- **Individual device programming** (Figure 2.2a**):** In this model, an application communicates directly with each device via APIs. This application can be centralized or directly integrated into the network device, enabling it to perform specific tasks.
- **Controller-based programmability** (Figure 2.2b **and c):** In this model, an application sends abstract, high-level instructions to a controller, which translates them into specific commands for the relevant network devices. This system is particularly popular, as it simplifies network management by masking its complexity. Different scenarios can be distinguished, depending on the type of instructions exchanged between the controller and the devices. Initially focused on data plane programmability (as with OpenFlow), more recent approaches adopt more abstract instructions, leaving devices free to optimize their implementation.
- **Programmability via a virtual network superimposed on the physical network** (Figure 2.2d**):** This model allows applications to create their own "Overlay" network, freeing themselves from the limitations imposed by the underlying physical network. The role of the latter is limited to providing basic connectivity between tunnel end nodes, while the overlay network manages all network services. This concept is also associated with network function virtualization, where components such as routers, switches, and firewalls are virtualized on servers. This process enables more flexible and scalable management of network resources.

2.4 Imperative and Declarative Programming Models

2.4.1 Introducing the Two Models

- **Imperative model:** In this model, a program is designed to know precisely every step required to complete a task. When applied to network programmability, this means that the program must define and apply all the states required on each network device to perform a specific action.
- **Declarative model:** In this model, the program focuses on the desired result, rather than on the steps required to achieve it. In the context of network programmability,

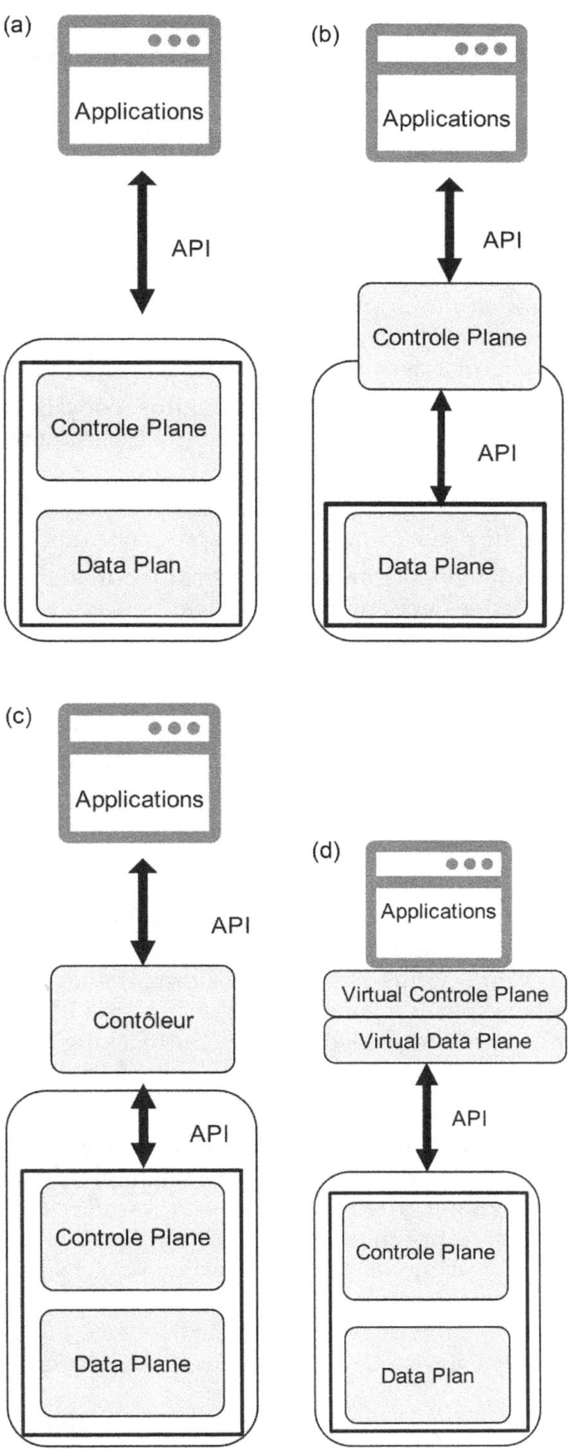

FIGURE 2.2
(a–d) Different models of network programmability.

each network element, when invoked by the program, takes the necessary actions to achieve the specified objective, sometimes making autonomous decisions. This model, therefore, allows for greater flexibility and adaptability in the network's responses to programmed requests.

The declarative model is increasingly favored due to several notable advantages:

- **Simplicity of implementation:** This model takes advantage of the intelligence already mastered by network teams, enabling equipment to make autonomous decisions. This is often faster and more reliable than depending on centralized commands. For example, a router making routing decisions locally can react more quickly than a system that depends on a central controller prone to failure.
- **Manufacturer preference:** Manufacturers favor this model because it allows them to open up access to the embedded intelligence in their equipment without compromising their control over the technology.
- **Scalability:** It makes it easy to adapt the network to changes by integrating global objectives, without the need for meticulous reprogramming.
- **Maintainability:** Adjustments or extensions can be made with fewer interruptions. Necessary changes are applied via global policies, rather than individual configurations for each piece of equipment.

2.4.2 Processing Example

To illustrate the difference between declarative and imperative models in network programmability, let's take the example of a task involving blocking communication between a PC and a server:

- **Imperative model:** In this model, the user is responsible for specifying every detail of the configuration. If the user wishes to block communication between a PC and a server, he or she must manually create and execute an access control list (ACL). The interface can simplify this process by guiding the user through the various ACL options, such as specifying source and destination IP addresses, ports, protocols, and other parameters needed to define the blocking rule. The user needs to know and decide on all these parameters to configure the ACL correctly.
- **Declarative model:** In the declarative model, the user focuses solely on the end goal, that is, blocking communication between the PC and the server. The user expresses this objective, and the system automatically determines the best parameters for achieving it. The router or system in charge of applying the ACL autonomously selects the optimum options for configuring the ACL according to the stated objective. This model can also be enhanced by artificial intelligence, enabling the user to express network objectives using natural language. For example, the user could simply write: "Block traffic between 'John's' PC and the data server", and the system automatically configures the necessary rules.

In short, the imperative model requires detailed knowledge and manual intervention to configure every aspect of the task, while the declarative model simplifies user interaction by focusing on the goal and letting the system determine the implementation details.

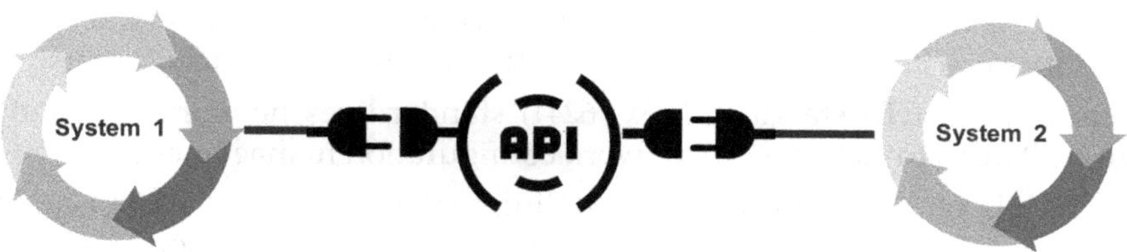

FIGURE 2.3
Fluid inter-system data exchange via API.

2.5 Application Programming Interfaces

2.5.1 API Presentation

APIs function as bridges enabling two distinct software applications or systems to interact and communicate. They define a set of rules and protocols for developing and interacting with software applications (Figure 2.3).

2.5.2 Standardized and Proprietary APIs

There are standardized APIs and proprietary APIs. Standardized APIs are designed according to established standards, often managed by standards bodies.

Proprietary APIs, on the other hand, are developed by companies or individuals and are generally not publicly available. They may be specific to a product or service.

2.5.3 APIs Used in SDN Architecture

As already seen in Chapter 1, in an SDN architecture, we can classify these APIs used in an SDN architecture into two essential categories:

- **Northbound APIs:** These connect SDN applications and orchestrators to the SDN controller. They enable applications to request network services or inform the controller of certain intentions or needs.
- **Southbound APIs:** These connect the SDN controller to physical or virtual network devices. These APIs control and collect information from devices, such as switches or routers, so that the controller can see the whole picture and manage the network centrally.

2.5.4 The Most Commonly Used Northern APIs

Here is a description of the northern APIs most commonly used in SDN network architectures:

- **CLI:** Accessible via telnet or SSH, this interface essentially serves as an API for network configuration. It focuses on the management plan.
- **RESTful API:** This API uses http/https commands to transmit instructions. It is characterized by its stateless approach, where each request constitutes an

independent action, without the need for a continuous connection. It is particularly popular with web developers and is frequently used in data centers.

- **Netconf:** This IETF standard (RFC 6241) standardizes network commands for devices. It aims to standardize network configuration management.
- **YANG:** A language dedicated to modeling network services, YANG enables, in conjunction with Netconf, the consistent configuration of various devices. This method is often adopted by service providers who want a degree of independence from manufacturers while still controlling the network.
- **SNMP:** A protocol used to manage and monitor network equipment.
- **Python API:** Programmable interfaces in Python that facilitate the automation and management of network configurations through scripting.

Other APIs, adapted to various uses, include BGP-LS, LISP, CAPWAP, and so forth.

Note that these are just a few examples of the multitude of programming interfaces available.

2.5.5 The Most Commonly Used Southern APIs

Here is an overview of some of the most commonly used south APIs on an SDN architecture:

- **OpenFlow:** OpenFlow is one of the first standardized APIs designed to facilitate communication between control plane controllers and data plane devices in an SDN network. It enables administrators to define traffic paths and manipulate data flows across the network in a dynamic, programmable way.
- **OpFlex:** OpFlex is an API developed by Cisco that works with a declarative control model. Unlike OpenFlow, which focuses on the meticulous configuration of network devices, OpFlex allows controllers to specify policies that are then interpreted and implemented by the devices themselves, offering greater flexibility and scale.
- **P4:** P4 (Programming Protocol-independent Packet Processors) is a programming language dedicated to describing how packets are processed by network devices. The associated API allows developers to precisely define and control packet processing, making network equipment more flexible and adapted to specific network functions.
- **OVSDB:** OVSDB (Open vSwitch Database Management Protocol) is a protocol for controlling the configuration of Open vSwitch instances, which is a multi-layer virtual switch. This API makes it possible to dynamically configure Open vSwitch instances and manage aspects of virtual networking directly through structured queries.

2.6 Network Automation via RESTful API

2.6.1 Presentation

REST (**Representational State Transfer**) is a set of architectural principles for designing web services. A RESTful API is an API that adheres to these rules. It enables communication between the client, such as a web or mobile application, and the server, using the http/https protocols (Figure 2.4).

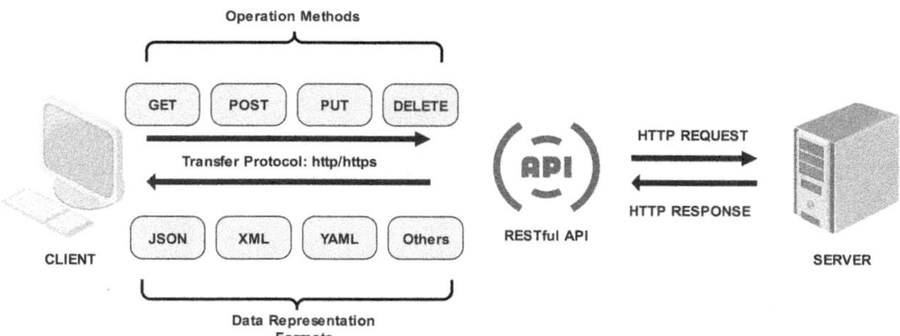

FIGURE 2.4
Methods and formats in API REST communication.

RESTful APIs offer several advantages:

- **Simplicity and flexibility:** Thanks to the use of http/https standards, they are easy to understand and implement.
- **Scalability:** The stateless nature of requests makes it easier to manage large volumes of clients. Each request to a server is entirely independent of others. The server retains no information on the state of the client's session after the request has been processed. This approach makes the system easier to scale, as the server does not need to store status information for each client, simplifying the management of large numbers of simultaneous requests.
- **Independence:** Client and server can be developed independently as long as they adhere to the rules defined by the API.

2.6.2 RESTful API Methods

The http/https methods commonly used in a RESTful API enable you to perform various operations on resources. Here's an overview of these methods and their typical uses:

- **GET:** Used to retrieve data from an element. In network automation, for example, this method can be used to obtain the current state of the network or to retrieve specific device configurations. It is designed to be a "risk-free" operation, not modifying the state of the resource.
- **POST:** Used to send data to a server to create a new resource. This is the method to use when the intention is to add a new resource to the system, such as a new user or a new item in a database.
- **PUT:** This method is used to update or completely replace an existing resource. It is ideal for cases where all the information on a resource needs to be updated. In a network context, it can be used to update entire device configurations.
- **DELETE:** Used to delete resources. It is definitive and deletes the resource specified by a unique identifier (URI) targeted by the HTTP request. This is a critical operation and must be used with caution to avoid accidental deletion of data.

These methods enable complete interaction with system resources, ensuring that RESTful APIs can handle any type of data management required by an application.

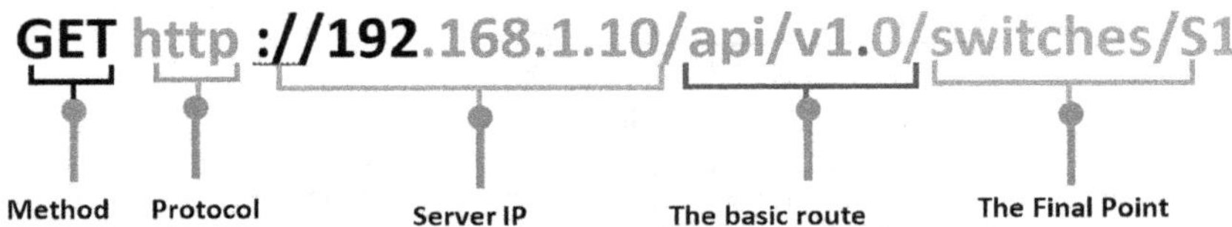

FIGURE 2.5
Anatomy of the RESTful API request.

2.6.3 Anatomy of a RESTful API Request

A RESTful API request generally consists of the following elements: the method used for the action, the transfer protocol, the target host, as well as the specific path to the resource and its parameters.

Let's take the GET request illustrated as an example to analyze its structure and understand how each part contributes to identifying and accessing the requested resource (Figure 2.5).

Here are the components of this query:

- **HTTP method: GET**—This is the method used to retrieve data from the server. In a RESTful API, **GET** is used to request a representation of a specific resource.
- **Protocol: HTTP**—This is the protocol used to transmit the request. Although **HTTP** is used in this example, for security reasons, **HTTPS** is generally preferred in production.
- **Host: 192.168.1.10**—This is the IP address of the server hosting the API. This address can also be a domain URL if the API is accessible over the Internet.
- **API path: /api/v1.0/switches/S1**—This is the API-specific path that details the location of the desired resource.
- **/api** usually indicates that the path leads to an API.
- **/v1.0** represents the API version, which is important for change management and backward compatibility.
- **/switchs/S1** specifies the path to the resource you wish to obtain, in this case, an element named **S1** in a **switchs** collection.

Each part of the URL is essential to guide the HTTP request to the appropriate resource and ensure that the correct HTTP method is applied for the desired action. In the case of our example, the request seeks information about element **S1** from the server. The response returned by the server will typically include an HTTP status (such as 200 OK for success), as well as the requested data, often in JSON or XML form.

2.6.4 RESTful API-Structured Representation Files

In RESTful APIs, data are often exchanged in a structured form that facilitates its interpretation and manipulation by computer programs. Three of the most commonly used formats are JSON, XML, and YAML (Table 2.1).

Here are some examples of responses in JSON, XML, and YAML formats (Table 2.2):

TABLE 2.1

Characteristics of the Three Formats: JSON, XML and YAML

Format Name	Features
JSON (JavaScript Object Notation):	Nature: Lightweight and easy for humans to read, it is based on JavaScript object notation. Use: This is the preferred format for web interfaces, as it is natively understood by browsers and is generally faster to parse and manipulate in JavaScript.
XML (eXtensible Markup Language):	Nature: More detailed than JSON and strict in terms of structure, it can be used to define customized schemas. Application: Often used in enterprise web services and configurations where precise data format validation is important.
YAML (YAML Ain't Markup Language):	Nature: Designed to be highly readable, it is often used for configuration files or files that need to be edited manually. Use: It's appreciated for its ability to represent hierarchical data and its absence of delimiters such as braces or commas.

TABLE 2.2

Example of RESTful API Structured Representation Files

JSON	XML	YAML

{
"id": "S1",
"name": "Switch Principal",
"type": "Layer 3 switch",
"IP address: "192.168.1.10",
"numberPorts": 24,
"modele": "Catalyst 9200",
"firmware": "v12.2",
"description": "Main switch used to manage internal network traffic."
}
	<?xml version="1.0" encoding="UTF-8" ?>
	<root>
	<id>S1</id>
	<name>Main switch</name>
	<type>Layer 3 switch</type>
	<IPaddress>192.168.1.10 </IPaddress>
	<numberPorts>24 </numberPorts>
	<modele>Catalyst 9200 </modele>
	<firmware>v12.2</firmware>
	<description>Main switch used to manage internal network traffic.</description>
	</root>
		--- 	
		id: S1
		name: Switch Principal
		type: Layer 3 switch
		IP address: 192.168.1.10
		numberPorts: 24
		model: Catalyst 9200
		firmware: v12.2
		description: Main switch used to manage internal network traffic.

Each of these formats has its own strengths and is suitable for different types of tasks. In RESTful APIs, JSON is generally the default format for data exchange due to its web compatibility and ease of handling, but XML and YAML are also used when their specificity brings additional advantages.

2.7 Using Python in Network Programming and SDN Architectures

2.7.1 Introduction

Python, due to its simplicity and flexibility, has become a popular choice for network programming, particularly in SDN architectures. This section explores how Python is used in network programming, with a particular focus on SDN architectures, highlighting its advantages, limitations, and interactions with network devices and controllers.

2.7.2 Advantages and Limitations of Python for Network Programming

The advantages of using Python for network programming include the following:

- **Simplicity and readability:** Python's clear, concise syntax makes code easier to write and maintain.
- **Rich library:** Python has an extensive standard library and third-party modules such as socket, scapy, and paramiko, which simplify network programming tasks.
- **Interoperability:** Python supports integration with other languages and technologies, which is crucial in heterogeneous environments.
- **Community and support:** The large community of Python developers offers excellent support and a wealth of learning and troubleshooting resources.

The limitations of using Python for network programming include the following:

- **Performance:** Python may be less performant than compiled languages like C or Java, particularly for large-scale data processing tasks.
- **Resource management:** Python automatically manages memory, which can lead to overloading and reduced performance in resource-constrained environments.

The use of Python in network programming and SDN architectures offers several significant advantages, not least its ease of use and the richness of its libraries. However, developers need to be aware of its limitations. As network technologies and Python continue to evolve, it's essential to stay informed and adapt your practices to make the most of the tools available.

2.7.3 Direct Interaction with Network Equipment

Python can interact directly with network devices via libraries that facilitate the management of network connections and protocols. For example, the **netmiko** library is used to automate the management of multi-vendor network devices via SSH/CLI.

Python also enables direct manipulation of network packets using tools like **Scapy**, which can be used to analyze or construct network packets (Figure 2.6a and b).

2.7.4 Interacting with an SDN Controller

In an SDN architecture, Python can interact with the SDN controller to orchestrate and automate the network. The controller, which acts as an intermediary layer between network applications and switching equipment, often exposes an API that Python can exploit.

- **REST API:** Many SDN controllers provide a REST API, allowing Python scripts to leverage libraries like **Requests** for programmatic network management.
- **OpenFlow:** Standardized protocol used in SDN, can be manipulated via Python to control the behavior of switches and routers in the network (Figure 2.7).

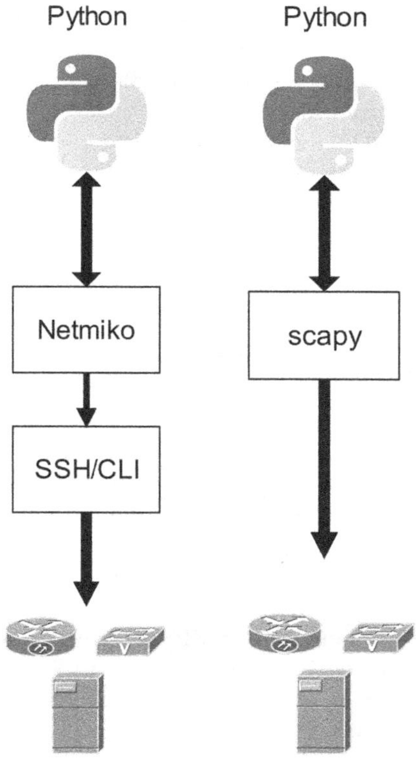

FIGURE 2.6A AND B
Using Netmiko and Scapy to interact with network devices.

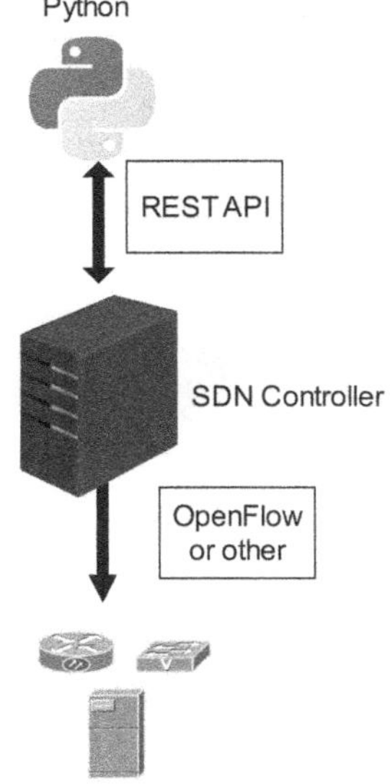

FIGURE 2.7
Integration of Python and REST API in SDN control.

Note: Although it is theoretically possible to ensure direct communication between Python and the OpenFlow protocol, the common and recommended practice is to use an SDN controller that acts as an intermediary between a Python script and the network devices to simplify programming and network management.

This takes advantage of the SDN model, where the controller takes care of network logic and the complexities of communicating with network devices, while the Python script interacts with the controller to implement policies, services, or perform analyses.

2.8 Chapter Conclusion

In conclusion, this chapter has explored the strategic dimension of network programmability in the context of SDN networks. We have examined the different models of network programmability, highlighting the distinctions between imperative and declarative approaches and their impact on network management. APIs have proved crucial in facilitating communication between different software components and network hardware. Among these APIs, RESTful APIs have played a fundamental role in standardizing access to network resources, thus contributing greatly to interoperability and the simplification of network management. Finally, we have highlighted the importance of Python, a powerful tool for network programming and SDN architectures, thanks to its simplicity and wealth of specialized libraries. Together, these elements define a new era where flexibility, automation, and operational efficiency are at the forefront of networking technologies.

Lab 3: Python Automation for VLAN Management

Objectives

- Program a script to configure network elements.

Case Study

This case study focuses on programming a script to configure network elements in an automated way. It explores the steps required to write, test, and deploy a script capable of managing the configuration of network devices, thereby improving the efficiency and consistency of operations in the network infrastructure.

Company ABC has several switches and routers. It wants to automate the creation of VLANs, among other tasks, using Python scripts.

Required Software

- **GNS3 or equivalent**

Network Topology

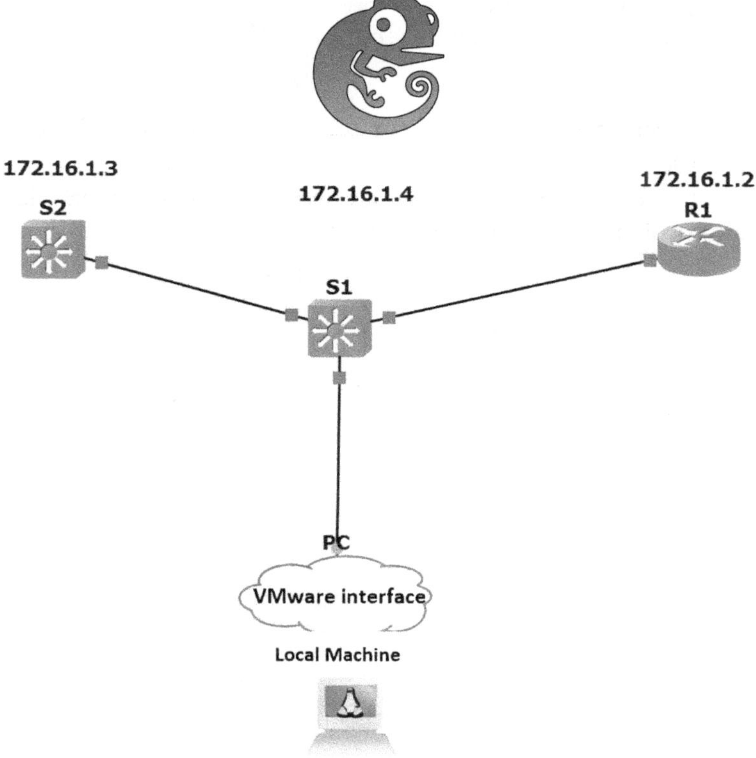

IP Address Table

Emulated Device	Device	Interface	IP Address/ Subnet Mask	Default Gateway
Cisco Router—C7200 (Dynamips, v15.2)	R1	G0/0	172.16.1.2/24	–
Cisco IOSvL2 Switch (v15.2(6))	S1	VLAN1	172.16.1.4/24	–
Cisco IOSvL2 Switch (v15.2(6))	S2	VLAN1	172.16.1.3/24	–
GNS3 Cloud	Local Machine	VMware Network Interface	172.16.1.1/24	–

Part A: Establish Basic Device Configuration

1. Create the network topology.
2. Assign IP addresses to device interfaces according to the addressing table.
3. Ping from the Local Machine to all network devices and ensure connectivity between elements.
4. On each network element
   a. Create a user "**cisco**" with password "**1234**".
   b. Set up the domain name "**cisco.com**".
   c. Generate an RSA key pair with a length of 1024 bits.
   d. Configure SSH access as follows

```
R1(config)# line vty 0 4
R1(config-line)# login local
R1(config-line)# transport input ssh
```

   e. Set the secret password "**1234**" for the *enable* mode (use the **enable secret** command).
5. On the Local Machine, check that you have access to each network element using the SSH protocol, using the **PuTTY** software.

Part B: Discover Network Programming with the Python Language

1. Launch a **Python** integrated development environment (IDE) (e.g., **Pyzo**) and make sure the **Netmiko** library is installed using the **pip show netmiko** command.
   - The aim of the **TP1.py** program is to establish a connection with Cisco switches in order to create VLANs.

```
from netmiko
import ConnectHandler

def configure_vlan(device, vlan_id, vlan_name):
    # Establish the connection with the required parameters
    connection = ConnectHandler(device_type=device['device_type'],
                                ip=device['ip'],
                                username=device['username'],
                                password=device['password'],
                                global_delay_factor=2,
                                secret=device['secret'])
    print ("start VLAN configuration" + device['ip'] + ":=>" +
  str(vlan_id))

    connection.enable()
    config_commands = [
        f'vlan {vlan_id}', # Create or modify VLAN
        f'name {vlan_name}', # Assign a name to the VLAN
    ]

    output = connection.send_config_set(config_commands)
    connection.disconnect() # Close connection after use
    print ("End of processing of " + device['ip'])
    #return vlan_output

devices = [

    {
        'device_type': 'cisco_ios',
        'ip': '172.16.1.3',
        'username': 'user1',
        'password': '1234',
        'secret': '1234' # Enable mode password
    },
    {
        'device_type': 'cisco_ios',
        'ip': '172.16.1.4',
        'username': 'user1',
        'password': '1234',
        'secret': '1234' # Enable mode password
    },
]

for device in devices:
    for vlan_id, vlan_name in [(10, 'V10'), (20, 'V20'),
  (30, 'V30')]:
        configure_vlan(device, vlan_id, vlan_name)
```

2. Open the **TP1.py** file
3. Fill in the connection variables for each switch:
   - ip: '172.16.1.3',
   - username: 'user1',
   - password: '1234',
   - secret: '1234
4. Run **TP1.py** to create VLANs 10, 20, and 30.
5. Verify that VLANs have been created.
6. Modify **TP1.py** to create VLANs 40 and 50. Check the result.
   - The purpose of the **TP2.py** program is to connect to Cisco switches, create VLANs, and configure interfaces in **'Access'** mode.

```
from netmiko import ConnectHandler

def configure_vlan(device, vlan_id, vlan_name):
    # Establish the connection directly with all the necessary
  details
    connection = ConnectHandler(device_type=device['device_type'],
                                ip=device['ip'],
                                username=device['username'],
                                password=device['password'],
                                global_delay_factor=2,
                                secret=device['secret'])
    print ("start VLAN configuration" + device['ip'] + ":=>" +
  str(vlan_id))
    connection.enable()
    config_commands = [
        f'vlan {vlan_id}', # Create or modify VLAN
        f'name {vlan_name}', # Assign a name to the VLAN
    ]

    output = connection.send_config_set(config_commands)
    connection.disconnect() # Close connection after use
    print ("End of VLAN configuration" + device['ip'])
    #return vlan_output

def configure_interfaces(device, interface, vlan_id):
    # Establish connection with device details
    connection = ConnectHandler(device_type=device['device_type'],
                                ip=device['ip'],
                                username=device['username'],
                                password=device['password'],
                                global_delay_factor=2,
                                secret=device['secret'])
```

```
    print("Start interface configuration on " + device['ip'] + ":=>"
  + interface)
    # Activate privileged mode
    connection.enable()

    # Configure interface commands
    config_commands = [
        'conf t',
        f'interface {interface}',
        switchport mode access',
        f'switchport access vlan {vlan_id}'
    ]

    # Send configuration commands
    output = connection.send_config_set(config_commands)

    # Close connection
    connection.disconnect()

    print("Configuration complete for " + device['ip'])

    # Return the output of the verification command
    #return interface_output
switchs = [

    {
        'device_type': 'cisco_ios',
        'ip': '172.16.1.3',
        'username': 'user1',
        'password': '1234',
        'secret': '1234' # Enable mode password
    },
    {
        'device_type': 'cisco_ios',
        'ip': '172.16.1.4',
        'username': 'user1',
        'password': '1234',
        'secret': '1234' # Enable mode password
    },
]

for device in switchs:
    for vlan_id, vlan_name in [(10, 'V10'), (20, 'V20'),
  (30, 'V30')]:
        configure_vlan(device, vlan_id, vlan_name)

for device in switchs:
    configure_interfaces(device, 'G0/1', 10)
    configure_interfaces(device, 'G0/2', 20)
```

7. Remove all previously configured VLANs before starting the next section.
8. Open the **TP2.py** file and fill in the connection variables.
9. Modify the **TP2.py** file to perform the following tasks:
   - Create VLANs: 10, 20, 30, and 40
   - Configure G0/3 to G0/8 interfaces in "**Access**" mode.

Part C: Introduction to Network Programming with the Python Language

- The purpose of the **TP3.py** program is to connect to Cisco elements, configure interfaces in **"Trunk"** mode, and perform inter-VLAN routing.

1. Using the configure_interfaces(device, interface, vlan_id) function in TP2.py as a reference, define the function configure_interfaces_Trunk(device, interface, vlan_id) to configure an interface in "Trunk" mode.
2. Save the result as a TP3.py file.
3. Run the TP3.py file to configure the appropriate interfaces in "Trunk" mode.
4. Check the result.
5. Define the **configure_vlan_routing (device, interface, vlan_id, ip_address)** function to configure inter-VLAN routing on router R1 and add it to the **TP3.py** file.
   For instance, calling **configure_vlan_routing(device, 'G0/0', 10, '192.168.10.1')** will produce the following results:
   - Create the G0/0.10 sub-interface.
   - Assign the sub-interface to VLAN 10.
   - Assign IP address 192.168.10.1 to the sub-interface.
6. Run the **TP3.py** script again to verify correct inter-VLAN routing between VLANs 10 and 20.
7. Check the result.
8. Add two Virtual PC Simulator (VPCS) hosts: PC1 assigned to VLAN10 and PC2 assigned to VLAN20, and make sure, once they've been configured, that communication is established among them.

Lab 4: SDN and RESTful API Integration

Objectives

- Understanding SDN architecture
- Understand and use RESTful APIs.

Case Study

This case study examines the foundations of an SDN architecture and explores the use of RESTful APIs to interact with programmable networks. It highlights how RESTful APIs enable network elements to be integrated and controlled in an automated way, offering greater flexibility and efficiency in the management of SDN network infrastructures.

Software to Use

- **GNS3 or equivalent**
- **Postman**

Network Topology

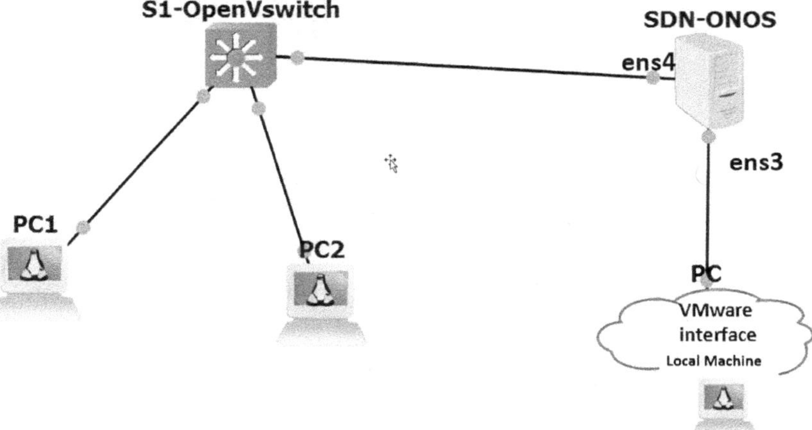

IP Address Table

Emulated Device	Device	Interface	IP Address/ Subnet Mask	Default Gateway
ONOS Controller (Ubuntu-based)	SDN-ONOS	ens3	172.16.1.10/24	–
ONOS Controller (Ubuntu-based)	SDN-ONOS	ens4	192.168.1.10/24	–
Open vSwitch (v2.4.90)	S1-OpenVswitch	br0	192.168.1.20/24	–
VPCS	PC1	NIC	192.168.1.100/24	–
VPCS	PC2	NIC	192.168.1.110/24	–
GNS3 Cloud	Local Machine	VMware Interface	172.16.1.1/24	–

Part A: Establish Basic Device Configuration

1. Create the network topology.
2. Assign IP addresses to device interfaces according to the addressing table.
   Note:
   - Use the command: ifconfig to configure an IP address on PC1, PC2, and SDN-ONOS. Example:

```
ifconfig ens3 192.168.1.10 netmask 255.255.255.0 up
```

   - To configure the S1-OpenVswitch, you can create and use a **configOVS.sh** file. Modify it and run it. The contents of **configOVS.sh** are as follows:

```
sudo ovs-vsctl add-br br0
sudo ovs-vsctl add-port br0 eth0
sudo ovs-vsctl add-port br0 eth1
sudo ovs-vsctl add-port br0 eth2
sudo ovs-vsctl add-port br0 eth3
sudo ifconfig br0 192.168.1.20 netmask 255.255.255.0
sudo ovs-vsctl set-controller br0 tcp:192.168.1.10:6633 # Connect
  OVS to the SDN controller (ONOS)
sudo ovs-ofctl -O OpenFlow13 show br0
sudo ovs-ofctl mod-flows br0 "priority=0,actions=normal"
sudo ovs-vsctl set bridge br0 other-config:datapath
  -id=0000000000000001
```

3. Verify the connectivity between all network devices by performing **ping** tests.
4. On the SDN-ONOS server, log in as "**root**" with a password "**root**". Start the SDN controller using the **onos.s'** script or appropriate commands.
5. On the Local Machine, open a web browser:
   a. Type in the URL: http://172.16.1.10:8181/onos/ui/

      Note: If the ONOS home page does not appear, please stop the ONOS service by pressing [Ctrl+D]. Then start ONOS with the following commands:

```
cd onos2/apache-karaf-3.0.8/bin # the 'bin' file path
./karaf clean
```

b. Enter login "**karaf**" and password "**karaf**".
c. Confirm that the S1-OpenVswitch appears correctly in the network topology.
d. Verify that both PCs are displayed in the "**Hosts**" list.

Note: After associating the switch with ONOS, **ping** communication will temporarily stop working.

Part B: Review the Basics of SDN Architecture and RESTful APIs

1. Place each element of the table according to its corresponding position on the following figure.

1- Management plane	2- Control plane	3- Data plane	4- NorthBound Interface
5- Southbound Interface	6- API NorthBound	7- API Southbound	8- SDN controller
9- SDN-ONOS	10 - S1-OpenVswitch	11- OpenFlow	12- Web browser
13- Postman	14- RESTful	15- CLI	16- Python

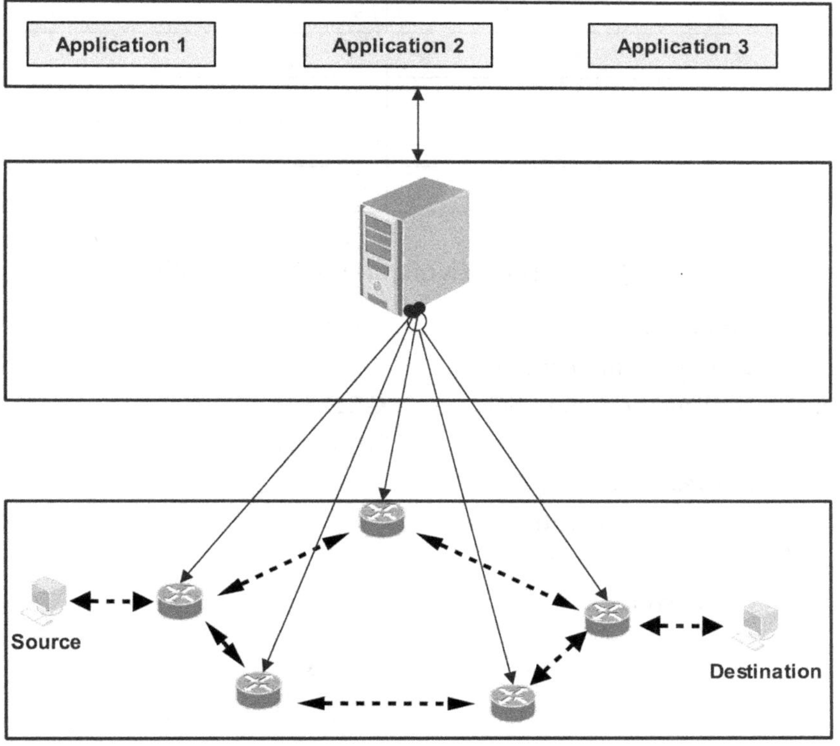

2. Recall three advantages of an SDN architecture.

1	
2	
3	

3. Which of the following characteristics are associated with RESTful APIs?
   - Use of standard http/https protocols
   - Permanent data storage on the server
   - Use flexible formats such as JSON, XML, and HTML
   - Use of client/server architecture
   - Each request is processed independently
   - RESTful Web services support caching
4. Match each RESTful method to its correct functionality

A	B	C	D	E
Create a new resource	Recover a resource	Delete a resource	Update an existing resource	Make partial updates to a resource

GET	
PUT	
POST	
DELETE	
PATCH	

Part C: Exploring RESTful Methods for Configuring and Controlling SDN Networks

1. Start the **Postman** software.
2. Set up a **GET** request in **Postman:**
   - In the REST method input field, select **GET**.
   - For the URL, enter http://172.16.1.10:8181/onos/v1/devices.
   - For **Authorization:**
     - Choose the **Basic Auth** type.
     - Enter Username: **karaf**.
     - Enter password: **karaf"**.

3. Analyze the result and identify the names of the fields shown in the figure below:


```
{
    "devices": [
        {
            "id": "of:0000000000000001",        1
            "type": "SWITCH",
            "available": true,
            "role": "MASTER",
            "mfr": "Nicira, Inc.",
            "hw": "Open vSwitch",
            "sw": "2.4.90",
            "serial": "None",
            "driver": "ovs",
            "chassisId": "1",
            "lastUpdate": "1702050206716",
            "humanReadableLastUpdate": "connected 6m32s ago",
            "annotations": {
                "channelId": "192.168.1.20:42129",
                "managementAddress": "192.168.1.20",        2
                "protocol": "OF_13"        3
            }
        }
    ]
}
```


4. Referring to the result obtained, what is the name of the data format used by the SDN controller to generate this response?
5. For each **RESTful URL** element listed in the first column, identify and note the corresponding part of the "GET http://172.16.1.10:8181/onos/v1/devices" request in the second column.

RESTful URL Element	**Corresponding Part of URL**
RESTful method	
Protocol	
SDN controller IP address	
Port	
API path base	
API version	
Resource or endpoint	

6. Retrieve and **show** the list of currently connected hosts (PC1 and PC2).
   Use the following **GET** request: http://172.16.1.10:8181/onos/v1/hosts/
7. Retrieve detailed information about host PC1.
   Use the following **GET** request: http://172.16.1.10:8181/onos/v1/hosts/ [PC1 ID]
   Note: The ID of PC1 should be extracted from the previously executed **GET** request (list of hosts). It corresponds to the MAC address of PC1.
8. Display **OpenFlow flow** on S1-OpenVswitch.
   Use the following **GET** request: http://172.16.1.10:8181/onos/v1/flows/ of:0000000000000001

9. Delete an **OpenFlow** rule on S1-OpenVswitch:
   - Identify the **arp** protocol and flow **Id**

```
"flows": [
        {
            "id": "281478909873038",      ⇐ flow Id
            ....
....

            },
            "selector": {
                "criteria": [
                    {
                        "type": "ETH_TYPE",
                        "ethType": "0x806"    ⇐ Arp protocol
                    }
                ]
            }
        },
```

   - Use the **DELETE** method.
   - Use the following URL:
     http://172.16.1.10:8181/onos/v1/flows/of:0000000000000001/[Flow ID]
     Note: The Flow ID must be extracted from a previously executed **GET** request that lists all flows. It corresponds to the unique identifier of the flow you want to retrieve.
   - Set up authentication in the Authorization section (Basic Auth).
   - Execute the query.
   - Confirm the flow deletion using a subsequent **GET** request.
   - Verify via the ONOS GUI that the flow has been successfully deleted.
10. Add an OpenFlow entry to S1-OpenVswitch:
    - Apply the **POST** method.
    - Use the following URL:
      http://172.16.1.10:8181/onos/v1/flows/of:0000000000000001
    - Set up authentication in the Authorization section (Basic Auth)
    - In the **"Body"** zone:
      - Select the **"raw"** option
      - In the drop-down box, change the "**text**" option to "**JSON**".

– In the text box, enter the following **JSON** text:

```
{
    "priority": 0,
    "timeout": 0,
    "isPermanent": true,
    "deviceId": "of:0000000000000001",
    "treatment": {
        "instructions": [
            {
                "type": "OUTPUT",
                "port": "NORMAL"
            }
        ]
    },
    "selector": {
        "criteria": [
            {
                "type": "ETH_TYPE",
                "ethType": "0x800"
            }
        ]
    }
}
```

- Run the query.
- Confirm the flow addition by using the following **GET** request.
- Verify via the ONOS GUI that the flow has been successfully added.

11. Add another **OpenFlow entry** on the S1-OpenVswitch, using the following **JSON** file:

```
{
    "priority: 10,
    "timeout: 0,
    "isPermanent": true,
    "deviceId": "of:0000000000000001",
    "treatment": {
        "instructions": [
            {
                "type": "OUTPUT",
                "port": "NORMAL
            }
        ]
    },
    "selector": {
        "criteria": [
```

```
                {
                    "type": "ETH_TYPE",
                    "ethType": "0x806"
                }
            ]
        }
    }
```

- Ensure that the flow has been added via the ONOS GUI.

12. Verify that the ping communication is restored between all network devices.

3

The OpenFlow Protocol

The OpenFlow protocol, the cornerstone of software-defined networking (SDN), represents a significant advance in the management and orchestration of computer networks. This chapter will detail the many facets of this protocol, first examining its intrinsic advantages in facilitating more flexible, centralized management of data flows. We will then explore the various versions of the OpenFlow protocol, highlighting the evolutions and improvements made over time.

OpenFlow's architecture and key components will be analyzed to understand how they integrate and function in a network environment. This will be followed by an in-depth discussion of OpenFlow's switch table management and the crucial role it plays in efficient packet routing.

Next, we'll look at the specifics of the flow table and flow entries, essential elements that enable OpenFlow to direct traffic dynamically and adaptively. OpenFlow messages, which facilitate communication between the various network components, will also be examined to illustrate their importance in the overall functioning of the protocol.

The section on how OpenFlow works will provide a detailed overview of operational processes, while the comparison with other SDN protocols will put OpenFlow's uniqueness and efficiency in the modern network ecosystem into perspective.

In short, this chapter aims to provide a comprehensive understanding of the OpenFlow Protocol, demonstrating its indispensable role in the SDN network revolution.

This chapter covers the following topics:

1. Introduction
2. Advantages of the OpenFlow protocol
3. OpenFlow protocol versions
4. Architecture and components of an OpenFlow architecture
5. Table management and role in OpenFlow switching
6. Flow table and flow entries
7. OpenFlow messages
8. How openflow works
9. OpenFlow ecosystem and switch management
10. Other SDN protocols
11. Conclusion.

DOI: 10.1201/9781003679394-3

3.1 Introduction

OpenFlow is a central protocol in the architecture of SDN. It enables a centralized SDN controller to communicate with network switches, facilitating the dynamic management and configuration of network traffic. A common misconception is that OpenFlow and SDN are interchangeable. In reality, OpenFlow is simply one of many protocols that enable the implementation of SDN technology, but it does not in itself define what an SDN network is. SDN is broader, encompassing concepts of network orchestration and control far beyond OpenFlow alone.

3.2 Benefits of the OpenFlow Protocol

One of the main advantages of OpenFlow is that it is an open standard, initially developed by Stanford University and subsequently managed by the Open Networking Foundation (ONF). This promotes a high level of interoperability among hardware manufacturers and software developers, driving continuous innovation in the networking industry.

The main advantages of the OpenFlow protocol include the following:

- **Increased interoperability:** As an open standard, OpenFlow enables harmonized communication between SDN controllers and switches from different manufacturers, reducing technological and commercial barriers.
- **Easier innovation:** OpenFlow's open, standardized nature encourages a dynamic community of developers and engineers, accelerating the development of new network functionalities and technologies.
- **Centralized management:** OpenFlow enables centralized management of network switches, facilitating network programming and configuration from a central point. This increases network efficiency and responsiveness to changes.
- **Adaptability:** OpenFlow's architecture enables networks to adapt quickly to the evolving needs of applications and services, providing greater flexibility to meet dynamic demands.

3.3 OpenFlow Protocol Versions

Since its introduction, OpenFlow has undergone several updates, each introducing new features and enhancements to meet the evolving needs of network management.

- **OpenFlow 1.0 (2008):** The very first version of the protocol. It laid the foundations for communication between controllers and switches.
- **OpenFlow 1.1 (2011):** This update introduced major enhancements, including support for multiple flow tables and improved support for port aggregation.

- **OpenFlow 1.2 (2011):** This release mainly strengthened and clarified some of the earlier specifications.
- **OpenFlow 1.3 (2012):** Probably one of the most popular and widely adopted versions. It introduced essential features such as support for switching groups, tunneling, and quality of service (QoS).
- **OpenFlow 1.4 (2013):** This release focused on operational robustness, with improvements for flow table management, controller synchronization, and the ability to identify and manage specific equipment characteristics.
- **OpenFlow 1.5 (2014):** Introduced advanced features, including enhanced packet processing, monitoring, and security.
- **OpenFlow 1.6 (2016):** Version 1.6 of OpenFlow, released in September 2016, brought significant improvements in terms of flow table management, support for multicasting, and advanced measurement features.

Each OpenFlow version has been designed to meet the changing needs of modern networks. Network administrators should familiarize themselves with the different versions to choose the one best suited to their specific needs.

3.4 Components of an OpenFlow Architecture

- We can distinguish three key components in an OpenFlow architecture (Figure 3.1):

- **The controller:** This is the network's central point. As such, it enables routing decisions and network management. It communicates with the switching devices using the OpenFlow protocol.
- **OpenFlow switches:** These hardware devices implement the directives transmitted by the controller. They are equipped with flow tables that establish procedures for processing and directing network traffic.
- **The flow table:** This comprises a set of rules and instructions that govern routing and actions within an OpenFlow switch. Each entry in the flow table defines the treatment to be applied to a given packet and determines its final destination.

3.5 Management and Role of Tables in OpenFlow Switching

In OpenFlow, optimal traffic management relies on a series of tables integrated in the switch's hardware or software. These tables are crucial for filtering, routing, and monitoring network traffic.

There are three types of tables in an OpenFlow system: flow table, group table, and statistics table (Figure 3.2).

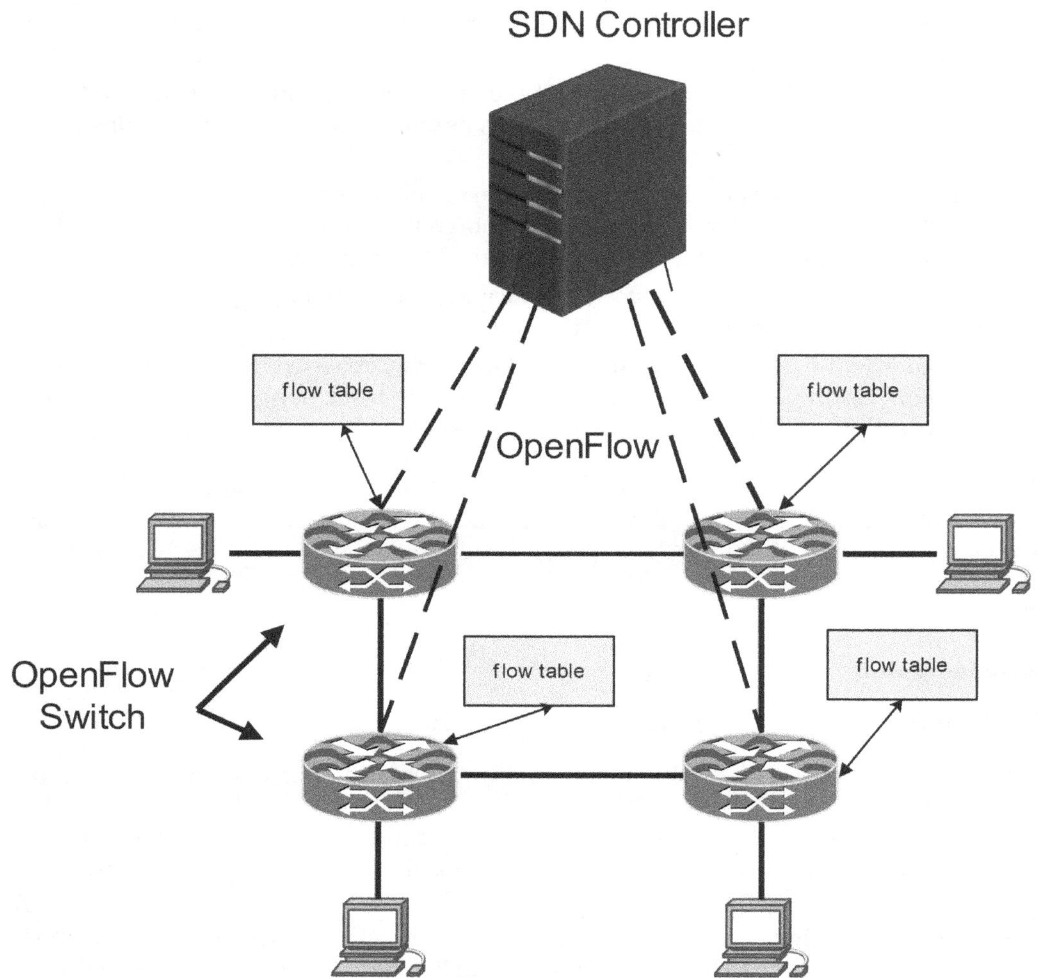

FIGURE 3.1
Centralized network flow management by the SDN controller.

- **Flow table:** At the heart of the system is the flow table. It contains "flow entries", which are essentially access rules. These rules are used to filter and process packets according to specific criteria, such as source IP address, port, and more. In an OpenFlow switch, there may be one or more flow tables. Each flow table is a collection of flow entries, which together define how the switch should handle incoming packets.
- **Group table:** This table offers additional flexibility in traffic management. It provides advanced methods for filtering and forwarding flows, enabling features such as broadcast and multicast. It is essential for efficient management of scenarios where a packet needs to be processed or forwarded to several destinations. Note that an OpenFlow switch can have one or more group tables.
- **Meter table:** This table plays a crucial role in monitoring and controlling network traffic. It gathers statistics on transferred data, providing an overview of network performance. It also supports various QoS operations, including essential

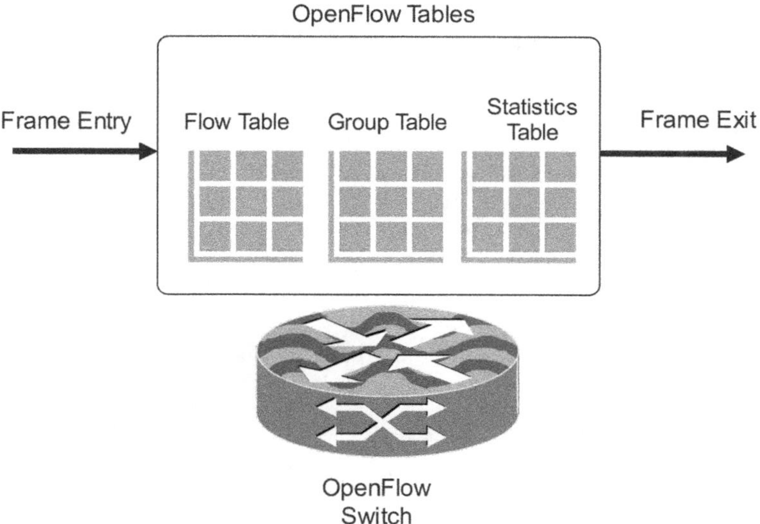

FIGURE 3.2
OpenFlow table structure.

functions such as rate limiting. This ensures that the network operates optimally and that resources are used efficiently.

The combination of these tables offers unrivalled granularity and flexibility in network traffic management, enabling OpenFlow to meet the complex and ever-changing needs of modern networks.

3.6 Flow Table and Flow Entries

3.6.1 Flux Inputs

Flow Entries are the fundamental elements of traffic management in an OpenFlow network. Each flow entry corresponds to a rule that specifies how incoming packets are to be handled and what actions are to be taken.

An incoming packet is first compared with the flow entry matching filters, and when it matches a specific rule, the action associated with that entry is executed. Actions can include forwarding, modifying, or deleting the packet. In addition, statistics are collected for each flow entry, enabling detailed analysis of network traffic and informed decision-making for future network management (Figure 3.3).

Each flow entry consists of several key components (Figure 3.4):

- **A match field:** Identifies certain attributes of the packet (such as source IP address, port, MAC address, etc.).
- **Action:** Determines how the packet is to be processed (transmitted, modified, deleted, etc.).

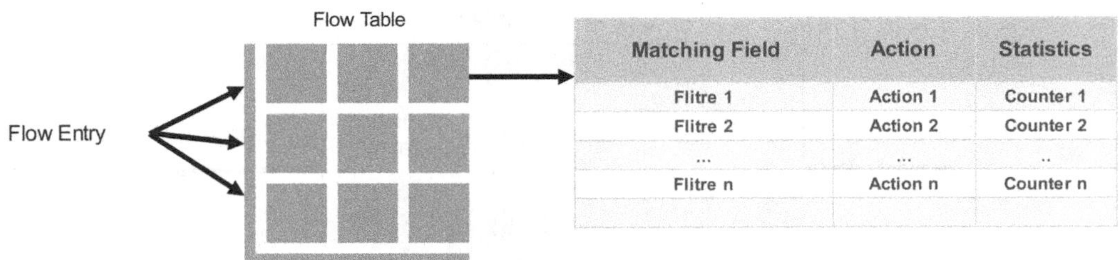

FIGURE 3.3
Internal structure of a flow table in OpenFlow.

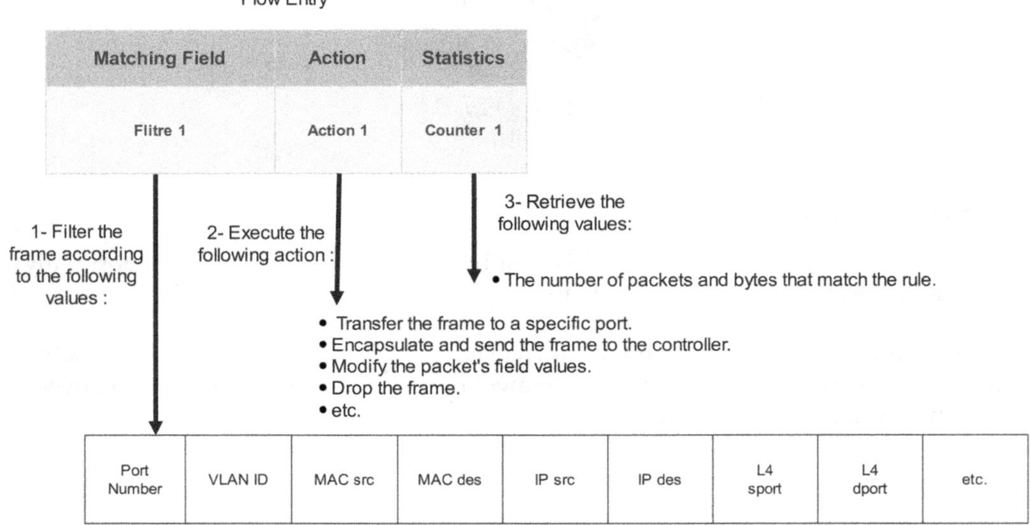

FIGURE 3.4
Structure of a flow input in OpenFlow.

- **Counters:** Keep statistics on the number of packets and bytes that match the rule. Priority can also be assigned to determine the order in which rules are applied.

In this way, flow inputs enable fine, precise traffic management, ensuring that each packet is processed in accordance with the network strategy.

3.6.2 Flux Tables

In the OpenFlow context, each switch contains one or more flow tables that dictate how packets are processed. They are organized hierarchically, enabling sequential routing of traffic through various rules. Each table has distinct capabilities, defined by specific actions or instructions. Together, they ensure that traffic is directed, modified, or filtered according to the precise needs of the network, while avoiding redundancy (Figure 3.5).

The idea behind using multiple flow tables in an OpenFlow switch is not necessarily to process more data, but rather to process data in a more organized and specialized way.

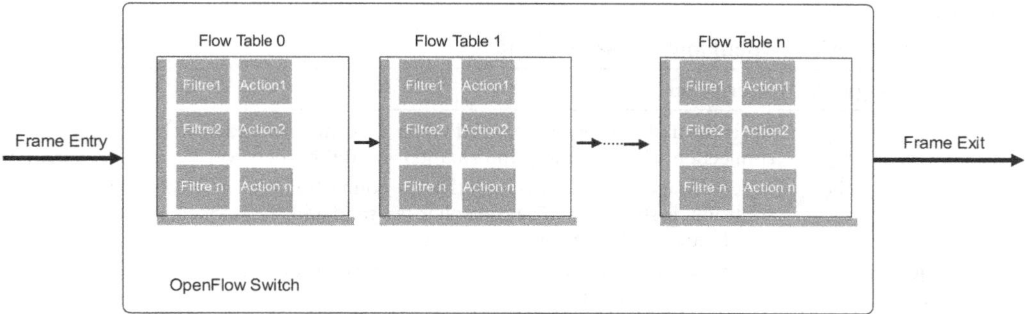

FIGURE 3.5
Flow table processing sequence in OpenFlow.

In fact, by having several flow tables, you can specialize each table to handle a certain type of traffic or perform a certain type of processing. For example, one table could focus on the initial classification of packets (determining whether they are voice, data, or video), another table could focus on routing, another on QoS policies for Voice over IP, and so on.

This offers great flexibility and enables fine-tuned traffic management. For example, if a packet is identified as voice, it could be treated with a higher priority or directed in a specific way thanks to the specialized table for voice traffic.

However, it is essential to note that the way these tables are organized and used depends on network policy and configuration.

3.7 OpenFlow Messages

3.7.1 OpenFlow Message Types

OpenFlow works using a series of messages that are exchanged between controllers and switches. These messages fall into four main categories:

- **Controller-to-switch messages:** These are directives sent by the controller to manage or query a switch. For example, a "Flow Mod" message is used to modify a switch's flow table.
- **Asymmetrical messages:** These are messages that can be sent at any time, unsolicited. An example is a "Packet-In" message, where a switch sends a packet to the controller for instructions.
- **Switch messages to the controller:** These messages are usually in response to a request from the controller. For example, a "Flow Removed" message informs the controller that a flow table entry has been removed.
- **Symmetrical messages:** These messages can be initiated by any party, switch, or controller, and have no direct correspondence. An example is the "Echo" message, used to check connectivity between the switch and controller.

These messages form the backbone of OpenFlow communication, facilitating seamless and dynamic interaction between controllers and switches.

TABLE 3.1

Description of the Main OpenFlow Messages

OpenFlow Message	Description
Hello Message	This is the first message exchanged when the controller and switch establish a connection. They exchange information about the OpenFlow versions they support.
Echo Request and Echo Reply	These messages are used to check that the connection between the switch and the controller is still active. The controller can send an Echo Request to the switch, which must reply with an Echo Reply.
Features Request and Features Reply	After the connection has been established, the controller asks for the switch's features, such as available ports, capacities, and so forth.
PACKET-IN	This message is sent from the switch to the controller when the switch receives a packet that it doesn't know how to handle (e.g., no matching flow is found). The controller then decides what to do with the packet.
FLOW-MOD	Sent from the controller to the switch to add, modify, or delete entries in the switch's flow table.
Error Message	In the event of an error, such as a badly formed message or an unsupported action, the switch or controller may send an error message.

3.7.2 OpenFlow Key Messages

OpenFlow communication between a switch and a controller is complex and varies according to the OpenFlow version used, the specific network configuration, and the programming parameters of the switch and controller. The following interactions represent typical examples of OpenFlow messages with a brief description of their role and operation (Table 3.1):

3.8 How OpenFlow Works

At the heart of the OpenFlow mechanism are the flow tables built into each switch. These tables contain defined rules that instruct the switch how to handle incoming packets. For each packet received, the switch searches for a matching rule in its flow tables, and if found, executes the associated action, such as forwarding, modifying or dropping the packet.

The "Table-miss" concept plays an essential role in OpenFlow's processing flow, acting as a safety net for packets that don't match any existing rules in the flow tables. When a packet fails to find a match, the "Table-miss" condition is applied. This condition usually results in the packet being sent to the SDN controller, indicating the absence of a predefined action for this packet. The controller can then decide either to process the packet immediately or to add new rules to the flow table to handle similar packets in the future.

The following diagram illustrates in detail the decision-making process adopted by an OpenFlow switch when a new packet arrives. It also includes an explanation of the interaction between the SDN controller and the switch, including the messages exchanged between them, which are crucial for efficient and responsive network management (Figure 3.6).

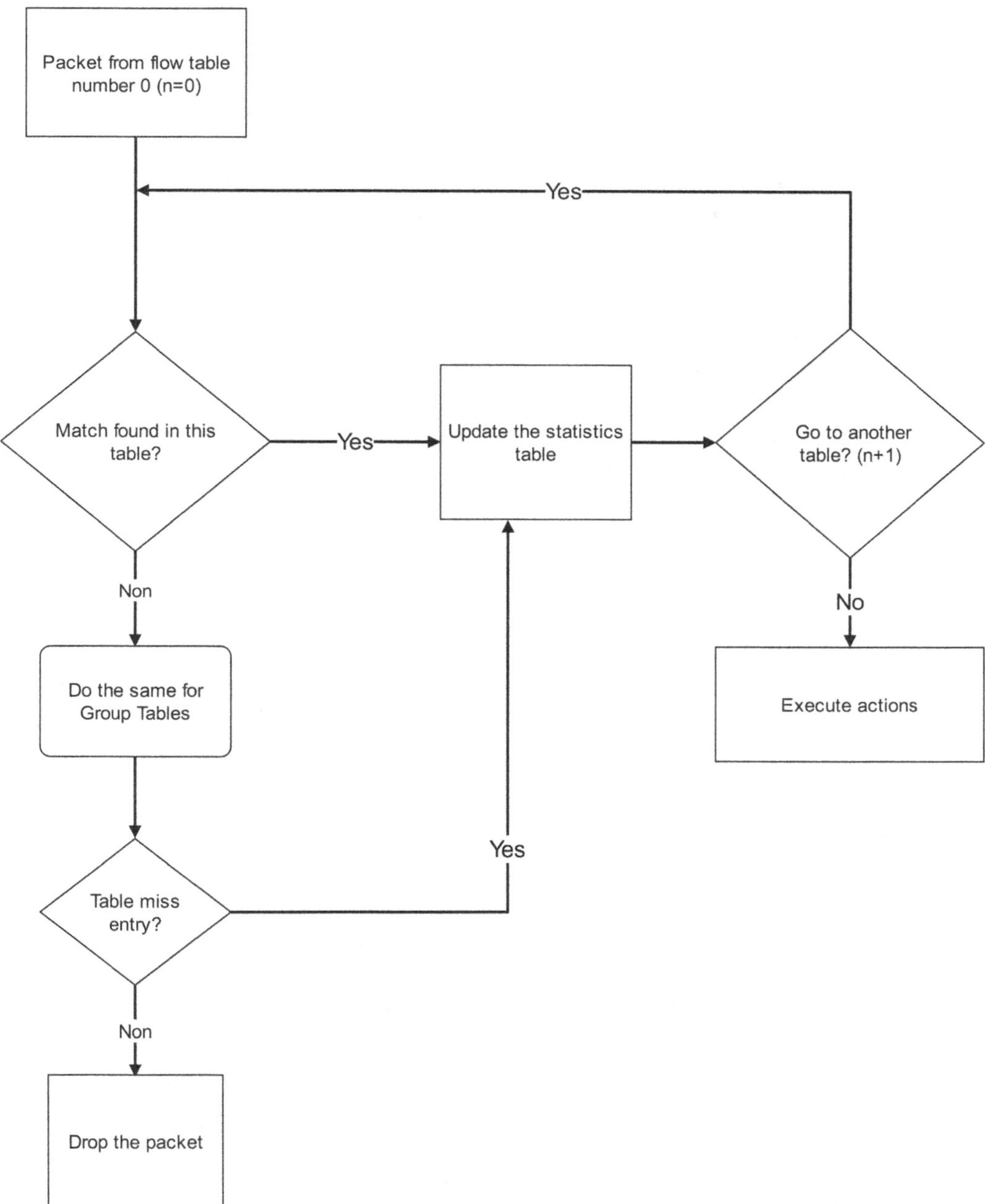

FIGURE 3.6
Packet processing flow diagram with OpenFlow.

1. **Packet arrival:** A packet arrives at the switch and is first processed by flow table 0.
2. **Match search:** The switch searches its flow tables for a rule that matches the packet headers. If a match is found in the current table (up to table n), it proceeds to the next step. Otherwise, it checks whether a 'Table-miss' instruction exists.

- **Match found:** If the packet matches an entry in the flow tables, the counters associated with this rule are updated. These counters can record the number of packets and bytes that have matched the rule.
- **Match not found in the flow table:** After completing processing with flow tables, the process continues with group tables to identify any matches and execute the specified actions.
- **Table-miss:** If there is no match and a 'Table-miss' instruction exists, the packet can be sent to the SDN controller. This is usually done via a PACKET-IN message. The controller then analyzes the packet and decides how to handle it, for example, by adding a new flow entry to the switch via a FLOW-MOD message.
- **No match or table-miss:** If no match is found and there is no table-miss entry, the packet is dropped. This means that the packet does not match any known rule and there is no directive to forward it to the controller, so it is discarded by the switch.

3. **Decision to go to another table:** If the corresponding flow rule contains an instruction to check another table, the packet is sent to this table for further evaluation. This process can be repeated several times, depending on the configuration of the flow and group tables.
4. **Execute actions:** If the packet is not to be sent to another table, or after traversing the necessary tables, the switch executes the actions specified by the last flow match found. These actions may include transmitting the packet to a specific port, modifying certain fields in the packet header, or encapsulating and sending the packet to the controller.

3.9 OpenFlow Ecosystem and Switch Management

3.9.1 Products Supporting the OpenFlow Protocol

With the rise of SDN, many manufacturers are adopting OpenFlow-compatible devices to leverage their advanced network management and programmability features. Here's a list of the main products supporting OpenFlow, each with a description of its features.

- **Open vSwitch (OVS):** This is a virtual switch specifically designed for data center environments, but it can also be installed on equipment dedicated to physical switching. It enables advanced traffic management and integration with various hypervisors such as Xen, KVM, and VMware. OVS is commonly used in software-defined networks (SDN) to offer greater flexibility and programmability. Google has adopted OVS in its SDN environment to optimize network operations and improve performance, contributing to its popularity and evolution.
- **HP 5400 zl switch series:** The HP 5400 zl switch series supports OpenFlow and offers high performance with a modular architecture. These switches are ideal for large enterprises and data centers, offering reliable, scalable connectivity.
- **Cisco Nexus 3000 series:** Cisco Nexus 3000 switches are high-performance data center devices that support OpenFlow. They are renowned for their low latency

and compatibility with SDN environments, making them a popular choice for modern networks.

- **Dell S4810:** The Dell S4810 is a high-density 10GbE switch that supports OpenFlow. It is suitable for modern data center networks, offering low latency and high switching capacity, while enabling flexible network management.
- **Juniper QFX5100:** This is a range of high-performance switches that support OpenFlow. They are used in data center environments and enterprise networks, offering high flexibility, high performance, and network programmability capabilities.
- **Huawei CloudEngine 12800:** Designed for large-scale data center networks, with support for OpenFlow. They deliver high performance, low latency, and high reliability, suitable for demanding environments.

All these devices offer increased flexibility and operational efficiency, meeting the needs of modern, dynamic network environments. In this document, however, we'll be focusing on the Open vSwitch (OVS) product, because of the features already mentioned, and the possibility of integrating it into practical work for educational purposes.

3.9.2 Open vSwitch Database Management Protocol

a. **Introduction to OVSDB**
   The Open vSwitch Database Management Protocol (OVSDB) protocol is a key component in the management of Open vSwitch (OVS) instances. It enables OVS virtual switches to be configured, managed, and monitored across a network, providing a standardized interface for interacting with network infrastructure components.

b. **OVSDB features**
   - **Configuration management:** OVSDB lets you configure various aspects of OVS instances, including interfaces, bridges, tunnels, and ports. This enables centralized, automated management of network configurations.
   - **Monitoring and statistics:** The protocol offers monitoring functions that track the performance and status of network elements managed by OVS, facilitating problem detection and resolution.
   - **Extensibility:** OVSDB is designed to be extensible, enabling network administrators to add new features and customize configurations to suit the specific needs of their infrastructure.

c. **Interaction with OpenFlow and OVS**
   - **Open vSwitch (OVS):** OVSDB is directly integrated with Open vSwitch, offering complete management of its instances. It enables the configuration and management of virtual switches that execute routing and packet-switching decisions.
   - **OpenFlow:** While OpenFlow is used to manage real-time data flows and control routing decisions, OVSDB supports configuration and status management of network elements. Together, they provide a complete solution for managing software-defined networks (SDN).

3.9.3 Open Vswitch Basic Commands

OVS comes with a set of utilities for configuration and administration. Here are the main command families for administering an OVS switch:

- **ovs-vsctl:** This is the main utility for configuring OVS. You can use it to add, modify, or delete bridges, ports, and interfaces. Some basic commands include the following:
  - **ovs-vsctl add-br:** Add a bridge.
  - **ovs-vsctl del-br:** Delete a bridge.
  - **ovs-vsctl add-port:** Add a port to a bridge.
  - **ovs-vsctl del-port:** Remove a port from a bridge.
  - **ovs-vsctl show:** Display current configuration.

Note: The term "bridge" in the series of commands refers to bridge equipment, which was the ancestor of the switch. The main difference between the two lies in the number of physical ports: the bridge had only two physical ports. In this context, the term "bridge" is still relevant to describe the basic function of connecting several network ports.

- **ovs-ofctl:** This utility is used to manipulate and query OpenFlow flow tables on OVS. Some common commands include the following:
  - **ovs-ofctl add-flow:** Add a flow rule.
  - **ovs-ofctl del-flows:** Delete one or more flow rules.
  - **ovs-ofctl dump-flows:** Display current flow rules.
  - **ovs-ofctl show:** Show ports and their status.
- **ovs-dpctl:** This tool is used to manage OVS datapaths. Although most administrators don't interact directly with ovs-dpctl that often, it is useful for advanced troubleshooting. The OVS datapath refers to the data plane responsible for processing and transmitting packets across the network.
  - **ovs-dpctl add-dp:** Add a datapath.
  - **ovs-dpctl del-dp:** Delete a datapath.
  - **ovs-dpctl dump-flows:** Display datapath flows.
- **ovs-appctl:** This is a utility for controlling running applications. It can be used to obtain status information, change certain configurations, or trigger specific actions.
  - **ovs-appctl fdb/show:** Display the FDB (Forwarding Database) table.
  - **ovs-appctl ofproto/trace:** Trace how a packet crosses flow tables.
- **ovsdb-tool:** This tool is used to manipulate and manage OVS databases. Although it is not generally used on a daily basis, it is crucial for tasks such as database upgrades.

3.10 Other SDN Protocols

3.10.1 Limitations and Challenges of the OpenFlow Protocol

Although the OpenFlow protocol has revolutionized network management by introducing unprecedented flexibility, it is not without its challenges and limitations. In what follows, we'll explore some of the main obstacles and concerns associated with OpenFlow adoption.

- **Performance:** OpenFlow is based on the principle of separating control and data planes. This can potentially introduce latencies, particularly when the controller has to process a large number of inputs and outputs.
- **Controller dependency problems:** With OpenFlow, routing logic is centralized on one controller. If this controller fails or becomes a bottleneck, it can compromise the integrity of the entire network.
- **Security:** OpenFlow controllers, if not properly secured, can become attractive targets for attackers.

3.10.2 Other Popular Protocols

While OpenFlow dominated the initial SDN landscape, other protocols have emerged to meet different or complementary requirements.

While OpenFlow focuses on managing packet flows, other protocols may focus on device configuration, topology information exchange, or network policy definition. This variety of approaches offers network engineers a palette of tools adapted to a multitude of scenarios.

In addition to OpenFlow, protocols such as OpFlex, Netconf, and P4, among others, have gained in popularity in the SDN field. Each of these protocols meets specific needs and has its own advantages and limitations.

3.10.3 Comparison between OpenFlow and OpFlex

Faced with the limitations of OpenFlow, Cisco has developed OpFlex. OpFlex offers greater flexibility in network configuration and aims to provide better integration with existing Cisco equipment and solutions. OpFlex is also more resilient and optimized for large-scale deployments. However, it is essential to note that the choice between OpenFlow and OpFlex will largely depend on the specific needs and network infrastructure preferences of each organization.

While Cisco introduced OpFlex in response to the challenges of OpenFlow, a key distinction lies in their fundamental approach to network management.

- **Imperative (OpenFlow):** OpenFlow follows an imperative approach where the controller dictates exactly how the switch should handle each packet, step by step. In other words, it gives precise instructions on how to handle the traffic.
- **Declarative (OpFlex):** OpFlex, on the other hand, takes a declarative approach. Rather than saying exactly how to do things, it simply describes what needs to be

achieved, leaving the details of implementation to the peripherals. It's like defining the objective or desired result without specifying the exact process for getting there.

When you define a high-level policy such as, for example, "**I want these two PCs to be able to communicate with each other only without any other access**", the SDN controller (which uses the OpFlex protocol) will interpret this policy and translate this objective into a series of actions and configurations for the network. This amounts to the following process:

- The administrator defines a declarative policy "I want these two PCs to be able to communicate with each other only".
- The SDN controller, using the OpFlex protocol, translates this declaration into a series of specific instructions for the network devices.
- These instructions could include:
  - Create a VXLAN extension (or other isolation mechanism) to segment the two PCs from the rest of the network.
  - Configure switches to add these two PCs to this specific VXLAN.
  - Establish access rules to ensure that only these two PCs can communicate with each other within this VXLAN, and block all other unwanted traffic.

The key idea is that the administrator simply defines the objective (the declarative approach) and the SDN controller, using protocols like OpFlex, takes care of the technical details to achieve that objective.

This contrast between imperative and declarative approaches is essential to understanding the fundamental differences between these two protocols.

3.11 Conclusion

In short, the OpenFlow Protocol is a crucial element of software-defined networks, offering flexibility and centralized management that are transforming the way networks are designed and operated. By exploring its versions, architecture, and components, we've been able to understand its strategic and technical importance. OpenFlow flow tables, flow entries, and messages play a central role in the fluidity and efficiency of data routing, underlining OpenFlow's ability to adapt to the growing demands of modern networks. By comparing OpenFlow with other SDN protocols, it becomes clear that this protocol is not just a component of today's network infrastructure, but also a vector for future network innovation. This chapter has thus enabled us to fully grasp the impact and possibilities offered by OpenFlow in the evolving landscape of network technologies.

Lab 5: SDN Architecture and Flow Control with OpenVSwitch and OpenFlow

Objectives

- Understand SDN architecture.
- Understand and use OpenVswitch commands.
- Understand the OpenFlow protocol.

Case Study

This case study explores the use of OpenVSwitch commands for virtual network management and examines the OpenFlow protocol, which enables precise control of data flows in SDN networks. It highlights how these tools and protocols facilitate flexible, centralized management of network infrastructures, while offering more granular control of network communications.

Software to Use

- **GNS3 or equivalent**

Network Topology

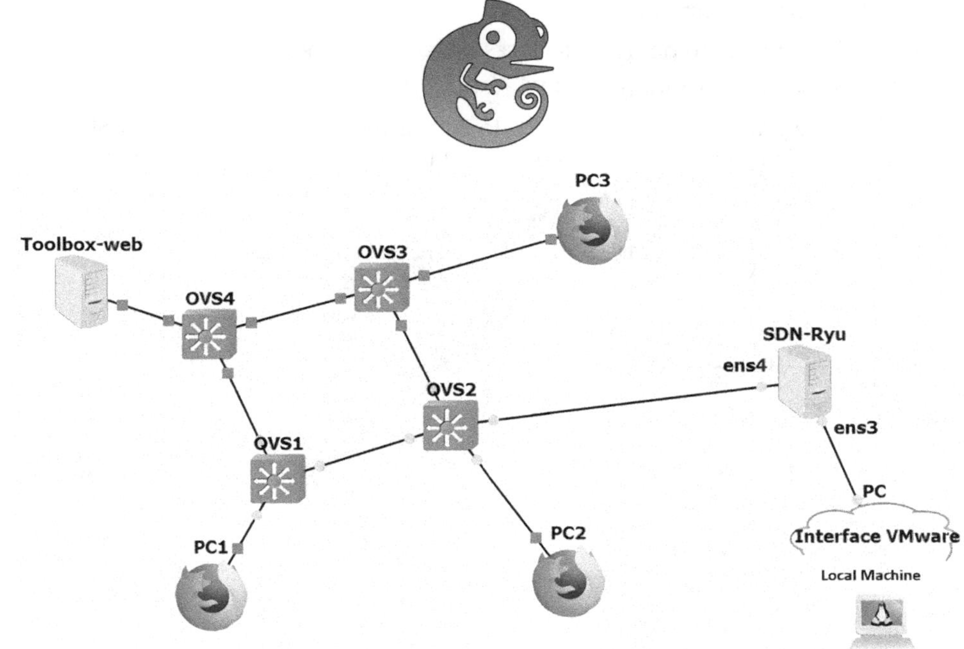

IP Address Table

Emulated Device	Device	Interface	IP Address/Subnet Mask
Ryu Controller (Ubuntu Linux, FlowManager)	SDN-Ryu	ens3	172.16.1.10/24
Ryu Controller (Ubuntu Linux, FlowManager)	SDN-Ryu	ens4	192.168.1.10/24
Docker OpenVswitch Or Open vSwitch (v2.4.90)	OVS1	br0	192.168.1.20/24
Docker OpenVswitch Or Open vSwitch (v2.4.90)	OVS2	br0	192.168.1.21/24
Docker OpenVswitch Or Open vSwitch (v2.4.90)	OVS3	br0	192.168.1.22/24
Docker OpenVswitch Or Open vSwitch (v2.4.90)	OVS4	br0	192.168.1.23/24
Docker Webterm	PC1	eth0	192.168.1.100/24
Docker Webterm	PC2	eth0	192.168.1.110/24
Docker Webterm	PC3	eth0	192.168.1.120/24
Docker Toolbox	Toolbox-web		192.168.1.200/24
GNS3 Cloud	Local Machine	VMware Interface	172.16.1.1/24

Part A: Establish Basic Device Configuration

1. Create the network topology.
2. Assign IP addresses to device interfaces based on the addressing table.
   a. IP address configuration on SDN-Ryu:

      Use the graphical user interface to configure the IP addresses on SDN-Ryu. You can also use the **ifconfig** command to configure them. For example:

```
ifconfig ens3 192.168.1.10 netmask 255.255.255.0 up.
```

```
# Static config for eth0
auto eth0
iface eth0 inet static
address 192.168.1.100
netmask 255.255.255.0
# gateway 192.168.0.1
```

b. Configuring OpenVswitch switches

Note: The commands presented below are intended for the **Docker Open vSwitch** environment. If you are using **Open vSwitch (v2.4.90)** or another installation, some commands may differ. In that case, please refer to **Lab 4** for appropriate instructions.

- Start OVS switches one by one to prevent STP loop.
- To assign an IP address to the br0 bridge:

```
sudo ifconfig br0 192.168.1.20 netmask 255.255.255.0. # for OVS1
```

Note: The IP address shown here is for OVS1. The IP addresses for the other OVS switches (e.g., OVS2, OVS3, etc.) are listed in the **IP Address Table** provided. Make sure to assign the correct IP for each switch according to that table.

- To connect this switch to the SDN controller:

```
sudo ovs-vsctl set-controller br0 tcp:192.168.1.10:6633.
```

- To assign a name and identify the switch OVS:

```
sudo ovs-vsctl set bridge br0 other-config:datapath-id=0000000000000
  00[id]
```

Note: The [id] should be replaced with a unique hexadecimal identifier (e.g., 1, 2, etc.) that distinguishes this switch OVS. This ID will be used by the ONOS controller to recognize the switch as of:000000000000000[id].

- Enable OpenFlow protocol version 1.3:

```
sudo ovs-ofctl -O OpenFlow13 show br0
```

- To activate the STP protocol:

```
sudo ovs-vsctl set Bridge br0 stp_enable=true
```

3. Ping the network elements and ensure connectivity between them.

4. On the SDN-Ryu server, start the SDN controller using the command:

```
ryu-manager ~/flowmanager/flowmanager.py ryu.app.simple_switch_13
```

Note: The Python runtime window must remain active during the test to ensure that the Ryu service is operational. We recommend using an SSH connection, via **PuTTY**, to run Ryu commands.

5. On Local Machine, launch a web browser:
   a. Enter the following URL: http://172.16.1.10:8080/home/index.html.
   b. Verify that all switches are displayed in the network topology.

Part B: Recall the Architecture and Components of an OpenFlow Architecture

1. Recall the three essential components of an OpenFlow architecture.
2. Link each item in the table with its corresponding definition.

1. Flow Table	A. It allows you to manage multicast and broadcast traffic more efficiently. It can be used to redirect packets to multiple destinations or to apply specific filtering rules.
2. Group Table	B. It collects information on the traffic passing through the switch. This information can be used to monitor the network, control quality of service, or optimize bandwidth utilization.
3. Statistics Table	C. It is a list of rules that determine how the switch should handle packets. These rules can be based on criteria such as source or destination IP address, TCP or UDP port, or data type.

3. Recall three advantages of an OpenFlow architecture:

1	
2	
3	

4. Explain components **1, 2,** and **3** of a Flux Input:

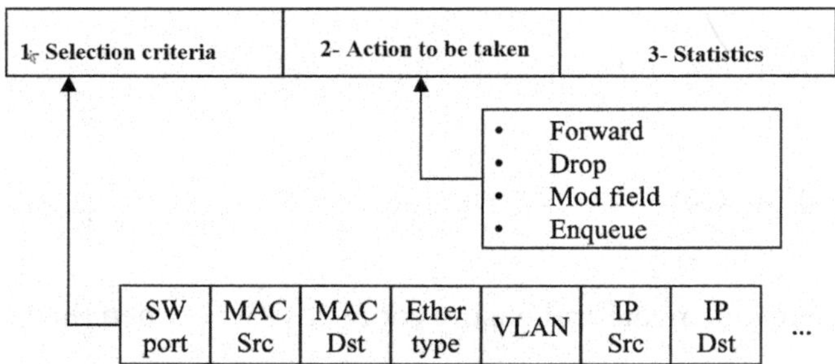

Part C: Handling and Managing Flow Tables in OpenFlow

1. Display the configuration of the OVS1 switch.
   On the **OVS1** switch, use the command:

```
ovs-vsctl show
```

2. Display the flow table of switch **OVS1.**
   On the **OVS1** switch, use the command:

```
ovs-ofctl dump-flows br0
```

3. Referring to the output of this command, associate each field with its corresponding field in the following table:

```
cookie=0x0, duration=44.013s, table=0, n_packets=33, n_bytes=2170,
  priority=1, in_port=eth2,dl_src=de:bf:a3:9b:4e:1b,dl_
  dst=06:7a:39:56:3c:ed actions=output:eth1
```

Flow Table number	
Criteria priority	
Selection criteria	
Action to be taken	
Number of packages matching this criterion	

4. Referring to the following output, associate each field with the corresponding category in the table:

```
cookie=0x0, duration=124.897s, table=0, n_packets=14, n_bytes=728,
  priority=0 actions=CONTROLLER:65535
```

Flow Table number	
Criteria priority	
Selection criteria	
Action to be taken	
Number of packages matching this criterion	

5. Add a flow rule on switch OVS1 to block **ping** requests between PC1 and Toolbox-web.
   a. Execute the following command on OVS1.

```
sudo ovs-ofctl add-flow br0 "priority=10, icmp, nw_src=192.168.1.100,
  nw_dst=192.168.1.200, actions=drop"
```

   b. On the Local Machine, use the web interface to check that the rule has been added to OVS1.
   c. On PC1, execute a **ping** command to verify that the communication between the two devices is blocked
   d. On PC1, check that you have access to the Toolbox-web web page by entering the following URL: http://192.168.1.200
6. Add a flow rule on switch OVS2 to block **TCP** requests to **80** from PC2 to Toolbox-web.
   a. Execute the following command on OVS2.

```
ovs-ofctl add-flow br0 "priority=10, tcp,nw_dst=192.168.1.200, tp_
  dst=80, actions=drop"
```

   b. On the Local Machine, use the web interface to check that the rule has been added to OVS2.
   c. On PC2, use a **ping** command to check that communication between the two elements is authorized.
   d. On PC2, verify that you can't access the Toolbox-web web page by entering the following URL: http://192.168.1.200
7. Add a flow rule on flow table number **1** of switch OVS3 to block TCP requests on port 80 from PC3 to Toolbox-web.
   a. Execute the following command on OVS3.

```
ovs-ofctl add-flow br0 " table=1, priority=10, tcp,nw_
  dst=192.168.1.200, tp_dst=80, actions=drop"
```

   b. On the Local Machine, use the web interface to check that the rule has been added to OVS3.
8. What is the purpose of using multiple flow tables in the OpenFlow protocol?
9. Create a "**Fast Failover**" OpenFlow group table on the OVS4 switch to enable redundancy between ports 2 and 3. This will ensure that if port 2 fails, the switch will automatically switch to port 3.

a. Execute the following command on OVS4

```
ovs-ofctl add-group br0 group_id=1,type=ff,bucket=watch_port:2,
  action=output:2, bucket=watch_port:3,action=output:3
```

b. On the Local Machine, use the web interface to check that the rule has been added to OVS4.

10. Create an OpenFlow group table of type "**Select**" on switch OVS2 to enable load balancing between ports 5 and 6.
   Execute the following command on OVS2.

```
ovs-ofctl add-group br0
  group_id=1,type=select,bucket=output:5,bucket=output:6
```

11. Route all traffic destined to the 192.168.2.0/28 network through ports 5 and 6, so that it is processed by the group table already created.
   a. Execute the following command on OVS2.

```
ovs-ofctl add-flow br0
  "priority=100,ip,nw_dst=192.168.2.0/28,actions=group:1
```

   b. On the **Local Machine**, use the web interface to verify that the two rules have been added to **OVS2**.

12. Configure **QoS** on port 4 of OVS3 to limit throughput to **100 Mbps** for the **172.16.1.0/24** network
   a. Execute the following command on OVS3 to create a **q0** queue and limit the bandwidth:

```
ovs-vsctl set port eth4 qos=@newqos -- --id=@newqos create qos
  type=linux-htb other-config:max-rate=100000000 queues=0=@q0 --
  --id=@q0 create queue other-config:min-rate=8000000
  other-config:max-rate=100000000
```

   b. Execute the following command on **OVS3** to apply the **q0** queue to the traffic of the 172.16.1.0/24 network:

```
ovs-ofctl add-flow br0 "table=2, priority=100, ip,
  nw_dst=172.16.1.0/24, actions=set_queue:0,normal"
```

   c. On the Local Machine, use the web interface to verify that the two rules have been added to **OVS2**.

13. In the context of OpenFlow and SDN networks, what is the description of a "**table-miss**" rule in an OpenVSwitch switch?
    a. A "table-miss" rule is a flow rule with the highest priority in the table, which processes the most important packets.
    b. A "table-miss" rule corresponds to a rule with very specific matching conditions and a defined action for particular types of traffic.
    c. A "table-miss" rule is a special rule that defines the action to be taken for packets that don't match any other rule in the flow table.
    d. A "table-miss" rule is used to redirect all incoming packets to a specific flow table, independently of other rules.
14. What is the "**table-miss**" value of OVS switches?
15. Referring to the roles of the **flow** and group tables you have studied, please create a flowchart illustrating the processing of a packet by the OpenFlow protocol.

Part D: OpenFlow Messages

Referring to the following log messages, indicate the corresponding OpenFlow message type for each line:

OpenFlow message type	Description
CTR => OVS	A message sent by the controller
OVS => CTR	A message sent by the OVS
CTR <=> OVS	A symmetrical message

Log messages	Message type
2023-09-28 14:15:03.257 [DEBUG] [org.ryu.openflowjava.protocol.impl] - Received OpenFlow HELLO message from OVS (192.168.1.20) to Controller (192.168.1.10). Version: OF_13	
2023-09-28 14:16:05.123 [DEBUG] [org.ryu.openflowjava.protocol.impl] - Received OpenFlow SET CONFIG message from OVS (192.168.1.20) to Controller (192.168.1.10). Configuration set to drop fragments.	
2023-09-28 14:16:18.556 [DEBUG] [org.ryu.openflowjava.protocol.impl] - Sent OpenFlow PACKET-OUT message from Controller (192.168.1.10) to OVS (192.168.1.20). Egress Port: 2, Data Length: 64 bytes.	
2023-09-28 14:16:12.890 [DEBUG] [org.ryu.openflowjava.protocol.impl] - Received OpenFlow PACKET-IN message from OVS (192.168.1.20) to Controller (192.168.1.10). Ingress Port: 1, Reason: NO_MATCH.	
2023-09-28 14:16:15.303 [DEBUG] [org.ryu.openflowjava.protocol.impl] - Sent OpenFlow FLOW-MOD message from Controller (192.168.1.10) to OVS (192.168.1.20). Match: Ingress Port 1, Action: Output Port 2.	
2023-09-28 14:16:21.897 [DEBUG] [org.ryu.openflowjava.protocol.impl] - Sent OpenFlow FLOW-MOD message from Controller (192.168.1.10) to OVS (192.168.1.20). Match: Source IP 192.168.1.100, Action: Drop.	
2023-09-28 14:16:05.123 [DEBUG] [org.ryu.openflowjava.protocol.impl] - Received OpenFlow SET CONFIG message from openflow:1 (br0) to Controller (192.168.1.10). Configuration set to drop fragments.	
2023-09-28 14:16:12.890 [DEBUG] [org.ryu.openflowjava.protocol.impl] - Received OpenFlow PACKET-IN message from openflow:1 (br0) to Controller (192.168.1.10). Ingress Port: 1, Reason: NO_MATCH.	

4

SD-WAN Technology

WANs are currently facing two major changes that require significant adaptation. Firstly, we are seeing a growing trend toward the migration of applications to the cloud, either as SaaS applications or via companies' private datacenters. This trend is forcing WANs to transform themselves to offer much more than just connectivity. Their role is now to ensure application performance and security.

SD-WAN is emerging as a key solution to these challenges. It reconfigures the use of the WAN, placing it explicitly at the service of applications while simplifying management. Moreover, SD-WAN redefines the traditional role of routers: beyond simply transferring packets, they are now designed to specifically route applications to ensure their efficiency and protection. This approach responds directly to the new requirements of modern enterprise networks, marking a significant evolution in WAN management.

In this chapter, we explore in detail the SD-WAN technology, a network solution increasingly valued for its flexibility and enhanced performance. We'll start with an overview of SD-WAN, describing its emergence as a superior alternative to traditional WAN networks. This will be followed by an analysis of the key features that distinguish SD-WAN, including its ability to dynamically manage bandwidth and prioritize network traffic according to business needs.

We'll also examine the architecture of SD-WAN, emphasizing the core components that support its deployment and management. Finally, we'll look at the issues and challenges associated with adopting this technology, such as the security concerns related to its Internet dependency, and the challenges of integrating with existing network infrastructures. This comprehensive overview aims to provide an in-depth understanding of SD-WAN, enabling companies to better assess its potential and implications for their network operations.

This chapter covers the following topics:

1. Introduction
2. Introducing SD-WAN
3. Key SD-WAN features
4. SD-WAN architecture
5. Issues and challenges of SD-WAN technology
6. Conclusion.

4.1 Introduction

The major challenges facing network architects in WANs mainly concern reliability and optimizing the use of available bandwidth. The high cost of long-distance connections makes bandwidth especially valuable in WANs, unlike LANs, where it is more readily

DOI: 10.1201/9781003679394-4

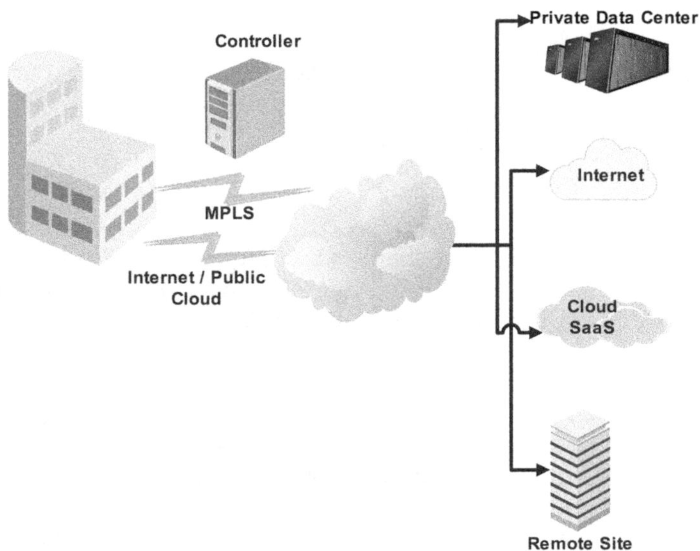

FIGURE 4.1
Example of a WAN architecture with a centralized controller.

available. In a context such as a LAN, it is possible to set up redundant connections without major financial considerations, given the low cost of cables. What's more, increasing bandwidth is generally a matter of adding extra ports and connections. However, this approach is not viable for WANs, where bandwidth costs are significantly higher due to distance, compared with a data center or campus. Adding redundant ports can worsen this issue. So it's crucial to maximize the efficiency and utilization of WAN links.

4.2 Introducing SD-WAN

SD-WAN is a network management approach that aims to optimize resource utilization by separating the control plane from the data plane. This separation enables centralized management and more intelligent orchestration of network traffic. Through a centralized controller, SD-WAN facilitates unified network management. This controller provides a comprehensive view of the network and enables the deployment of network policies across various branch offices (Figure 4.1).

4.3 Key SD-WAN Features

SD-WAN allows companies to manage link failure and bandwidth more effectively, optimize various traffic types and respond quickly to evolving customer requirements while keeping costs manageable. These features are particularly appreciated by organizations that depend on extensive network connections to carry out their operations (Figure 4.2).

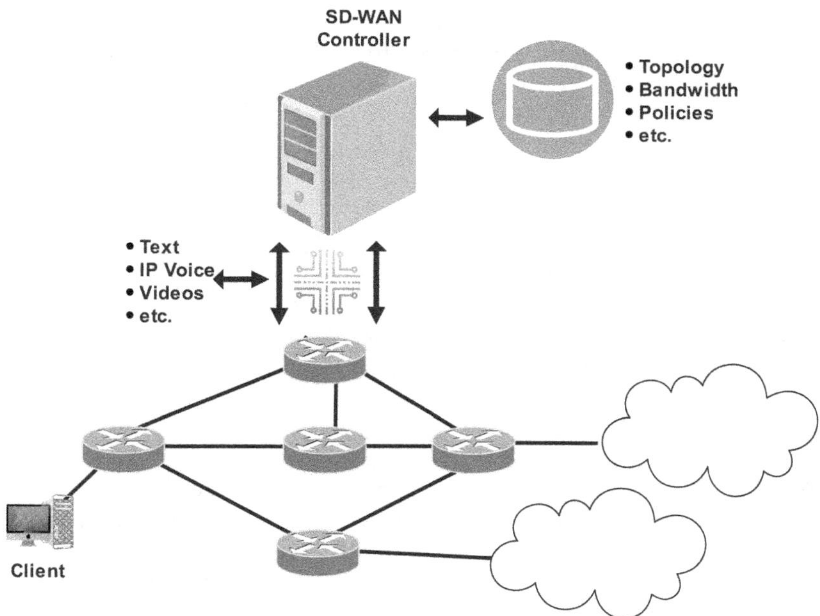

FIGURE 4.2
SD-WAN network management via a central controller.

4.3.1 Link Failure Management

In a traditional WAN configuration, when a link failure occurs, the network must reconverge. During this process, all routers attempt to reroute traffic to an available link. This rerouting is managed autonomously by each router along the route, using a routing protocol to establish a new path and reserve the necessary bandwidth. This mechanism is non-deterministic, as it is impossible to predict which router will be the last to successfully reroute its traffic in a given scenario. This uncertainty illustrates the difficulties encountered in WANs without software-defined networking (SDN) solutions when a router fails.

In a network equipped with SD-WAN technology and a centralized controller, the challenges of reconvergence in the event of link failure can be resolved much more efficiently. This central controller has a global view of all possible routes and available bandwidth, enabling it to optimize traffic more strategically. It relies on traffic engineering applications to compute the optimal path allocation in the network. This solution can be calculated once and then applied simultaneously to all network devices. The advantage of this SDN-based approach is that it is deterministic: the same process will produce the same result every time, guaranteeing predictable and efficient traffic management in the event of failure.

4.3.2 Growing Bandwidth Management

Service providers are faced with the need to manage ever-increasing bandwidth, due to network expansion and growing user demand. SD-WAN, with its dynamic bandwidth management capabilities, offers an efficient solution. It enables traffic to be intelligently distributed over various links (such as the public Internet, MPLS, etc.) according to availability and cost.

By doing so, it minimizes the need for significant investments in increasing bandwidth on dedicated links, enabling service providers to meet growing demands without proportionately increasing costs.

4.3.3 Diversity of Traffic Types

SD-WAN efficiently manages different types of traffic, such as VoIP and video, which require specific levels of service. Using Quality of Service (QoS) policies, SD-WAN can prioritize critical traffic, such as VoIP calls and video conferences, ensuring the necessary quality without resorting to bandwidth over-provisioning. This ability to differentiate and prioritize traffic based on its importance and resource needs avoids congestion and maximizes the use of available network resources.

4.3.4 Flexible and Responsive Services

SD-WAN offers remarkable flexibility when it comes to managing changes in service requirements. For example, if a customer wants higher priority or higher speeds for their traffic, service providers can adjust network policies quickly through the centralized SD-WAN controller. These adjustments can be made without disrupting existing traffic flows, which is essential for maintaining customer satisfaction and loyalty. What's more, these changes can be managed automatically in line with service level agreements, making services more adaptive to changing needs.

4.4 SD-WAN Architecture

The SD-WAN architecture typically comprises three main components:

- **Edge equipment:** These are deployed at sites and are responsible for transmitting and receiving network traffic.
- **SD-WAN controllers:** They determine the optimal paths for traffic, based on defined policies and the current state of the network.
- **Management portal:** It provides a unified interface for network configuration and monitoring, simplifying management and administration.

The SD-WAN operating principle can be summarized as follows: the controller selects the optimal path for each data packet based on the established policies and current network conditions, thereby optimizing performance and cost.

4.5 Issues and Challenges of SD-WAN Technology

Although SD-WAN offers many advantages, it also presents certain challenges that need to be taken into account:

- **Security:** While SD-WAN provides enhanced security features, its open architecture and reliance on the Internet can introduce new security challenges that require careful management.
- **Complexity and initial costs:** Deploying an SD-WAN solution can be initially complex and expensive, requiring considerable investment in hardware and expertise.
- **Integration with existing infrastructures:** Integrating SD-WAN with existing network infrastructure can be complex, requiring careful planning and rigorous technical execution.

4.6 Conclusion

In conclusion, SD-WAN represents a significant advance in enterprise network management, offering improved security features, more flexible bandwidth management and better overall performance compared to traditional WAN solutions. However, despite its many advantages, SD-WAN adoption is not without its challenges. Companies have to navigate between technical complexity, potential up-front costs, and obstacles associated with integrating existing systems. By taking these factors into account and carefully planning their transition to SD-WAN, organizations can maximize the benefits of this technology to more effectively meet their network connectivity and security needs.

Lab 6: Optimizing WAN Traffic with SD-WAN and FortiGate Configuration

Objectives

- Understand SD-WAN technology
- Configure a FortiGate device.

Case Study

This case study explores how SD-WAN technology optimizes data transmission across WAN links in IT networks. It highlights how this solution improves routing efficiency while reducing costs, intelligently exploiting available network resources, and ensuring centralized management of data flows.

Company ABC has three WAN links: An ADSL line, a fiber optic line, and a 5G link. It wants Office 365 users to use the fiber optic line, VPN users to use the 5G link, and the ADSL line to be reserved for all other internet use.

Required Software

- **GNS3 or equivalent**

Network Topology

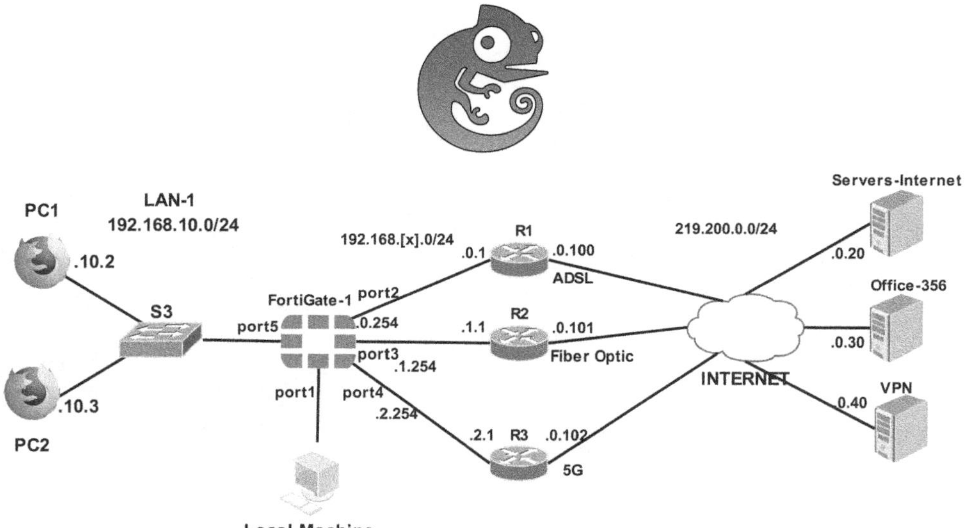

IP Address Table

Emulated Device	Device	Interface	IP address/ subnet mask	Default Gateway
FortiGate Virtual Appliance (v7.2.4.2)	FortiGate-1	port1	172.16.1.10/24	–
FortiGate Virtual Appliance (v7.2.4.2)	FortiGate-1	port2	192.168.0.254/24	–
FortiGate Virtual Appliance (v7.2.4.2)	FortiGate-1	port3	192.168.1.254/24	–
FortiGate Virtual Appliance (v7.2.4.2)	FortiGate-1	port4	192.168.2.254/24	–
FortiGate Virtual Appliance (v7.2.4.2)	FortiGate-1	port5	192.168.10.1/24	–
Cisco Router – C7200 (Dynamips, v15.2)	R1	F0/0	219.200.0.100/24	–
Cisco Router – C7200 (Dynamips, v15.2)	R1	G1/0	192.168.0.1/24	–
Cisco Router – C7200 (Dynamips, v15.2)	R2	F0/0	219.200.0.101/24	–
Cisco Router – C7200 (Dynamips, v15.2)	R2	G1/0	192.168.1.1/24	–
Cisco Router – C7200 (Dynamips, v15.2)	R3	F0/0	219.200.0.102/24	–
Cisco Router – C7200 (Dynamips, v15.2)	R3	G1/0	192.168.2.1/24	–
Docker Container – Webterm	PC1	eth0	192.168.10.2/24	192.168.10.1
Docker Container – Webterm	PC2	eth0	192.168.10.3/24	192.168.10.1
Docker Container –Toolbox	Internet Servers	eth0	219.200.0.20/24	–
Docker Container –Toolbox	Office-365	eth0	219.200.0.30/24	–
Docker Container –Toolbox	VPN	eth0	219.200.0.40/24	–
GNS3 Cloud Node	Local Machine	VMware Interface	172.16.1.1/24	–
Ethernet Switch	INTERNET	–	–	–

Note: It is important to note that the FortiGate Virtual Appliance (v7.2.4.2) is not an SDN controller. It has been used in this context for the following reasons:

a. It natively supports SD-WAN technology, allowing the simulation of certain dynamic routing logics.

b. It requires minimal hardware resources, making it suitable for lightweight virtual environments such as GNS3 or EVE-NG.

c. It is easy to deploy and configure, which simplifies hands-on lab activities.

This choice was therefore made for the sake of simplification within the scope of this lab. However, using a real SDN controller (such as ONOS, OpenDaylight, etc.) is also possible for more realistic SDN experiments.

Students are encouraged to understand that FortiGate is not part of the SDN controller solutions, but is used here as a pedagogical substitute based on the constraints and objectives of the lab.

Part A: Establish Basic Device Configuration

1. Create the network topology.
2. Assign IP addresses to PC, Servers, and Router interfaces according to the addressing table.
   a. Configuring router IP addresses:

      Use the **Cisco IOS** command to configure the router's IP address.

   b. Configure IP addresses on PCs and Servers.

Using the element GUI, modify the configuration file to assign an IP address: For example:

```
# Static config for eth0
auto eth0
iface eth0 inet static
address {element IP address}
netmask 255.255.255.0
gateway {Element gateway
```

Note: The values {element IP address} and {element gateway} must be replaced with the correct IP address and gateway assigned to the element. These addresses are available in the **IP Address Table** provided.

3. Assign IP addresses to **FortiGate-1** interfaces
   a. Basic configuration:
      - Log on to FortiGate-1 with login **"admin"** and no password. Update password to **"123456"**.
      - Use the following commands to configure the IP address for port1:

```
config system interface
edit port1
set mode static
set ip 172.16.1.10 255.255.255.0
append allowaccess http
end
```

   b. Configure IP addresses for other interfaces, port2, port3, port4, and port5:
      - On the Local Machine, open a web browser.
      - Enter the URL: http://172.16.1.10, and connect to the FortiGate interface.
      - In the "**Network > Interface**" menu, double-click on the interface to be configured.
      - Assign the appropriate IP address to the interface.
      - Set the alias as ADSL, Optical Fiber, 5G, and LAN, respectively.
      - Define the role of port5 as **LAN** and the other ports as **WAN**.
      - Allow **pinging** on all interfaces.
4. **Ping** the elements on the same network and ensure connectivity among them. On FortiGate, to **ping** an element, use the command:

```
execute ping {IP}
```

Note: Replace {IP} with the appropriate IP address of the target element (e.g., Servers, Routers, and Hosts). All IP addresses are listed in the **IP Address Table**. This step verifies that all devices within the same subnet can communicate with each other.

5. Configure **PAT** (NAT overload) on Cisco routers.

```
(config)#int f0/0
(config-if)# ip nat outside
(config)#int g1/0
(config-if)# ip nat inside
(config)# access-list 1 permit any
(config)#ip nat inside source list 1 interface f0/0 overload
```

6. Add access rules to FortiGate-1 to authorize Internet access.
   - Using FortiGate's graphical interface, click on the menu: "**Policy & Object > Firewall Policy**".
   - Add access rules for each type of connection, based on the parameters shown below.

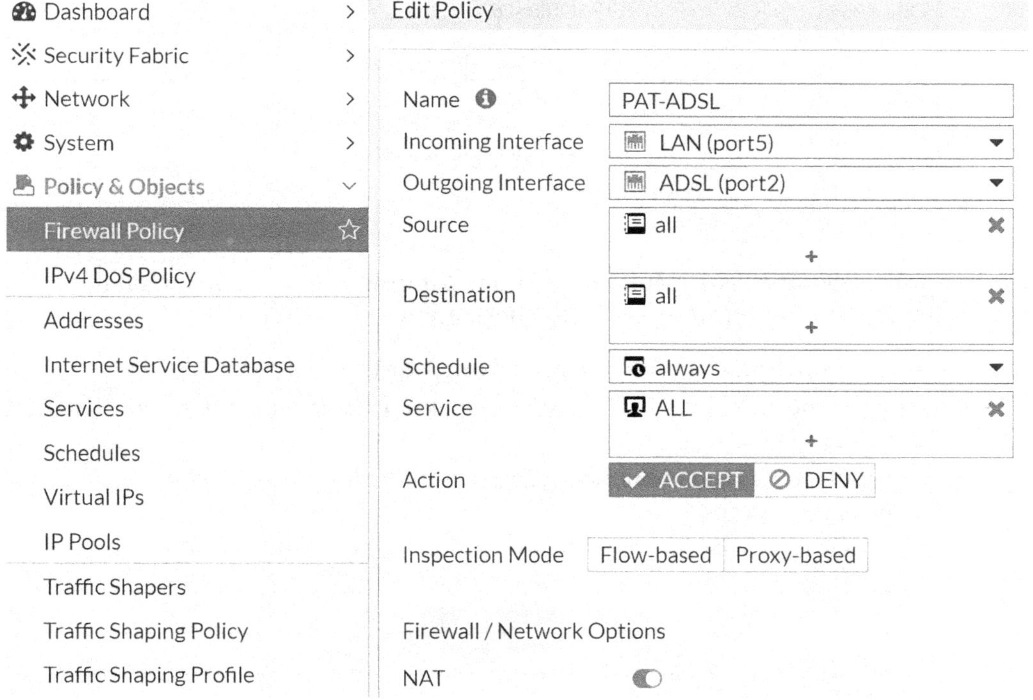

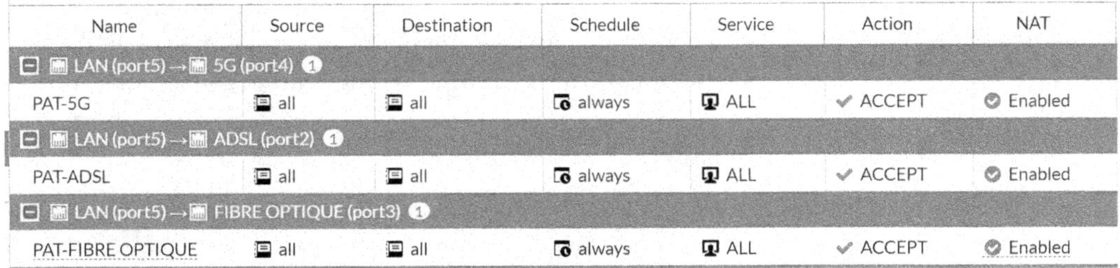

Name	Source	Destination	Schedule	Service	Action	NAT
LAN (port5) → 5G (port4) 1						
PAT-5G	all	all	always	ALL	ACCEPT	Enabled
LAN (port5) → ADSL (port2) 1						
PAT-ADSL	all	all	always	ALL	ACCEPT	Enabled
LAN (port5) → FIBRE OPTIQUE (port3) 1						
PAT-FIBRE OPTIQUE	all	all	always	ALL	ACCEPT	Enabled

7. Configure web pages on servers.
    - Open the server console.
    - Access the **"/var/www/html"** directory using the **cd** command.
    - Access the **"index.html"** file using the **nano** command.
    - Replace the HTML code between the tags "**< title>... </ title>**" and "**<h1>... </h1>**" with the following:

Web server	**HTML code**
Internet servers	<title>Internet servers </title> .. <h1 style="text-align: center;"> Internet-Servers </h1>
Office-365	<title>Office-365</title> ... <h1 style="text-align: center;"> Office-365</h1>
VPN	<title>VPN</title> ... <h1 style="text-align: center;"> VPN </h1>

    - Save the file.

Part B: Application of Classic Multi-Technology Internet Connection Techniques with Static Routing and Preference Parameterization

1. Configure **multi-route static routing** on FortiGate-1.
    - Using FortiGate's graphical interface, click on the menu: "**Network > Static Routes**".
    - Add static routes based on the parameters in the following tables:
        - **Route 1: ADSL**

Destination	0.0.0.0/0.0.0.0
Gateway/Address	192.168.1.1
Interface	ADSL (port2)
Administration Distance	30
Comments	ADSL

- **Route 2: Fiber Optics**

Destination	0.0.0.0/0.0.0.0
Gateway/Address	192.168.2.1
Interface	OPTICAL FIBER (port3)
Administration Distance	20
Comments	OPTICAL FIBER

- **Route 3: 5G**

Destination	0.0.0.0/0.0.0.0
Gateway/Address	192.168.3.1
Interface	5G (port4)
Administration Distance	10
Comments	5G

2. Explain the role and importance of administrative distance in route management and selection within the context of the current network topology.
3. On **PC1**, check that you can access the **Server-Internet** and **Office-365** web pages.
4. On **PC1**, execute the following command: **traceroute 219.200.0.20** to determine the network path used to reach the server. Identify the connectivity technology used.

```
root@PC1:~# traceroute 219.200.0.20
traceroute to 219.200.0.20 (219.200.0.20), 30 hops max, 60 byte
  packets
 1 192.168.10.1 (192.168.1.1) 10.336 ms 10.333 ms 10.327 ms
 2 192.168.2.1 (192.168.2.1)  22.768 ms 25.809 ms 26.027 ms => Via 5G
  Line
 3 219.200.0.20 (219.200.0.20) 39.071 ms 39.359 ms 39.436 ms
```

5. Analyze and justify the result obtained from the previous exercise. Next, discuss the disadvantages associated with using traditional methods of connecting to a WAN network in general.
6. Remove the **5G** link from **port 4** of the FortiGate-1. Then, from **PC1**, run a check to confirm that access to the web pages of the **Server-Internet** and **Office-365** servers is still possible.
7. Justify the result obtained.

Part C: Applying SD-WAN Techniques for Internet Connection Management

1. Provide a brief definition of SD-WAN technology.
2. Delete all previously created configurations:
   - Delete access rules.
   - Remove static routing.
3. Using the FortiGate-1 graphical interface, click on the menu: "**Network > SD-WAN Zones**".
   - Create a new **SD-WAN** Zone named **SD-WAN.**
   - Create **SD-WAN Members** based on the parameters in the following tables:
     - **SD-WAN Member 1: ADSL**

Interface	ADSL (port2)
SD-WAN Zone	SD-WAN
Gateway/Address	192.168.0.1
Cost	30

     - **SD-WAN Member 2: Fiber Optics**

Interface	OPTICAL FIBER (port3)
SD-WAN Zone	SD-WAN
Gateway/Address	192.168.1.1
Cost	20

     - **SD-WAN Member 3:4G/5G**

Interface	5G (port4)
SD-WAN Zone	SD-WAN
Gateway/Address	192.168.2.1
Cost	10

Interfaces	Gateway	Cost
virtual-wan-link		
SA-WAN		
5G (port4)	192.168.2.1	10
FIBRE OPTIQUE (port3)	192.168.1.1	20
ADSL (port2)	192.168.0.1	30

4. Create a default route to the Internet via the SD-WAN interface.
   - Using FortiGate-1's graphical interface, click on the "**Network > Static Route**" menu.

- Add a default route based on the parameters in the following table:

Destination	0.0.0.0/0.0.0.0
Interface	SD-WAN
Comments	SD-WAN

5. Add access rules to FortiGate-1 to authorize Internet access.
   - Using FortiGate-1's graphical interface, click on the menu: **Policy & Object > FirewallPolicy**.
   - Add access rules for each type of connection, based on the parameters shown below.

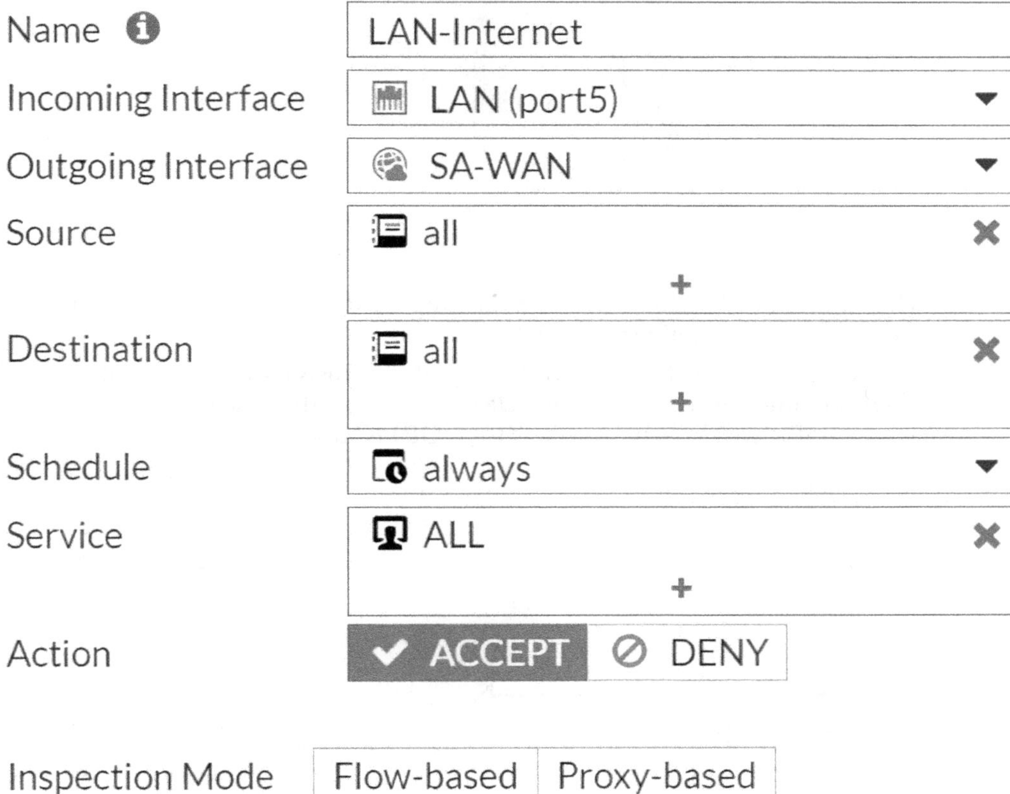

6. On PC1, check that you can access the Server-Internet and Office-365 web pages.
7. Analyze the various SD-WAN load balancing parameters.
   - Using the FortiGate-1 GUI, click on the menu: **Network > SD-WAN Rules**.

- Double-click on the default rule named **SD-WAN**.

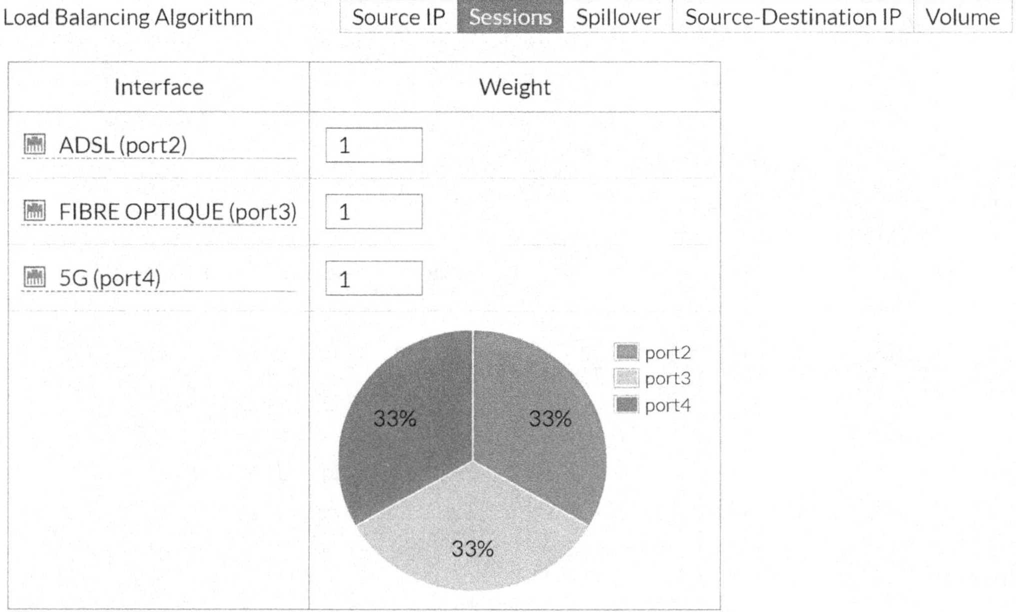

- What is the role of each tab in load balancing configuration, and how can these roles be used to optimize network traffic?

8. Create a new SD-WAN rule named **SERVERUR-INTERNET** that routes all traffic to the **Server-Internet** server via the **ADSL** line, unless this line is unavailable, in which case traffic will be sent via the **FIBRE-OPTIC** line.

9. Explain each of the strategy options for selecting output interfaces, and how these options can be used to optimize network traffic.

Select a strategy for how outgoing interfaces will be chosen.

- ○ **Manual**
  Manually assign outgoing interfaces.
- ● **Best Quality**
  The interface with the best measured performance is selected.
- ○ **Lowest Cost (SLA)**
  The interface that meets SLA targets is selected. When there is a tie, the interface with the lowest assigned cost is selected.
- ○ **Maximize Bandwidth (SLA)**
  Traffic is load balanced among interfaces that meet SLA targets.

10. Create another SD-WAN rule named "**Office-356**" that routes all traffic to the Office-356 server via the **FIBRE-OPTICAL** line, unless this line is unavailable, in which case traffic will be sent via the **ADSL** line.
11. Create another SD-WAN rule named "**VPN**" which authorizes only **PC2** to route all traffic to the **VPN** server via the **5G** line, unless the latter is unavailable, in which case traffic will be sent via the **FIBRE-OPTIC** line.
12. Execute the command **traceroute 219.200.0.20** on PC1 to determine the network path used to reach the server. Identify the connectivity technology used.

```
root@PC1:~# traceroute 219.200.0.20
traceroute to 219.200.0.20 (219.200.0.20), 30 hops max, 60 byte
  packets
 1 192.168.10.1 (192.168.1.1) 10.336 ms 10.333 ms 10.327 ms
 2 192.168.0.1 (192.168.0.1)  22.768 ms 25.809 ms 26.027 ms =>  via
  ADSL Line
 3 219.200.0.20 (219.200.0.20) 39.071 ms 39.359 ms 39.436 ms
```

13. Execute the command **traceroute 219.200.0.30** on PC1 to determine the network path used to reach the server. Identify the connectivity technology used.

```
root@PC1:~# traceroute 219.200.0.30
traceroute to 219.200.0.20 (219.200.0.20), 30 hops max, 60 byte
  packets
 1 192.168.10.1 (192.168.1.1) 10.336 ms 10.333 ms 10.327 ms
 2 192.168.1.1 (192.168.0.1)  22.768 ms 25.809 ms 26.027 ms =>  via
  Fiber Optic Line
 3 219.200.0.20 (219.200.0.20) 39.071 ms 39.359 ms 39.436 ms
```

5

SDN Technology Applied to Campus Networks: SD-LAN and Group-Based Policy Management

At the heart of the digital transformation of educational institutions and businesses lie campus networks, complex ecosystems where unprecedented demands for security, performance, and flexibility converge. This chapter explores how software-defined networking (SDN) technology is revolutionizing campus infrastructure management through the concept of software-defined local area network (SD-LAN) and group-based policy management (GBP).

In this context, we will begin with an overview of campus networks, highlighting their crucial role and the unique challenges they present. We will then analyze the key requirements for their optimization, where reliability, security, and adaptability emerge as essential imperatives to meet the evolving needs of end-users.

The following section will focus on SD-LAN technology, an evolution of SDN specifically designed for campus environments. We'll look at its various aspects, from macro- and micro-segmentation to the overall architecture, as well as the basic components that enable agile and secure network management. Particular attention will be paid to AAA servers and their integration with various authentication solutions, illustrating their central role in securing network access.

Subsequently, we will explore GBP, a key pillar for implementing granular security strategies. This discussion will include micro-segmentation combined with GBP and the adoption of "Zero Trust" architecture, highlighting how these approaches can coexist and reinforce each other to deliver optimal security.

Finally, we will conclude with an overview of the solutions available on the market that implement the general SD-LAN concepts presented in this chapter.

This chapter aims to provide an in-depth understanding of SDN innovations applied to campus networks, offering readers the knowledge they need to grasp these technologies.

This chapter covers the following topics:

1. Introducing campus networks
2. Key requirements for campus network optimization
3. SD-LAN technology
4. Group-based policy management
5. Automated campus network solutions
6. Conclusions based on the Groups

 DOI: 10.1201/9781003679394-5

5.1 Introducing Campus Networks

A campus network consists of a set of LANs located within a defined geographical area. Typically, the network equipment and communication links are owned by the entity managing the campus, be it a university, private company, or government institution, among others. Campus end-users can connect to the network via wireless access points or wired connections, using desktops, laptops, shared computer workstations, or mobile devices such as tablets and smartphones. These devices may belong to the organization or to the individuals themselves. Additionally, these personal devices may either run access control software supplied by the IT department or operate independently.

5.2 Key Requirements for Campus Network Optimization

Campus networks must meet specific requirements that extend well beyond the basic functionality of a computer network. They have to manage a wide range of users, devices, and applications, while guaranteeing security, performance, and reliability. Here are just a few of the key requirements that campus networks must meet:

- **Setting up differentiated access levels:** It's crucial that campus networks can manage different levels of access for different users and their specific needs. For example, students or employees may have access to different resources than guests or external service providers. These differentiated access levels can result in specific restrictions (i.e., what they can or cannot access) and quality of service management, including traffic prioritization and bandwidth limitations. This management requires the use of advanced technologies, beyond VLANs, and traditional firewall configurations to control traffic flows.
- **BYOD (Bring Your Own Device) policy support:** With increasing numbers of employees and students using their own personal devices (smartphones, tablets, and laptops) to connect to the campus network, it's imperative that networks can accommodate them securely and efficiently. This includes appropriate authentication, authorization, and access control.
- **Access control and security:** Campus networks need to be protected against intrusions, malicious attacks, and data leakage. Robust security measures are essential, including firewalls, intrusion detection systems (IDS), and intrusion prevention systems. It is also crucial to establish strict security policies and make users aware of the risks associated with IT security.
- **Service discovery:** It's important that users of campus networks can easily locate and access necessary services, such as printers, file servers, and web applications. To achieve this, an efficient service discovery system must be in place, using technologies such as Domain Name System or Dynamic Host Configuration Protocol (DHCP).

5.3 SD-LAN Technology

5.3.1 Introduction

SD-LAN technology involves applying SDN principles to LANs. In an SD-LAN, network control is centralized and programmable, allowing for more flexible and dynamic management of network resources. Tasks such as switch and router configuration, performance management, and network monitoring can be automated and optimized using central software.

5.3.2 Types of Segmentation on an SD-LAN Network

In the SD-LAN architecture, macro-segmentation and micro-segmentation play crucial roles in ensuring security and efficient network management. These two concepts are pillars of the security and access control strategy in an SD-LAN, enabling organizations to segment and isolate network traffic according to operational and security needs.

5.3.2.1 Macro Segmentation

Macro-segmentation refers to the division of a network into sub-networks or logical segments, each operating as an isolated entity with its own security and routing policies. This segmentation can be achieved in several ways, of which the following are the most commonly used:

- **Virtual Local Area Network (VLAN) segmentation:** VLANs are the classic type of segmentation used in traditional networks. A VLAN enables devices to be grouped together within the same logical network, even if they are physically dispersed. This method is particularly useful for separating groups of users or services while maintaining centralized network management.
- **Segmentation by Virtual Extensible LAN (VXLAN):** VXLAN is a technology used primarily in data center environments to overcome the limitations of VLANs in terms of number of IDs and scalability. With VXLAN, hundreds of thousands of network segments can be created, providing enhanced traffic isolation. This technology also supports the mobility of virtual machines across network segments without interrupting ongoing services.
- **Segmentation by the routing domain (Virtual Routing and Forwarding, VRF):** In this form of segmentation, each routing domain has its own routing table and broadcast domain, ensuring complete isolation of data flows. This makes it possible to create several independent logical networks within a single physical infrastructure. Each domain can enforce its own security, access, and routing policies, providing stronger isolation compared to traditional VLANs.

5.3.2.1.1 Key Features of Segmentation

- **Isolating traffic domains:** By segmenting the network, companies can isolate traffic from different departments, services, or user groups. For instance, traffic from

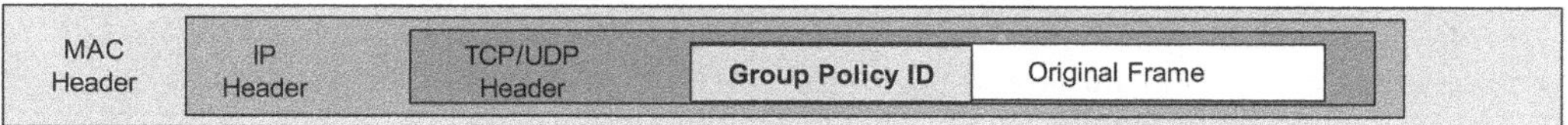

FIGURE 5.1
Extended frame structure for network micro-segmentation.

the finance team can be isolated from the development team's traffic, minimizing the risk of unauthorized access or interference.

- **Application of specific policies:** Each network segment can enforce its own security, quality of service (QoS), and traffic management policies, adapted to the specific needs of users or applications within that segment.

5.3.2.2 Micro-Segmentation

Micro-segmentation takes the concept of segmentation one step further, offering even finer granularity. While traditional segmentation divides the network into logical sub-networks, micro-segmentation isolates traffic within a single sub-network. It applies security policies directly to individual users, devices, or applications by inserting a specific tag into each frame.

This tag, distinct from traditional segment identifiers such as the VLAN ID, uniquely identifies the group to which a user or device belongs, facilitating more precise and secure access management and policy enforcement (Figure 5.1).

5.3.2.2.1 Key Features of Micro-Segmentation

- **Flexibility and adaptation to dynamic environments:** Micro-segmentation is particularly useful in dynamic environments where users and devices move frequently. Security policies track the identities of users or devices, rather than their IP addresses, ensuring continuous protection wherever the user or device connects to the network.
- **Granular access control:** With micro-segmentation, each user, device, or traffic flow can be isolated, even within the same segment. This makes it possible to apply very specific security policies, depending on identities or traffic types, ensuring that interactions between users and services are strictly controlled.
- **Reduced attack surface:** By restricting potential communications within network segments, micro-segmentation minimizes the attack surface exposed to insider threats or intrusions. For example, even if a device is compromised, micro-segmentation can prevent malware from spreading to other parts of the network.
- **Support for sensitive applications:** Some critical applications require additional protection to ensure they run smoothly without interference or unauthorized access. Micro-segmentation protects these applications by strictly limiting the communication flows they can receive or transmit.
- The following table compares segmentation and micro-segmentation in terms of granularity, complexity, and typical use cases (Table 5.1).

TABLE 5.1

Comparative Segmentation and Micro-Segmentation: Granularity, Complexity, and Use Cases

	Granularity Level	Complexity of Implementation	Use Cases
Segmentation	Traditional segmentation operates at a macro level, dividing the network into logical segments based on criteria such as department or function.	Traditional segmentation is generally simpler to implement, as it involves fewer rules and exceptions.	Segmentation is often used to isolate the main functional areas of the network.
Micro-segmentation	Micro-segmentation, on the other hand, operates at a micro level, enforcing specific policies on individual users or devices.	Micro-segmentation, although more complex, offers much finer-grained security tailored to the specific needs of organizations.	Micro-segmentation is employed to protect critical applications, mitigate insider threats, and guarantee granular security in highly dynamic environments.

Adding a tag to a network frame to identify a specific type of traffic or segment can go by different names, depending on the technology or provider:

- **Security Group Tags (SGTs):** As previously mentioned, this term is specific to Cisco TrustSec. It is used to tag packets to facilitate segmentation and the enforcement of security policies in a Cisco environment.
- **NSX Security Tags:** VMware NSX uses its own security tags to enforce micro-segmentation policies in a virtual environment. These tags are used to define and segment network traffic within a data center.
- **Security Labels:** In other environments, we may also speak of "security labels" or "policy tags", depending on the technologies used. These labels or tags are used to enforce similar security policies, although the underlying mechanisms may differ.
- **Palo Alto Networks Tags:** Utilized in Palo Alto firewalls to categorize and enforce security policies on resources.
- **Micro-Segmentation Policies (Illumio):** Illumio uses labels for adaptive, application-based micro-segmentation.

5.3.3 SD-LAN Architecture

Traditionally, LANs are based on a three-tier or three-layer architecture consisting of the Access, Distribution, and Core layers. The Access layer is closest to the end-user, where computers, wireless access points, and other peripherals are connected. The Distribution layer acts as an intermediate point for aggregating traffic from the various access switches while applying security and traffic management policies. Finally, the Core layer ensures fast, efficient routing of traffic between different parts of the network and to external networks (Figure 5.2).

However, this traditional architecture presents several limitations, particularly in flexibility, scalability, and security policy management. It can become complex to manage as the number of connected devices and traffic requirements increase. Moreover, enforcing consistent security policies across all network layers is often challenging and requires extensive manual configuration. These challenges are one of the main reasons why the SD-LAN architecture was developed to overcome the limitations of traditional LANs by offering automation, simplified segmentation, and centralized management.

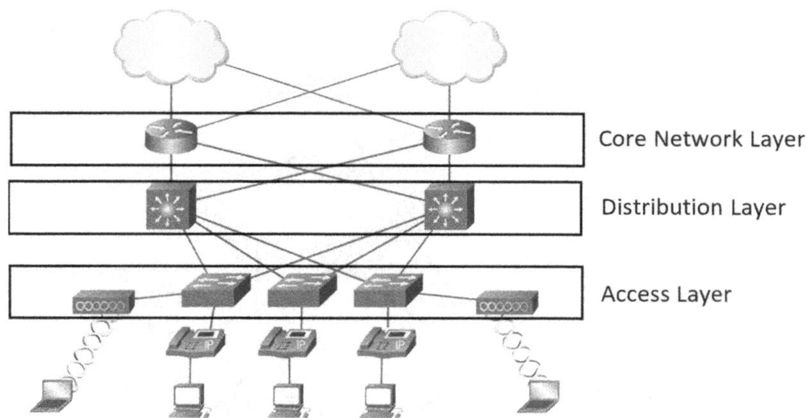

FIGURE 5.2
Three-layer LAN architecture.

5.3.4 Basic SD-LAN Components

- **SD-LAN controller:** The heart of the SD-LAN architecture is the controller, which functions as the brain of the network. This controller centralizes the management of the entire network, enabling complete visibility and precise control of network resources. It orchestrates network policies, device configurations, and real-time monitoring, ensuring that traffic management decisions are consistently made in a centralized manner (Figure 5.3).
- **AAA server:** AAA servers are designed to ensure that only authorized users and devices can access specific network resources. The concept of an AAA server is based on three key components:
    - **Authentication (Who):** This process verifies the user or device attempting to connect to the network. This may include verifying information such as login credentials or digital certificates.
    - **Authorization (What):** Once a user is authenticated, authorization determines which resources they can access. For example, a marketing department employee might be authorized to access marketing files, but not financial databases.
    - **Accounting:** Accounting logs network activities, creating event logs to show when, how, and where access took place. These data are essential for security audits and compliance.
- **Switches and routers:** In an SD-LAN, switches and routers act as physical or virtual endpoints, centrally managed by the SD-LAN controller. These devices are programmable and can dynamically adjust their configurations in response to controller directives, enabling flexible traffic management and improved network performance.
- **Wireless access points:** Wireless access points in an SD-LAN are also under the control of the central SDN controller or delegated to a dedicated Wi-Fi controller, enabling unified management of wireless and wired networks, usually via a

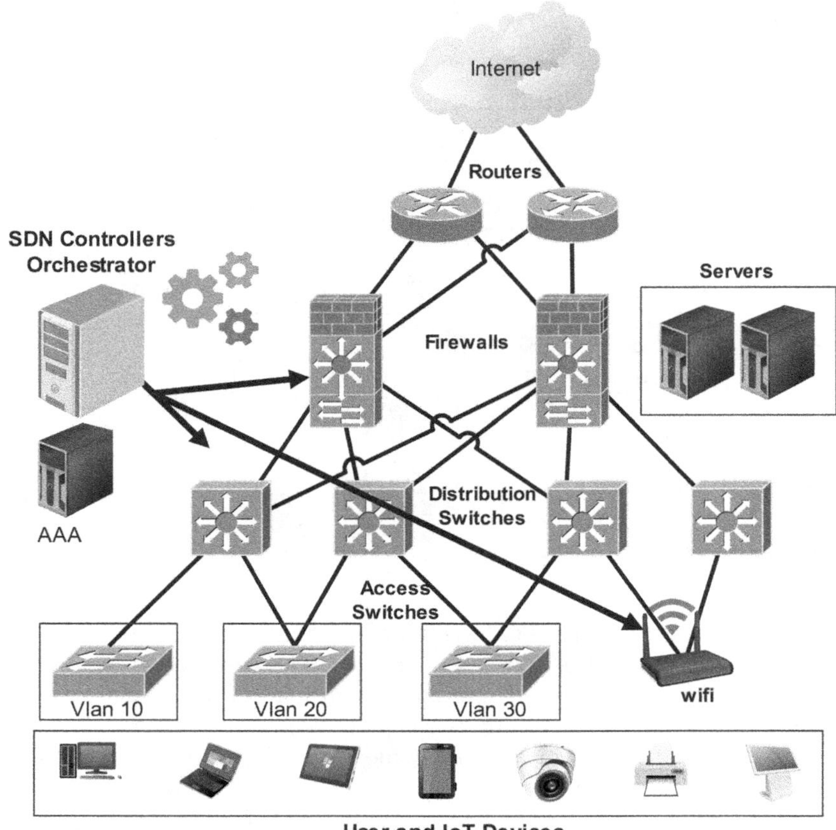

FIGURE 5.3
General SD-LAN network components.

protocol such as CAPWAP or equivalent. This is crucial in campus environments where users frequently switch between wired and wireless connections.

- **Orchestrator:** The SDN orchestrator adds a higher layer to the SDN model, enabling network policy to be managed and unified across all devices, especially when several SDN controllers coexist in the network, as in the case of networks hosting fault-tolerant SDN controllers, high-availability controllers, Wi-Fi controllers, and so on. This additional layer also makes it possible to manage and automate various devices other than routers and switches, such as servers, firewalls, or equipment from different vendors. One chapter is dedicated to a detailed exploration of the relationship between SDN and orchestrator, to better understand their interaction and impact on modern network management.

One of the main advantages of SD-LAN is its ability to scale easily with the addition of new devices or switches, without requiring a major overhaul of the network architecture. Centralized management allows network administrators to rapidly deploy new access points or switches and configure them remotely via the SD-LAN controller. This flexibility is essential in dynamic campus networks, where network requirements can change rapidly in line with new academic projects or evolving technologies.

5.3.5 AAA Servers

5.3.5.1 Presentation

The evolution of modern networks has made it essential to implement robust solutions to guarantee access security and compliance. Among these solutions, AAA servers play a central role in managing secure access to IT networks.

In addition to these three standard tasks, an AAA server can perform additional checks on several key aspects in advanced scenarios.

- **What:** It thoroughly examines the type of equipment or device attempting to access the network, identifying if it is a computer, smartphone, or tablet, to determine whether the device is authorized to connect.
- **When:** The server logs and evaluates the precise time of the connection attempt, allowing for the definition of authorized access windows and the identification of suspicious attempts outside these periods.
- **Where:** It verifies the physical or geographical location of the device based on its IP address or other location data, ensuring that access is made from secure or approved locations.
- **How:** The server guarantees that the connection method used, whether wired (LAN), wireless (WLAN), or through a virtual private network (VPN), adheres to corporate security policies and is properly secured.

5.3.5.1.1 RADIUS and TACACS: Authentication Protocols

Two major protocols are used by AAA servers to manage authentication: RADIUS (Remote Authentication Dial-In User Service) and TACACS (Terminal Access Controller Access-Control System).

- **RADIUS:** Designed to manage user authentication over wireless networks, VPN, or modem connections, RADIUS combines authentication and authorization processes in a single transaction. It is commonly used for network connections requiring user IDs and passwords, such as VPN or Wi-Fi access.
- **TACACS:** Unlike RADIUS, TACACS separates authentication, authorization, and accounting functions, enabling more granular access management. TACACS is often preferred in environments requiring tighter control over who can access which resources. TACACS+, an enhanced version developed by Cisco, is a more secure, flexible, and advanced version of TACACS.

Here is a table comparing the RADIUS and TACACS+ protocols (Table 5.2):

5.3.5.2 AAA Servers and Integration with Active Directory (AD) and Azure AD

AAA servers don't usually operate in isolation, but often interact with other servers to verify user credentials. One of the most common cases is integration with AD or Azure AD, centralized databases used by Microsoft to manage users, groups, and resources.

When AAA is coupled with AD, it can authenticate users by verifying their credentials in the AD or Azure AD database.

TABLE 5.2

Comparison of RADIUS and TACACS+ Protocols

Features	RADIUS	TACACS+
Acronym	Remote Authentication Dial-In User Service	Terminal Access Controller Access Control System Plus
Default port	UDP 1812 (authentication), UDP 1813 (accounting)	TCP 49
Protocols used	UDP	TCP
Encryption	Partial encryption (password only)	Full packet encryption
Authentication	Combining authentication and authorization in the same package	Separation of authentication, authorization, and audit (AAA)
Main application	Network access (WLAN, VPN, Dial-up, etc.)	Network equipment administration
Interoperability	Standard, widely supported protocol	Cisco proprietary protocol
Scalability	Supports more simultaneous users	Less suitable for large environments
Order support	No	Yes, support for detailed equipment commands
Separation of AAA functions	No	Yes
Performance	Faster but less secure	Slower but more secure
Open or proprietary standard	Open (RFC 2865 and 2866)	Owner Cisco

5.3.5.3 Authentication Standards

AAA servers often work in conjunction with various authentication standards and protocols to ensure that devices accessing the network are authentic and authorized. Among the most widely used standards, we distinguish the following:

- **802.1X:** This is an authentication protocol for both wired and wireless networks. It establishes a framework for authenticating users or devices through an authentication server.
- **Extensible Authentication Protocol (EAP):** EAP is a flexible authentication protocol that allows for the exchange of different authentication methods between the client and the authentication server. The most common EAP variants include:
  - EAP-TLS (Transport Layer Security): This method uses digital certificates to authenticate both client and server. This is one of the most secure methods.
  - EAP-PEAP (Protected EAP): This method encapsulates EAP within a TLS tunnel, providing secure authentication, commonly used with username/password credentials.
  - EAP-TTLS (Tunneled TLS): Similar to EAP-PEAP, but offers greater flexibility for internal authentication methods.
- **MAC Authentication Bypass (MAB):** This authentication method is employed when the client device does not support 802.1X. It relies on the device's MAC address as an identifier.
- **WebAuth Definition:** WebAuth is another web-based authentication mechanism. When a user attempts to connect to the network, they are redirected to a web page where they must enter their credentials to be authenticated.

5.4 Group-Based Policy Management

5.4.1 Presentation

Traditional network access management relies on assigning users or devices to dedicated VLANs, creating DHCP pools, and configuring access control lists to enforce appropriate access policies on edge devices. Although these approaches are functional, they present several challenges. With the evolution of endpoints, smart devices, IoT, and BYOD, it becomes necessary to create new VLANs and DHCP extents, as well as to add these new IP subnets to access control lists. However, a growing number of access control list (ACL) entries can lead to an increased administrative burden and greater complexity with new security requirements, while also expanding the potential attack surface due to the growing sophistication of endpoints, increasing the IT burden associated with infrastructure maintenance.

GBP is a network management approach that enables access and security policies to be defined on the basis of group membership, regardless of location or IP addresses. Groups can be defined according to various criteria, such as user role, device type, department, or other criteria chosen by the administrator.

GBP takes advantage of micro-segmentation to associate defined groups with tags inserted in user frames. Together, these technologies provide a strengthened security architecture capable of dealing with modern threats.

This approach, combined with SDN, offers a new way of managing access on campus networks. SDN makes it possible to centralize group management for micro-segmentation, and to define dynamic access policies based on groups of users, devices, applications, or any other type of traffic.

5.4.2 Micro-Segmentation Combined with GBP

Micro-segmentation inserts a tag into each frame to identify and segregate traffic from different groups within the network. This tagging mechanism facilitates fine-grained control over data flows between specific applications, services, or users, ensuring the application of tailored security policies from the network entry point. This approach is particularly effective in campus networks, where traffic can be complex and varied.

This method extends deeper into the network, enabling access policies to be applied not only to switches, routers, or access points but also to all elements processing frames, such as firewalls, IDS, and more.

As micro-segmentation and GBP are international standards, devices from various vendors can interoperate to ensure effective implementation of network policies.

When integrated with micro-segmentation, GBP may be referred to differently depending on the vendor. Below are some examples of terms used by different vendors for similar concepts:

- **Security Group ACLs (SGACLs):** Used by Cisco SD-Access to enforce group-based security policies.
- **NSX DFW (Distributed Firewall):** Employed by VMware NSX, it enforces security policies based on the security tags associated with virtual machines.
- **AWS Identity-Based Policies:** In AWS, group-based policies are implemented through roles and security policies linked to IAM groups.

- **Azure Network Security Groups (NSGs):** Azure leverages NSGs to enforce network filtering policies based on user groups or virtual resources.
- **Juniper Contrail Policy Groups:** Juniper implements group-based policies within its SDN network solutions through Contrail Security.
- **Palo Alto Networks Dynamic Address Groups:** Palo Alto Networks employs Dynamic Address Groups to enforce dynamic policies based on groups of IP addresses linked to specific tags.

Each vendor uses its own terminology to describe group-based policies combined with micro-segmentation, yet the concept remains largely consistent: The concept is to secure and segment networks by enforcing specific rules on groups of objects (devices, users, and applications) rather than on individual entities.

This demonstrates that mechanisms may differ depending on the technology or product, but they all share the common objective of controlling access and segmenting networks at a granular level based on roles or security groups.

5.4.3 Zero Trust Approach: Foundations and Implementation with GBP

5.4.3.1 Introducing Zero Trust Architecture

The "Zero Trust" architecture is founded on the core principle of never trusting by default and always verifying every access attempt, regardless of whether it originates from inside or outside the network.

Here are the main principles of this architecture:

- **Continuous, dynamic verification:** Every access attempt, whether internal or external, is subjected to identity and device compliance checks.
- **Minimal privilege model:** Users and devices are provided only with the access rights necessary to perform their tasks, minimizing risks in the event of a compromise.
- **Network segmentation:** The network is divided into distinct security zones, reducing potential attack surfaces and restricting lateral movement in the event of an intrusion.
- **Evidence-based trust:** Access decisions are based on factors such as location, device, activity, and context, rather than mere network membership.

5.4.3.2 "Zero Trust" Architecture with GBP

Two fundamental concepts that enable Zero Trust architecture in modern networks are GBP and micro-segmentation. The integration of these two elements within a network establishes a "Zero Trust" architecture, providing the following benefits:

- **Inter-segment and extra-segment communication:** Micro-segmentation establishes strict boundaries between elements within the same network segment, ensuring that communication flows are tightly controlled through GBP-defined policies. Inter-segment communication is regulated to permit only explicitly authorized interactions, preventing unauthorized access to critical resources. Additionally, for communication flows exiting the network to external systems (extra-segment), specific security policies are enforced to maintain the continuity of the "Zero Trust" principle. This guarantees that each flow is authenticated and authorized, minimizing the risks of intrusions or data breaches.

- **Granular, adaptive security:** Each user, device, or application is governed by specific policies, restricting access to essential resources and reducing the risk of exposure.
- **Resilience in the face of cyberthreats:** By restricting communications between segments, micro-segmentation prevents attacks from spreading, even if a segment is compromised.
- **Flexible, centralized management:** Thanks to GBP, security policies can be dynamically adapted based on user or device behavior. Segments created through micro-segmentation are continuously monitored and regulated to maintain a secure environment.

5.4.4 Key Components of GBP

The main components of GBP are as follows:

- **Entity groups:** This component encompasses the classification of users, devices, or resources that require specific management. These groups are defined to streamline the assignment and application of policies and services.
- **Services to be provided:** This component outlines the specific functions and capabilities that will be applied to different groups of entities based on security policies. Services may include various elements such as specific applications, traffic type management, QoS, content filtering, monitoring, and other critical network and security functions. They play a crucial role in guaranteeing that security policies are not only theoretically defined but also effectively enforced.
- **Security policies (contract):** These are the rules that define the authorizations, restrictions, and behaviors applicable to each group. These policies define which actions are permitted or prohibited for group members within the network.

5.4.5 GBP Management with an SDN Controller

For further clarification, let's take the example of a user who wishes to connect to a campus wireless network. The wireless access points are set up to utilize an AAA authentication server (Figure 5.4).

The following steps generally describe the process of connecting a user to an SD-LAN. The network relies on GBP combined with micro-segmentation. The process consists of the following steps:

Step 1:

1. **Detection and Connection:**
   - A user or device attempts to connect to the network through a wireless access point (or switch).
   - The 802.1X protocol, often paired with other protocols, is used to capture user or device credentials.

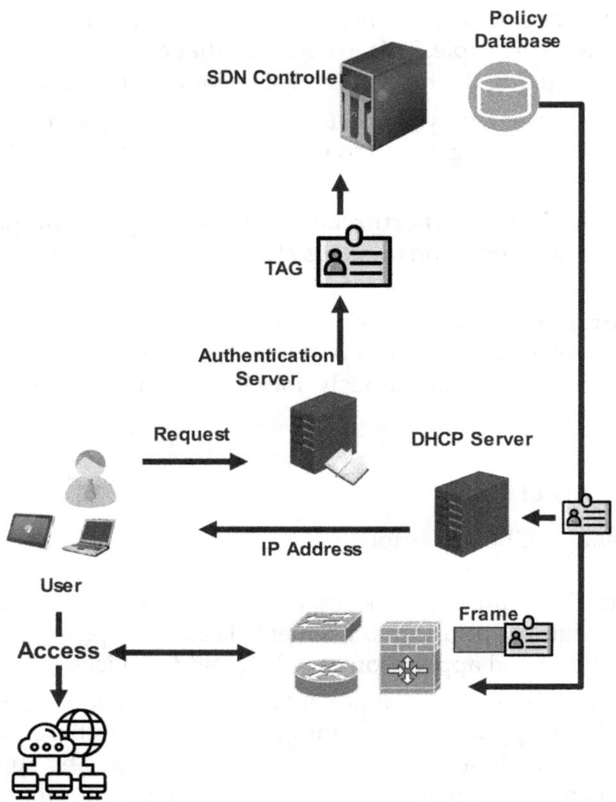

FIGURE 5.4
General authentication and user access process in an SD-LAN network.

  - If the 802.1X protocol is not supported by the device, an alternative, such as MAB, can be employed.

2. **Authentication request:**
   - The credentials captured by the access point or switch are transmitted to the AAA server through the RADIUS or TACACS protocol.
3. **Identity validation via the AAA server:**
   - The AAA server validates the identity of the user or device by querying an identity directory, such as AD or a certificate server.
   - This identification process can be performed in several ways:
     - Physical: Use of a physical device, such as a smart card, to guarantee the physical presence of the user or device.
     - Digital certificate: This method verifies the identity of a user or device through a certificate issued by a trusted Certification Authority.
     - Credentials: Providing a username and password through an authentication window, often complemented by additional security measures such as two-factor authentication.

4. **Assessment of Access and Compliance Policies:**

   Furthermore, access may be conditioned by various additional factors to enhance security and optimize network management:

   - **Time restriction:** Access may be restricted based on a predefined connection schedule. For example, certain users or groups may be authorized to access the network only during working hours or at specific times of the day.
   - **Geographical restriction:** Policies may include location-based login strategies, permitting access exclusively from specific locations. This approach is particularly effective for preventing access from unsecured or off-campus locations.
   - **Device type:** Access can also be restricted according to the type of device used. Certain resources may be reserved exclusively for specific equipment, restricting access from non-compliant or less secure devices.
   - **Compliance status:** The AAA server also evaluates the device's compliance status, for instance, by verifying that it is up-to-date with security requirements such as antivirus and encryption policies.

5. **Assigning a Security Tag:**

   If the device or user is successfully authenticated and complies with security policies, the AAA server assigns a tag to the user or device. These tags are used to apply specific security policies and determine what level of access is granted to the network.

Step 2:

1. **Policy enforcement via the SDN Controller:**
   - Once authentication is successfully completed, the SDN controller assumes network management and enforces the defined GBPs. These policies are established based on the tags assigned by the AAA server.
   - Micro-segmentation is enforced at this stage, restricting user or device access to specific segments of the network. These segments are defined according to the roles or groups to which the user or device belongs.
   - The application of the access policy can extend not only to switches, routers, or access points, but also to all elements that process frames, such as firewalls, IDS, routers from other vendors, and more. The SDN controller, via dedicated libraries, can automate policy enforcement on these elements. The SDN controller, via dedicated libraries, can automate the application of the policy to these elements.
2. **Assigning an IP address:**
   - After authentication, the user or device is assigned an IP address, often in a specific VRF domain, depending on the tags. This ensures that the user remains within a predefined network segment, even when changing connection points within the network (mobility).

Step 3:

1. **Access Control and Surveillance:**
   - As the user or device uses the network, the SDN controller continuously monitors activity. At the same time, the AAA server re-evaluate policies based on changes in behavior or emerging risks.
   - If suspicious activity is detected or the device becomes non-compliant, the AAA server can restrict access in real-time by adjusting access policies or placing the user in a quarantine segment.
2. **Audit and reporting:**
   - Network activities are logged for security audits and performance analysis. These logs can be used to identify unauthorized access attempts, evaluate the effectiveness of applied policies, and optimize configurations for improved performance.

5.5 Automated Campus Network Solutions

The following is a non-exhaustive list of solutions available on the market that apply the general SD-LAN concepts explained in this chapter. However, each solution has its own specific characteristics and presents certain differences.

- **Cisco SD-Access:** Cisco SD-Access is a campus network solution based on automation and centralized management using Cisco DNA Center. It enables dynamic micro-segmentation, group-based security policy, and simplified network management.
- **Aruba ESP (Edge Services Platform):** Aruba ESP is a unified platform offering automated campus network management capabilities with cloud-based intelligence. It enables advanced micro-segmentation and adaptive security policies for enterprise networks.
- **Juniper Mist AI:** This solution uses artificial intelligence to automate and optimize campus networks, offering simplified management and real-time analysis. It enables dynamic segmentation of users and devices while ensuring policy-based security.
- **Extreme Networks Fabric Connect:** An SD-LAN solution for campus networks that simplifies configuration and management through automation and dynamic segmentation. It offers reliable, secure connectivity with granular security policies for users and applications.
- **Huawei CloudCampus:** It offers centralized management and automation capabilities for campus networks, allowing for dynamic and secure segmentation. It streamlines network operations and enhances efficiency through artificial intelligence and integrated analytics.
- **Fortinet Secure SD-Branch:** Fortinet Secure SD-Branch brings advanced security capabilities to campus networks by integrating security and automation through

centralized control. It enables segmentation and protection of remote branches while maintaining consistent security policies throughout the entire campus network.

These solutions focus on automation, centralized management with micro-segmentation capabilities, and group-based security policy management.

5.6 Conclusion

To conclude this chapter, we explored innovative technologies that are redefining campus network architectures, with a particular emphasis on SD-LAN and GBP. This exploration has demonstrated how these technologies can address the growing demands for performance, security, and flexibility in modern networks.

By introducing a layer of programmability and automation, SD-LAN aims to simplify campus network management while enhancing its operational efficiency. SD-LAN's flexible and adaptive architectures allow administrators to swiftly respond to evolving user and application needs, marking a significant step toward more agile and resilient IT infrastructures.

Furthermore, the adoption of GBP provides a robust approach to securing networks by dynamically aligning access and security policies with user groups and traffic types. The integration of GBP with SDN controllers unlocks new possibilities for even finer, context-aware network management.

Lab 7: Implementing SD-LAN Segmentation and Group Policies via OpenFlow

Objectives

- Understand SD-LAN architecture.
- Understand segmentation.
- Apply segmentation combined with GBP to control access in an SD-LAN network
- Use a Python script to configure OpenVswitch devices.
- Analyze the OpenFlow protocol instructions.

Case Study

The primary objective of this study is to combine traditional segmentation with GBP to effectively control access to the SD-LAN network. In particular, it aims to demonstrate that it is possible, in uncomplicated cases, to use traditional access management methods to secure an SD-LAN network. To this end, we will explore the use of Python scripts, via the Ryu SDN controller, to configure access rules on OpenVswitch devices and analyze OpenFlow protocol instructions.

ABC would like to deploy an SD-LAN network to benefit from centralized, programmable management.

Required Software

- **GNS3 or equivalent**

Network Topology

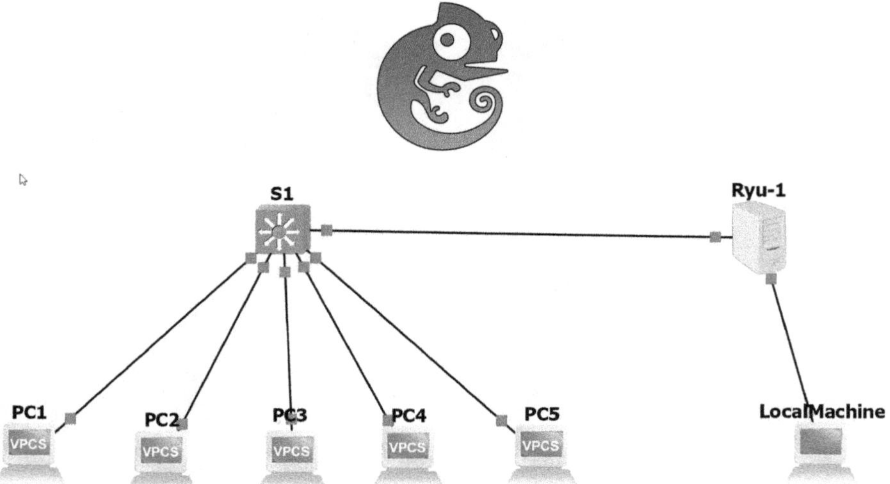

IP Address Table

Emulated Device	Device	Interface	IP Address/ Subnet Mask	Default Gateway
Ryu Controller (Ubuntu Linux, FlowManager)	SDN-Ryu	ens3	172.16.1.10/24	–
Ryu Controller (Ubuntu Linux, FlowManager)	SDN-Ryu	ens4	192.168.1.100/24	–
Open vSwitch (v2.4.90)/ Docker OpenVswitch	S1	br0	192.168.1.200/24	–
VPCS	PC1	eth0	192.168.1.10/24	–
VPCS	PC2	eth0	192.168.1.20/24	–
VPCS	PC3	eth0	192.168.1.30/24	–
VPCS	PC4	eth0	192.168.1.40/24	–
GNS3 Cloud	Local Machine	VMware Interface	172.16.1.1/24	–

Part A: Establishing Basic Device Configuration

1. Create the network topology.
2. Assign IP addresses to device interfaces according to the addressing table.
   a. Set SDN-Ryu's IP address.
   b. Set the IP addresses of PC1, PC2, PC3 and PC4.
   c. Configure the OpenVswitch switch as follows:

```
ifconfig br0 192.168.1.200 netmask 255.255.255.0
ovs-vsctl set-controller br0 tcp:192.168.1.100:6633
ovs-ofctl -O OpenFlow13 show br0
ovs-ofctl mod-flows br0 "priority=0,actions=normal"
ovs-vsctl set bridge br0 other-config:datapath-id=0000000000000001
```

3. **Ping** the network elements and ensure connectivity among them.
4. On the SDN-Ryu server, start the SDN controller:
   a. Use the **PuTTY** tool (or an equivalent SSH client) to connect to the Ryu controller.
   b. Execute the following command to start the SDN service and its graphical interface:

```
ryu-manager ~/flowmanager/flowmanager.py ryu.app.simple_switch_13
```

5. On the local Machine, launch a web browser:
   a. Enter the URL: http://172.16.1.10:8080/home/index.html.
   b. Verify that the switch appears correctly in the network topology view.

Part B: Using Classic Segmentation Combined with GBP to Manage Access on an SD-LAN Network

1. Recall the essential components of the GBP.
2. Create a Python script on the Ryu controller.
   a. Close the **PuTTY** window, then reconnect to the Ryu server.
   b. Create the file **micro_segmentation_V1.py** on the Ryu server.

```
nano micro_segmentation_V1.py
```

   c. Paste the contents of the Python script provided by the trainer into the **macro_segmentation_V1.py** file. The contents of the latter should be as follows:

```
from ryu.base import app_manager
from ryu.controller import ofp_event
from ryu.controller.handler import CONFIG_DISPATCHER, MAIN_DISPATCHER
from ryu.controller.handler import set_ev_cls
from ryu.ofproto import ofproto_v1_3
class GBPPolicyApp(app_manager.RyuApp):
    OFP_VERSIONS = [ofproto_v1_3.OFP_VERSION]

    def __init__(self, *args, **kwargs):
        super(GBPPolicyApp, self).__init__(*args, **kwargs)
        # Endpoints defined by IP addresses
        self.endpoints = {'PC1': '192.168.1.10', 'PC2':
  '192.168.1.20', 'PC3': '192.168.1.30'}
        # Endpoint groups
        self.endgroups = {'Gr1': ['PC1', 'PC2'], 'Gr2': ['PC3']}
        # Providers defined by IP addresses
        self.providers = { 'F1': '192.168.1.40', 'F2':
  '192.168.1.50'}
        # Access policy: which group can access which provider
        self.access_policy = {'Gr1': ['F1', 'F2'], 'Gr2': ['F2']} #
  Example policy
"""This block defines the data structures for endpoints, endgroups,
  providers, and access policies, including the IP addresses of PCs
  and providers, the division of PCs into groups, and the rules
  specifying which groups can access which providers."""
    def is_access_allowed(self, endpoint, provider):
        for group, providers in self.access_policy.items():
            if endpoint in self.endgroups[group] and provider in
  providers:
                return True
        return False
```

```
    def add_flow(self, datapath, priority, match, actions,
  buffer_id=None):
        ofproto = datapath.ofproto
        parser = datapath.ofproto_parser
        inst = [parser.OFPInstructionActions(ofproto.OFPIT_APPLY_
  ACTIONS, actions)]

        if buffer_id:
            mod = parser.OFPFlowMod(datapath=datapath,
  buffer_id=buffer_id,
                                    priority=priority, match=match,
                                    instructions=inst)
        else:
            mod = parser.OFPFlowMod(datapath=datapath,
  priority=priority,
                                    match=match, instructions=inst)
        datapath.send_msg(mod)

    def implement_policy(self, datapath):
        ofproto = datapath.ofproto
        parser = datapath.ofproto_parser

        for provider_name, provider_ip in self.providers.items():
            for endpoint_name, endpoint_ip in self.endpoints.items():
                if not self.is_access_allowed(endpoint_name,
  provider_name):
                    # If access is not allowed, drop the packets
                    match = parser.OFPMatch(eth_type=0x0800,
                                            ipv4_src=endpoint_ip,
                                            ipv4_dst=provider_ip)
                    actions = [] # No actions mean drop
                    self.add_flow(datapath, 100, match, actions)
"""This method enforces defined access policies by adding flow rules
  that block unauthorized traffic between access points and
  providers. If access is not authorized, a flow rule is added to
  drop the corresponding packets."""

    @set_ev_cls(ofp_event.EventOFPSwitchFeatures, CONFIG_DISPATCHER)
    def switch_features_handler(self, ev):
        datapath = ev.msg.datapath
        self.implement_policy(datapath)
```

Script Algorithm Explanation: In summary, this program is a Ryu controller script designed to implement GBP in a network using OpenFlow. It initializes access policies by defining end devices (PCs), service providers, and groups, along with the corresponding access rules. The script automatically blocks any unauthorized traffic between user groups and providers by adding flow suppression rules to the OpenFlow switch, ensuring that only authorized flows can traverse the network.

Note: It is important to note that the learner is not required to know the purpose of every command and library used in this script.

3. Run the Ryu controller combined with the Python script.

```
ryu-manager ~/flowmanager/flowmanager.py
ryu.app.simple_switch_13 ./ macro_segmentation_V1.py
```

4. On the Local Machine, open a web browser:
   c. Type in the URL: http://172.16.1.10:8080/home/index.html.
   d. On the **"Flow"** tab, check that the flows are correctly registered.

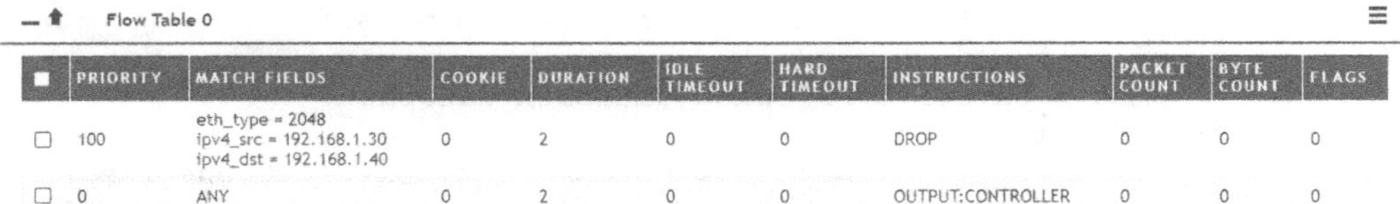

Flow Table 0

	PRIORITY	MATCH FIELDS	COOKIE	DURATION	IDLE TIMEOUT	HARD TIMEOUT	INSTRUCTIONS	PACKET COUNT	BYTE COUNT	FLAGS
☐	100	eth_type = 2048 ipv4_src = 192.168.1.30 ipv4_dst = 192.168.1.40	0	2	0	0	DROP	0	0	0
☐	0	ANY	0	2	0	0	OUTPUT:CONTROLLER	0	0	0

5. Referring to the explanation of the algorithm in the Python script, explain the recorded filtering rule.

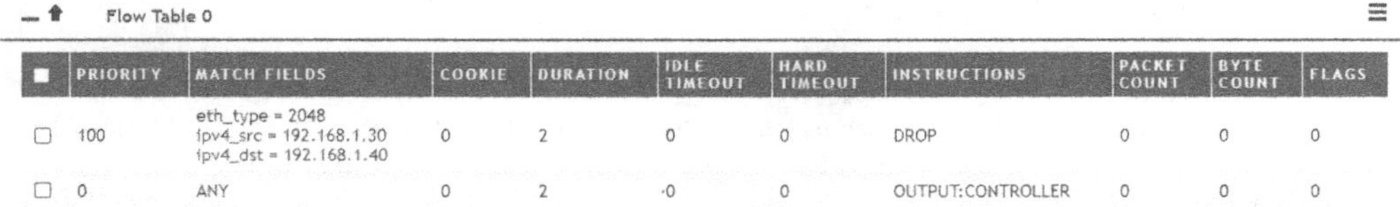

Flow Table 0

	PRIORITY	MATCH FIELDS	COOKIE	DURATION	IDLE TIMEOUT	HARD TIMEOUT	INSTRUCTIONS	PACKET COUNT	BYTE COUNT	FLAGS
☐	100	eth_type = 2048 ipv4_src = 192.168.1.30 ipv4_dst = 192.168.1.40	0	2	0	0	DROP	0	0	0
☐	0	ANY	0	2	0	0	OUTPUT:CONTROLLER	0	0	0

6. On PC3, check that you can **ping** PC3.
7. Create the Python file **macro_segmentation_V2.py** on the Ryu controller. The contents of this file differ from the previous one by the following block:

```
...
    def __init__(self, *args, **kwargs):
        super(GBPPolicyApp, self).__init__(*args, **kwargs)
        # Load configuration from JSON file
"""This block is used to load endpoints, endgroups, providers and
  access policies from the 'config.json' file."""
        with open('config.json', 'r') as config_file:
            config = json.load(config_file)
        self.endpoints = config['endpoints']
        self.endgroups = config['endgroups']
        self.providers = config['providers']
        self.access_policy = config['access_policy']
 ...
```

8. Create the Python file **config.json** on the Ryu controller. The contents of this file are as follows:

```
{
    "endpoints": {
        "PC1": "192.168.1.10",
        "PC2": "192.168.1.20",
        "PC3": "192.168.1.30"
    },
    "endgroups": {
        "Gr1": ["PC1", "PC2"],
        "Gr2": ["PC3"]
    },
    "providers": {
        "F1": "192.168.1.40",
        "F2": "192.168.1.50"
    },
    "access_policy": {
        "Gr1": ["F1", "F2"],
        "Gr2": ["F2"]
    }
}
```

9. Run the Ryu controller combined with the Python script **macro_segmentation_V2.py** and check the result.
10. Create the Python file **macro_segmentation_V3.py** on the Ryu controller and fill it with the content provided by the trainer.

> Explanation of the script algorithm: This Python script uses the Ryu controller to implement advanced GBP in an SDN. It reads and interprets access rules from two JSON files, which define connection policies between various endpoints and providers, according to criteria such as source IP address, destination IP address, protocol used, and port involved. The script translates these policies into OpenFlow flow rules for an OVS switch, allowing or blocking network traffic according to the specifications. Defined actions (allowing or blocking traffic) are applied dynamically, offering flexible customization of security and traffic control within the SD-LAN network.

11. Create the **policies.json** and **data.json** files on the Ryu controller and fill them with the content provided by the trainer.

12. Run the Ryu controller combined with the Python script **macro_segmentation_V3.py** and check the result.

☐	100	eth_type = 2048 ipv4_src = 192.168.0.10 ipv4_dst = 192.168.0.40 ip_proto = 6 udp_dst = 80	0	0	0	0	OUTPUT:NORMAL	0	0	1
☐	100	eth_type = 2048 ipv4_src = 192.168.0.20 ipv4_dst = 192.168.0.40 ip_proto = 6 udp_dst = 80	0	0	0	0	OUTPUT:NORMAL	0	0	1
☐	100	eth_type = 2048 ipv4_src = 192.168.0.10 ipv4_dst = 192.168.0.40 ip_proto = 6 udp_dst = 22	0	0	0	0	DROP	0	0	1
☐	100	eth_type = 2048 ipv4_src = 192.168.0.20 ipv4_dst = 192.168.0.40 ip_proto = 6 udp_dst = 22	0	0	0	0	DROP	0	0	1
☐	100	eth_type = 2048 ipv4_src = 192.168.0.30 ipv4_dst = 192.168.0.50 ip_proto = 6 udp_dst = 80	0	0	0	0	OUTPUT:NORMAL	0	0	1
☐	100	eth_type = 2048 ipv4_src = 192.168.0.30 ipv4_dst = 192.168.0.40 ip_proto = 6 udp_dst = 80	0	0	0	0	DROP	0	0	1

Lab 8: Programmable Micro-Segmentation in SD-LAN Using Ryu and OpenVSwitch

Objectives

- Understand SDN-LAN architecture.
- Understand the principles of micro-segmentation.
- Apply micro-segmentation combined with GBP to manage access in a network.
- Use a Python script to configure OpenVswitch devices.
- Analyze OpenFlow protocol instructions.

Case Study

The primary objective of this study is to integrate micro-segmentation with GBP in order to effectively control access to the SD-LAN network. To achieve this, we will explore the use of Python scripts, via the Ryu SDN controller, to insert a tag indicating the user's group in frames. In addition, the script will be used to configure access rules on OpenVswitch devices and analyze OpenFlow protocol instructions. The aim of this study is to provide a practical and theoretical understanding of these concepts for optimized and secure network management.

ABC would like to deploy an SD-LAN network to benefit from centralized, programmable management. It also plans to set up differentiated access levels for its users.

Required Software

- **GNS3 or equivalent**

Network Topology

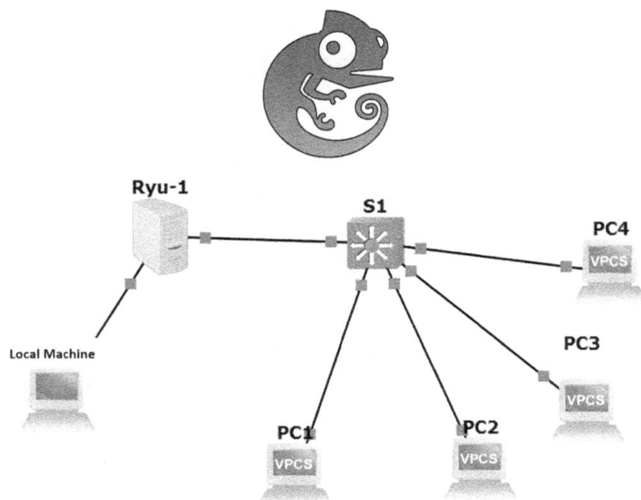

IP Address Table

Emulated Device	Device	Interface	IP Address/ Subnet Mask	Default Gateway
Ryu Controller (Ubuntu Linux, FlowManager)	SDN-Ryu	ens3	172.16.1.10/24	–
Ryu Controller (Ubuntu Linux, FlowManager)	SDN-Ryu	ens4	192.168.1.100/24	–
Open vSwitch (v2.4.90)/ Docker OpenVswitch	S1	br0	192.168.1.200/24	–
VPCS	PC1	eth0	192.168.1.10/24	–
VPCS	PC2	eth0	192.168.1.20/24	–
VPCS	PC3	eth0	192.168.1.30/24	–
VPCS	PC4	eth0	192.168.1.40/24	–
GNS3 Cloud	Local Machine	VMware Interface	172.16.1.1/24	–

Part A: Establishing Basic Device Configuration

1. Create the network topology.
2. Assign IP addresses to device interfaces according to the addressing table.
   a. Set SDN-Ryu's IP address.
   b. Set the IP addresses of PC1, PC2, PC3, and PC4.
   c. Configure the OpenVswitch switch as follows:

```
ifconfig br0 192.168.1.200 netmask 255.255.255.0
ovs-vsctl set-controller br0 tcp:192.168.1.100:6633
ovs-ofctl -O OpenFlow13 show br0
ovs-ofctl mod-flows br0 "priority=0,actions=normal"
ovs-vsctl set bridge br0 other-config:datapath-id=0000000000000001
```

3. **Ping** the network elements and ensure connectivity among them.
4. On the SDN-Ryu server, start the SDN controller:
   a. Use the **PuTTY** tool (or an equivalent SSH client) to connect to the Ryu controller.
   b. Execute the following command to launch the SDN service and its graphical interface:

```
ryu-manager ~/flowmanager/flowmanager.py ryu.app.simple_switch_13
```

5. On the Local Machine, launch a web browser:
   a. Enter the following URL: http://172.16.1.10:8080/home/index.html
   b. Verify that the switch appears correctly in the network topology view.

Part B: Theoretical Background on SD-LAN Architecture

1. Recall the essential components of an **SD-LAN** architecture.
2. Link each item in the table with its corresponding definition.

1. Group-based policy management (GBP)	A. A server that manages authentication, authorization, and accounting for users and devices on the network.
2. Macro-segmentation	B. A tool or platform that automates and manages the configuration, deployment, and coordination of network resources in an SDN environment.
3. Orchestrator	C. The division of a network into large logical segments to isolate different traffic or application areas.
4. AAA server	D. A network security method that divides network segments into smaller, more specific units, inserting a specific tag for each frame.
5. Micro-segmentation	E. A system that applies network policies according to user or device groups, enabling granular control of traffic flows and security.

Part C: Using Micro-Segmentation Combined with GBP to Manage Access on an SD-LAN Network

1. Create the Python file on the Ryu controller.
   a. Close the **PuTTY** window and then reconnect to the Ryu server using SSH.
   b. Create the file "micro_segmentation.py" on the Ryu server.

```
nano micro_segmentation.py
```

   c. Paste the contents of the Python script provided by the trainer into the **micro_segmentation.py** file. The contents should be as follows:

```
import socket
from ryu.base import app_manager
from ryu.controller import ofp_event
from ryu.controller.handler import CONFIG_DISPATCHER, set_ev_cls
from ryu.ofproto import ofproto_v1_3
from ryu.lib.packet import ethernet, ether_types, ipv4

def ip_to_int(ip):
    """Convert an IP string to integer."""
"""This block defines a function to convert textual IP addresses
  into integers, optimizing storage in metadata fields."""
    return int.from_bytes(socket.inet_aton(ip), 'big')
class GroupBasedSegmentation(app_manager.RyuApp):
    OFP_VERSIONS = [ofproto_v1_3.OFP_VERSION]
```

```
"""This method initializes the class and defines a dictionary that
  associates each IP address with a specific group for group-based
  segmentation."""
    def __init__(self, *args, **kwargs):
        super(GroupBasedSegmentation, self).__init__(*args,
  **kwargs)
        self.ip_to_group = {
            '192.168.1.10': 1, # Group 1
            '192.168.1.20': 1, # Group 1
            '192.168.1.30': 2, # Group 2
            '192.168.1.40': 2  # Group 2
        }

    @set_ev_cls(ofp_event.EventOFPSwitchFeatures, CONFIG_DISPATCHER)
    def switch_features_handler(self, ev):
        datapath = ev.msg.datapath
        ofproto = datapath.ofproto
        parser = datapath.ofproto_parser

        # Setup table-miss flow entry in table 0
        match = parser.OFPMatch()
        actions = [parser.OFPActionOutput(ofproto.OFPP_CONTROLLER,
  ofproto.OFPCML_NO_BUFFER)]
        self.add_flow(datapath, 0, match, actions, table_id=0)

        # Setup metadata and reg0 write rules in table 0
        for ip, group in self.ip_to_group.items():
            ip_int = ip_to_int(ip) # Convert IP address to integer
            match = parser.OFPMatch(eth_type=ether_types.ETH_TYPE_IP,
  ipv4_src=ip)
            instructions = [
                parser.OFPInstructionWriteMetadata(metadata=ip_int,
  metadata_mask=0xffffffff),
                parser.OFPInstructionActions(ofproto.OFPIT_APPLY_
  ACTIONS, [parser.OFPActionSetField(reg0=group)]),
                parser.OFPInstructionGotoTable(1)
            ]

"""For each IP, converts the address to an integer, stores this
  value in the metadata field, defines the group in reg0, and
  directs the flow to the next table. This prepares the switch to
  apply rules based on IP address and group."""
            self.add_flow(datapath, 100, match, [], instructions,
  table_id=0)
        # Setup group communication rules in table 1
```

```
        for ip, group in self.ip_to_group.items():
            match = parser.OFPMatch(eth_type=ether_types.ETH_TYPE_IP,
  ipv4_dst=ip, reg0=group)
            actions = [parser.OFPActionOutput (ofproto.OFPP_NORMAL)]
            instructions = [parser.OFPInstructionActions(ofproto.
  OFPIT_APPLY_ACTIONS, actions)]
            self.add_flow(datapath, 200, match, [], instructions,
  table_id=1)

"""Configures table 1 to enable communication between members of the
  same group, based on the destination IP address and the registered
  group."""

        # Default drop rule in table 1 to block other communications
        match = parser.OFPMatch()
        self.add_flow(datapath, 1, match, [], table_id=1) # No
  actions means drop

    def add_flow(self, datapath, priority, match, actions,
  instructions=None, buffer_id=None, table_id=0):
        ofproto = datapath.ofproto
        parser = datapath.ofproto_parser
        if instructions is None:
            instructions = [parser.OFPInstructionActions(ofproto.
  OFPIT_APPLY_ACTIONS, actions)]
        mod = parser.OFPFlowMod(datapath=datapath, priority=priority,
  match=match,
                                       instructions=instructions,
  table_id=table_id)
        datapath.send_msg(mod)
```

Explanation of the script algorithm: In brief, this program is a Ryu controller script designed to implement group-based network micro-segmentation using the OpenFlow protocol. It starts by associating each IP address with a specific group, thus establishing the rules for packet processing on SDN switches. When a switch connects, the controller sets up rules in the flow table to record source IP addresses as metadata and store the corresponding group in the reg0 register of each frame. It then configures rules in a subsequent table to allow communication exclusively between PCs in the same group, rejecting all other communications by default to reinforce network micro-segmentation.

Note: It is important to note that the learner is not required to know the purpose of every command and library used in this script.

2. Run the Ryu controller combined with the Python script.

```
ryu-manager ~/flowmanager/flowmanager.py
  ryu.app.simple_switch_13 ./ micro_segmentation.py
```

3. On the Local Machine, open a web browser:
   a. Enter the following URL: http://172.16.1.10:8080/home/index.html
   b. On the **"Flow"** tab, check that the flows are correctly registered.

Flow Table 0

PRIORITY	MATCH FIELDS	COOKIE	DURATION	IDLE TIMEOUT	HARD TIMEOUT	INSTRUCTIONS	PACKET COUNT	BYTE COUNT	FLAGS
100	eth_type = 2048 ipv4_src = 192.168.1.10	0	2	0	0	SET_FIELD: reg0:1 WRITE_METADATA:0xc0a8010a/0xffffffff GOTO_TABLE:1	0	0	0
100	eth_type = 2048 ipv4_src = 192.168.1.20	0	2	0	0	SET_FIELD: reg0:1 WRITE_METADATA:0xc0a80114/0xffffffff GOTO_TABLE:1	0	0	0
100	eth_type = 2048 ipv4_src = 192.168.1.30	0	2	0	0	SET_FIELD: reg0:2 WRITE_METADATA:0xc0a8011e/0xffffffff GOTO_TABLE:1	0	0	0
100	eth_type = 2048 ipv4_src = 192.168.1.40	0	2	0	0	SET_FIELD: reg0:2 WRITE_METADATA:0xc0a80128/0xffffffff GOTO_TABLE:1	0	0	0
0	ANY	0	2	0	0	OUTPUT:CONTROLLER	0	0	0

Flow Table 1

PRIORITY	MATCH FIELDS	COOKIE	DURATION	IDLE TIMEOUT	HARD TIMEOUT	INSTRUCTIONS	PACKET COUNT	BYTE COUNT	FLAGS
200	eth_type = 2048 ipv4_dst = 192.168.1.10 reg0 = 1	0	2	0	0	OUTPUT:NORMAL	0	0	0
200	eth_type = 2048 ipv4_dst = 192.168.1.20 reg0 = 1	0	2	0	0	OUTPUT:NORMAL	0	0	0
200	eth_type = 2048 ipv4_dst = 192.168.1.30 reg0 = 2	0	2	0	0	OUTPUT:NORMAL	0	0	0
200	eth_type = 2048 ipv4_dst = 192.168.1.40 reg0 = 2	0	2	0	0	OUTPUT:NORMAL	0	0	0
1	ANY	0	2	0	0	DROP	0	0	0

4. Referring to the explanation of the Python script algorithm, explain the role of the following instructions:

PRIORITY	MATCH FIELDS	COOKIE	DURATION	IDLE TIMEOUT	HARD TIMEOUT	INSTRUCTIONS	PACKET COUNT	BYTE COUNT	FLAGS
100	eth_type = 2048 ipv4_src = 192.168.1.10	0	2	0	0	SET_FIELD: reg0:1 WRITE_METADATA:0xc0a8010a/0xffffffff GOTO_TABLE:1	0	0	0

SET_FIELD: reg0:1	
WRITE_METADATA:0xc0a8010a/0xffffffff	
GOTO_TABLE:1	

5. Referring to the explanation of the algorithm in the Python script, explain the following filtering rule:

PRIORITY	MATCH FIELDS	COOKIE	DURATION	IDLE TIMEOUT	HARD TIMEOUT	INSTRUCTIONS	PACKET COUNT	BYTE COUNT	FLAGS
200	eth_type = 2048 ipv4_dst = 192.168.1.10 reg0 = 1	0	2	0	0	OUTPUT:NORMAL	0	0	0

eth_type=2048 ipv4_dst=192.168.1.10 reg0=1	
OUTPUT: NORMAL	

Part E: Testing and Analysis of Results

1. On **PC1**, check that you can **ping PC2**.
2. On **PC3**, check that you can **ping PC4**.
   Note: It is possible to integrate subgroups within the same group (e.g., subgroups **1-1**, **1–2**, etc.) in order to manage access among them. To do this, simply add an additional value, "**reg1**", to the frame.
3. Referring to the theoretical part and this practical work, please describe the algorithm that explains the steps involved in implementing micro-segmentation in combination with GBP to manage access in an SD-LAN network. Please also explain the role of the AAA server in this context.

Lab 9: Cisco Micro-Segmentation with SGT and CTS

Objectives

- Configure Cisco devices to leverage micro-segmentation combined with GBP to control access within an SD-LAN network.

Case Study

This study aims to integrate micro-segmentation with GBP for effective access control in an SD-LAN network composed of Cisco devices.

ABC intends to deploy a Cisco SD-LAN network to establish differentiated access levels for its users.

Required Software

- **GNS3 or equivalent**

Network Topology

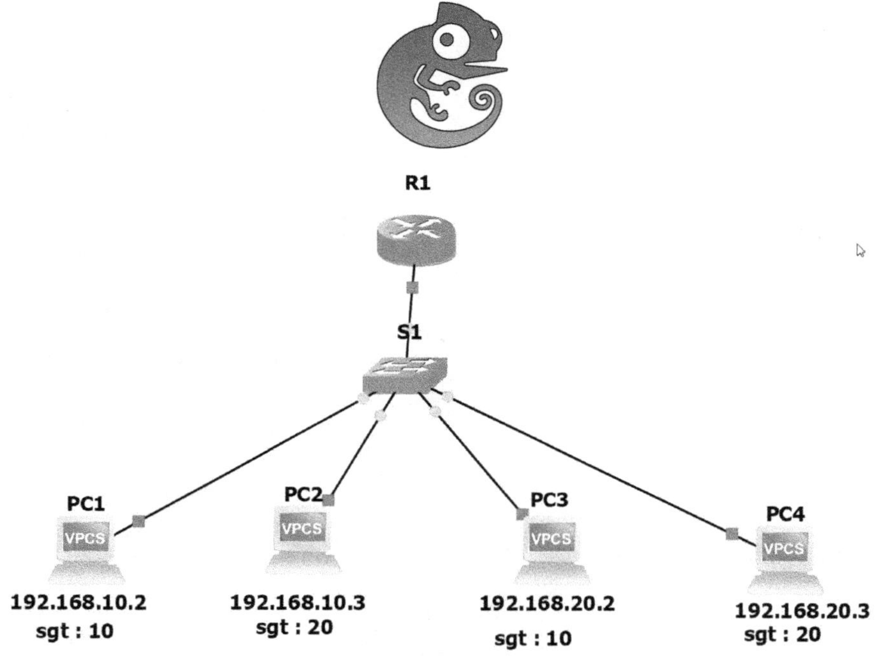

IP Address Table

Emulated Device	Device	Interface	IP Address/ Subnet Mask	Default Gateway
Cisco CSR1000v (IOS XE v17.3.1a, QEMU)	R1	G1.10	192.168.10.1/30	–
Cisco CSR1000v (IOS XE v17.3.1a, QEMU)	R1	G1.20	192.168.20.1/30	–
VPCS	PC1	eth0	192.168.10.2 (VLAN10)	192.168.10.1
VPCS	PC2	eth0	192.168.10.3 (VLAN10)	192.168.10.1
VPCS	PC3	eth0	192.168.20.2 (VLAN20)	192.168.20.1
VPCS	PC4	eth0	192.168.20.2 (VLAN20)	192.168.20.1

Part A: Establish Basic Device Configuration

1. Recall the definition of **SGACLs**.
2. Configure the PCs' IP addresses, then assign them to the appropriate VLANs after configuring switch S1.
3. On R1, set sub-interface IP addresses.
4. Activate **CTS** functionality.

```
(config)# cts role-based enforcement
```

5. Define one SGT value per IP address.

```
cts role-based sgt-map 192.168.10.2 sgt 10
cts role-based sgt-map 192.168.10.3 sgt 20
cts role-based sgt-map 192.168.20.2 sgt 10
cts role-based sgt-map 192.168.20.3 sgt 20
```

Note: On Cisco, users can be grouped and statically assigned SGTs. Grouping can be done according to different values, such as IP addresses, subnets, VLANs, or Layer 2 and Layer 3 interfaces. In our case study, we used an SGT mapping by IP address.

6. On R1, display the security groups created

```
R1#sh cts role-based sgt-map all
Active IPv4-SGT Bindings Information

IP Address SGT Source
============================================
192.168.10.2 10 CLI
192.168.10.3 20 CLI
192.168.20.2 10 CLI
192.168.20.3 20 CLI
```

```
IP-SGT Active Bindings Summary
============================================
Total number of CLI bindings = 4
Total number of active bindings = 4
```

7. Create two ACLs named "deny_ip" and "permit_ip" to define access permissions between different network elements:

```
(config)# ip access-list role-based deny_ip
 10 deny ip
(config)# ip access-list role-based permit_ip
 10 permit ip
```

8. Apply the ACLs to regulate traffic between user groups.

```
(config)# cts role-based permissions from 10 to 10 permit_ip
(config)# cts role-based permissions from 20 to 20 permit_ip
(config)# cts role-based permissions from 10 to 20 deny_ip
```

9. Verify the configuration of the ACLs that you have created.

```
R1#sh cts role-based permissions from 10 to 10
IPv4 Role-based permissions from group 10 to group 10 (configured):
        permit_ip
RBACL Monitor All for Dynamic Policies: FALSE
RBACL Monitor All for Configured Policies: FALSE
R1#sh cts role-based permissions from 10 to 20
IPv4 Role-based permissions from group 10 to group 20 (configured):
        deny_ip
RBACL Monitor All for Dynamic Policies: FALSE
RBACL Monitor All for Configured Policies: FALSE
```

Part E: Test and Analysis of Results

1. On **PC1**, verify that you can **ping PC3**.
2. On **PC2**, verify that you can **ping PC4**.
3. On **PC1**, verify that you can't **ping PC4**.

   Note: You cannot perform **ping** tests between PC1 and PC2, nor between PC3 and PC4, as switch S1 does not support Cisco's micro-segmentation capability. It is important to note that the simulation of SGT functionalities is currently not supported on VIOS-L2 switches.

6

The Convergence of NFV and SDN for a Modern Network Infrastructure

In the digital age, the demand for more flexible, scalable, and efficient network infrastructures continues to grow. Network functions virtualization (NFV) and software-defined networking (SDN) technologies are critical technologies for addressing these requirements. By decoupling network functions from physical hardware and centralizing network control, NFV and SDN provide a transformative approach to network design, deployment, and management. This chapter explores the synergy between NFV and SDN, demonstrating how their convergence can transform modern network infrastructures.

The first section of this chapter introduces NFV, explaining its fundamental principles and highlighting its significance in network function virtualization. We also discuss the standards and architectures defined by entities such as the European Telecommunications Standards Institute (ETSI) and the OpenNFV project, which facilitate NFV adoption and interoperability.

The following section highlights the impact of NFV in data centers, describing how it optimizes operations and improves the efficiency of IT services. We also look at how NFV contributes to reducing costs and improving the flexibility of data infrastructures.

The heart of the chapter is dedicated to the interaction between NFV and SDN. This section explores how these two technologies can be integrated to create more robust and agile networks. Specific examples of synergy in cloud service provider networks and inline network functions will be presented, illustrating the benefits of this integration in real-life scenarios.

Finally, we'll conclude with a discussion of where it's most beneficial to combine NFV and SDN, highlighting the practical considerations and challenges associated with their convergence.

Through this chapter, we aim to provide an in-depth understanding of how NFV and SDN can be jointly leveraged to revolutionize network infrastructures, providing professionals and organizations with the means to effectively navigate the evolving landscape of network technologies.

This chapter covers the following **topics:**

1. Introduction to NFV
2. Network virtualization standards
3. Data center optimization through nfv
4. Interaction between NFV and SDN
5. When to combine NFV and SDN?
6. Conclusion.

DOI: 10.1201/9781003679394-6

6.1 Introduction to NFV

NFV is revolutionizing the telecommunications sector by converting functions traditionally performed on dedicated hardware into software running on standard servers. This innovation offers increased flexibility and the possibility of significantly reducing operating and maintenance costs.

This technology allows nearly all network functions to be virtualized, enhancing management agility and cost-effectiveness. The ETSI presents several NFV use cases, including single and multilayer switches, routers, and security solutions such as enterprise firewalls, next-generation firewalls, and intrusion detection and prevention systems.

By consolidating traditional network functions into software platforms, NFV promotes more efficient resource management, reduced costs, and an enhanced ability to innovate rapidly in the face of changing market requirements.

6.2 Network Virtualization Standards

With the rise of this technology, establishing standards to guide and standardize virtualization practices in the industry has become essential. ETSI and OpenNFV are at the forefront of these initiatives, playing a key role in harmonizing approaches to network function virtualization.

6.2.1 European Telecommunications Standards Institute

ETSI is an internationally recognized standards organization, playing a pivotal role in the development of telecommunications standards, including those for NFV. ETSI's NFV initiative was launched in 2012 by several leading telecom operators. The aim was to establish international standards and architectures to foster innovation and collaboration between the various stakeholders.

6.2.1.1 ETSI Architecture and Standards

- ETSI NFV defines a reference infrastructure that divides network functions into three main areas (Figure 6.1).
- **NFV infrastructure (NFVI):** Includes the physical and virtualized resources required to support VNF virtualized network functions. This includes compute, storage, and network hardware, as well as virtualization software.
- **VNF manager:** Responsible for VNF lifecycle management, including initialization, scaling, modification, and termination of VNF instances.
- **NFV orchestration:** Manages NFVI resources across different domains and orchestrates network services on the NFVI.

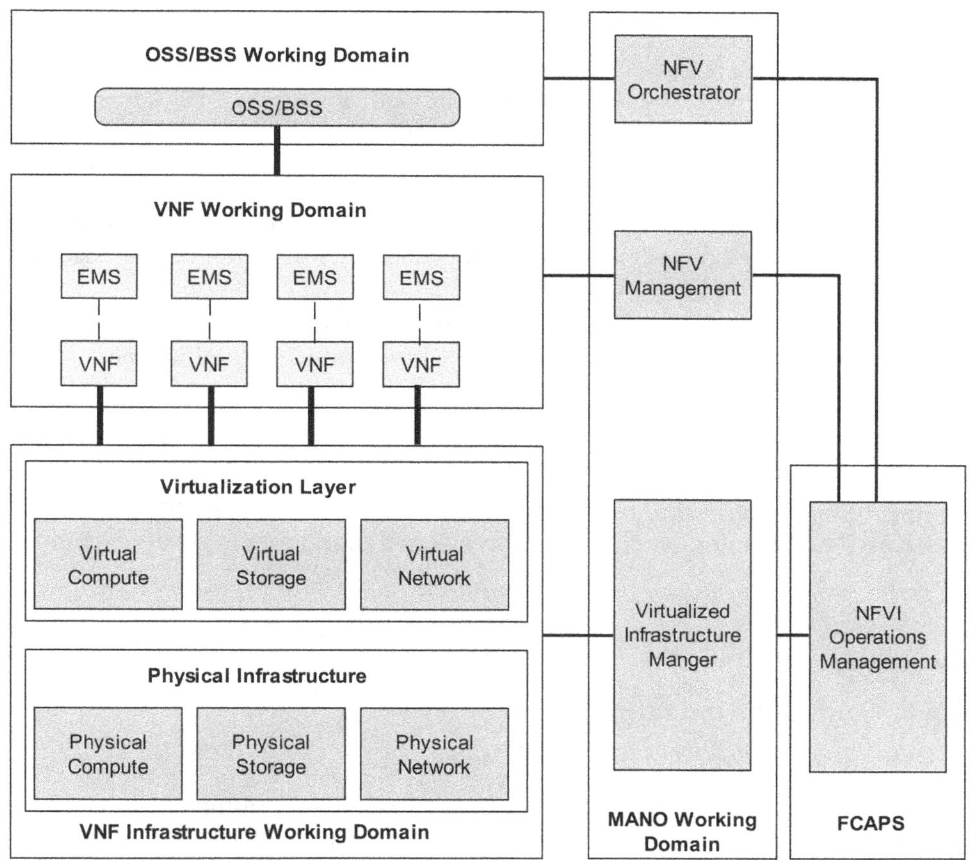

FIGURE 6.1
Architecture of virtualized networks according to ETSI standards.[1]

6.2.1.2 ETSI Standards and Specifications

ETSI's work includes the definition of technical specifications and group reports to guide NFV implementation. These documents cover aspects such as security, network management, and interoperability between products from different manufacturers. These documents are available for download from the official ETSI website: https://www.etsi.org.

6.2.2 OpenNFV Project

OpenNFV is a project launched by the Linux Foundation to accelerate innovation in NFV. Unlike ETSI, which focuses on the creation of standards and specifications, OpenNFV emphasizes the implementation of these standards through open source projects.

6.2.2.1 *Platform and Contributions*

OpenNFV provides a continuous integration and testing platform for NFV technologies. By collaborating with standards defined by bodies such as ETSI, OpenNFV helps ensure that the various NFV components can work together effectively. Key elements of OpenNFV include:

- **Integration of various open source elements:** Use of components such as OpenStack for virtualization resources, or Kubernetes for container management, integrated into an NFV environment.
- **Testing and validation:** OpenNFV carries out regular tests to validate the interoperability and performance of NFV solutions based on ETSI specifications.

6.2.2.2 *Collaboration and Interoperability*

One of OpenNFV's strengths is its ability to bring together diverse market players, from software developers to service providers, to collaborate on common NFV solutions. This has facilitated greater interoperability and accelerated the adoption of NFV technologies.

6.3 Data Center Optimization through NFV

6.3.1 Definition and Function of a Data Center

A data center is a physical infrastructure designed to house IT equipment, including servers, storage systems, and network components. This facility is specially designed to guarantee the security, redundancy, and high availability of IT resources.

These features are essential for efficient and secure management, and we'll look at them in more detail in the following sections.

- **Security management:** Data centers implement rigorous security measures, including biometric access controls, camera surveillance systems, and advanced network security solutions. These measures are vital to guard against physical and digital intrusions, preserving data integrity and confidentiality.
- **Monitoring and maintenance:** The robustness of data center infrastructures is maintained through continuous monitoring and maintenance. Operating around the clock, these monitoring processes detect and respond to any technical or security problems, which is crucial to preventing service interruptions and minimizing downtime. Preventive maintenance is carried out on a regular basis to keep equipment in optimum working order, thus guaranteeing the continuity of the services offered by the center.
- **Support for cloud computing:** The reliability and capacity of data centers to withstand high operational loads enable them to play an essential role in supporting cloud computing services. By providing the necessary computing power and storage capacity, data centers facilitate cloud operations, enabling companies to deploy and operate large-scale applications and services flexibly and efficiently.

- **Enterprise application hosting:** The ability of data centers to centrally and securely manage mission-critical applications and data is particularly valuable for large enterprises. Not only does this enable efficient management, it also enhances security, a benefit derived directly from the rigorous infrastructure and security practices implemented within data centers.

6.3.2 Impact of NFV on Data Center Efficiency

Data centers are thus critical to the modern digital economy, supporting both daily business operations and technological innovations. They continue to evolve through advanced technologies, such as network function virtualization and automation, to enhance efficiency and reduce operational costs.

Adopting NFV in data centers brings many benefits, including:

- **Optimized resource utilization:** Virtualization enables several network functions to be grouped together on a single physical server, improving resource utilization and reducing hardware footprint.
- **Greater flexibility and scalability:** VNFs can be easily deployed, resized, and relocated on demand, enabling data centers to adapt quickly to changing workloads and new business requirements.
- **Lower costs:** NFV can reduce investment (CapEx) and operating (OpEx) costs by eliminating the need for dedicated network hardware and simplifying infrastructure management.
- **Increased agility:** NFV enables data centers to deploy new network services more quickly and easily, giving them a competitive edge.

Let's take the example of a telecom operator wishing to deploy one or more virtual firewalls in its data center. With NFV, the operator can install the virtual firewalls on a generic server, rather than purchasing several dedicated physical firewall devices. This saves the operator money and increases the flexibility of its network infrastructure. What's more, the NFV orchestrator can automate the deployment and management of virtual firewalls, saving the operator time and reducing errors.

6.4 Interaction between NFV and SDN

6.4.1 Overview of NFV-SDN Interactions

While NFV and SDN are distinct technologies, their objectives are complementary. NFV facilitates the rapid, on-demand deployment of network services, while SDN offers centralized control and optimized management of these services. Together, they enable harmonious orchestration that can dynamically allocate network resources according to real-time needs.

The aim of SDN is to provide the fastest, most flexible service execution possible, while NFV aims to reduce the cost and time required to deploy network functions.

The combination of SDN and NFV offers many advantages for network management:

- **Agility and flexibility:** The combination of NFV and SDN enables networks to adapt quickly to changes, such as sudden increases in bandwidth demand or the deployment of new services.
- **Cost reduction:** By reducing dependency on expensive hardware and optimizing resource utilization, NFV and SDN can significantly reduce operational and investment costs.
- **Enhanced security:** The ability to deploy and manage security functions dynamically and centrally helps to respond more effectively to emerging threats.
- **Easier innovation:** The flexibility offered by NFV and SDN encourages innovation, enabling operators to test and launch new services quickly and at lower risk.
- **Better visibility and control:** SDN centralizes network management, providing a unified overview and facilitating decision-making. NFV enables granular monitoring of VNFs, optimizing their performance.

SDN and NFV are two complementary technologies that are revolutionizing network management. Far from being a question of exclusive choice, it's a question of understanding how to exploit them together to effectively meet today's needs. The key to this synergy lies in seamless communication between SDN and NFV, enabling them to coordinate actions and monitor network status.

6.4.2 NFV-SDN Synergies for Cloud Service Providers

A compelling example of their combined use is in cloud service provider networks, which host thousands or even millions of NFVs in data centers. The complexity of managing, monitoring, and orchestrating this number of NFVs and their service chains underlines the need for coordination.

The framework defined by ETSI indicates that an NFV manager can create, activate, or deactivate an NFV. However, if this NFV is essential for an active customer service, the infrastructure, represented by the SDN controller, must not interrupt it without prior coordination. For this, a common repository accessible to both SDN and NFV is needed to monitor and understand the current state of services.

Ideally, this repository should include a status management system that enables NFVs to be tracked individually or collectively, facilitating integrated, coordinated management. Operators can thus use SDN technology to manage the flow of data across virtualized infrastructures, while NFV can rapidly deploy services such as security and network optimization, tailored to changing customer needs.

6.4.3 Network Infrastructure Configuration Topology based on SDN and NFV

The following topology illustrates the architecture of a solution integrating SDN and NFV concepts. Here is an explanation of the various elements shown in the topology (Figure 6.2):

- **SDN controller:** The heart of the SDN infrastructure, the SDN controller centralizes network management and makes intelligent decisions about how traffic is directed across the network. It interacts directly with SDN applications and physical network devices such as routers and switches. It is connected to a number of

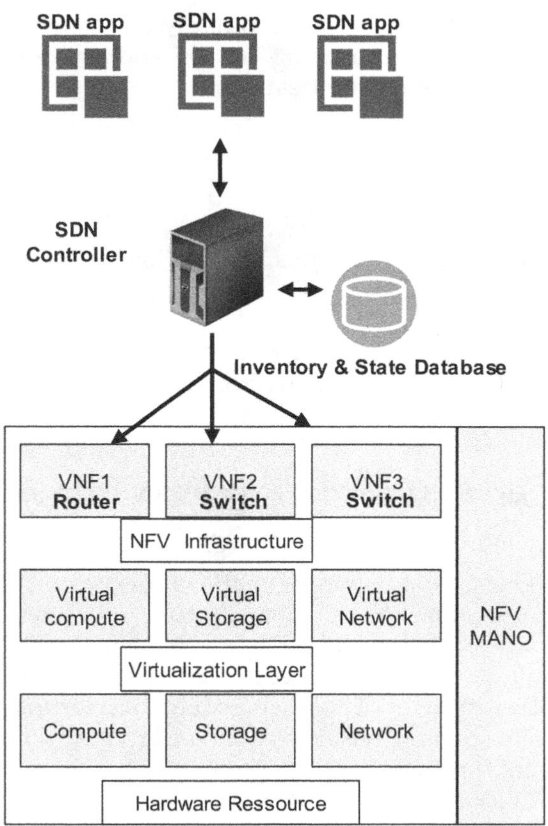

FIGURE 6.2
Example of an architecture unifying SDN and NFV.

SDN applications that use the controller's API to obtain the necessary network services and influence network behavior.

- **SDN applications:** These applications are developed to perform specific network functions such as traffic analysis, network security, and path optimization. They communicate with the SDN controller to obtain network information and request network configuration changes.
- **Virtual network functions (VNFs):** VNFs are instances of network functions traditionally performed by dedicated hardware, such as firewalls, load balancers, and VPN routers, virtualized as software. They are positioned on the NFVI to process network traffic in accordance with policies defined by the SDN controller and SDN applications.
- **NFVI:** Provides the environment required to run VNFs. It comprises virtualized computing, storage, and network resources. These components are as follows:
  - **Virtual compute:** Computing resources for running applications and services.
  - **Virtual storage:** Storage resources for data and applications.
  - **Virtual network:** Virtualized network components that connect VNFs to each other and to the external network.

- **Hardware resources:** This is the physical hardware on which the virtualization layer is built. It provides the computing, storage, and network connectivity capacity needed to support the virtual infrastructure.
- **NFV MANO (Management and Orchestration):** Manages and orchestrates NFV resources and VNFs. It is responsible for the setup, configuration management, healing, and scaling of virtual resources and network services. Interacts with the inventory and status database to track and manage network resources and services.
- **Inventory and state database:** It stores information on the current state and configuration of network resources, VNFs, and NFV infrastructure.

This **infrastructure** enables considerable flexibility and scalability in network management by moving network logic and functions from physical devices to configurable, automated software.

6.4.4 NFV-SDN Synergies for Optimizing Network Routing Services

6.4.4.1 Virtual Routing and Forwarding Technology

In an environment where several network functions coexist on the same infrastructure, it becomes essential to guarantee the isolation of traffic and routes between different network functions or instances. Virtual Routing and Forwarding (VRF) technology makes it possible to create multiple routing instances on a single physical or virtual router, each operating as an independent entity. This ensures that each virtualized network function (or client in a multi-tenant scenario) has its own isolated routing domain, preventing traffic and routes from different functions or clients from intermingling

The main features of VRF can be summarized as follows:

- **Routing isolation:** Each VRF is completely isolated from other VRFs, which means that routes in one VRF cannot be accessed, or can be accessed according to access rules, from another VRF. This isolation is essential in multi-tenant environments where several customers or services share the same physical infrastructure. It is a form of network segmentation into logical sub-networks or segments.
- **Separate routing tables:** Each VRF has its own routing table, enabling several clients or services to use the same IP addresses without any risk of address conflicts. For example, two different clients can use the same private address space without interference between their respective networks.
- **Flexibility and scalability:** VRF enables network operators to create new network segments dynamically, according to customer or service requirements. This flexibility is particularly useful in NFV environments, where new network functions can be deployed rapidly and require dedicated routing space.
- **Multi-protocol support:** VRF supports several routing protocols, including Border Gateway Protocol (BGP), Open Shortest Path First (OSPF), and Enhanced Interior Gateway Routing Protocol (EIGRP). This allows for great flexibility in the way routes are propagated and managed within each VRF.

6.4.4.2 Centralization of Routing Tables with Locator/ID Separation Protocol

Locator/ID Separation Protocol (LISP) is a network architecture protocol that separates endpoint identifiers (EIDs), which identify network nodes, from their routing locators (RLOCs), which specify their network locations.

This separation makes it possible to centralize and simplify routing table management, offering greater flexibility and scalability in complex network environments. In the context of NFV and SDN Synergies, LISP plays a crucial role in facilitating more dynamic, centralized management of network resources.

6.4.4.2.1 LISP Protocol Presentation

LISP is a routing and encapsulation protocol developed to improve the scalability and flexibility of IP networks. Traditionally, in IP networks, a single IP address serves as both identifier and locator for a device. This means that if a device moves within the network, its IP address must change, complicating routing management.

LISP solves this problem by separating these two functions:

- **ID:** It represents the unique identity of a device or network node. It can be an IP address assigned to a machine, independent of its position in the network.
- **Locator** indicates the current location of this device on the network. This is usually the IP address of the router or access point where the device is connected.

This separation enables a device to retain its unique identifier even if it physically moves within the network, while the locator can change according to the device's new position. This concept is analogous to a mobile phone network, where a device retains its number regardless of its location, and its network identifier depends on two parameters: a fixed identity and a dynamic locator.

6.4.4.2.2 LISP's Contribution to Centralizing and Simplifying Routing Table Management

LISP centralizes routing table management, shifting the complexity of locator management to centralized servers called Map-Servers (MS) and Map-Resolvers (MR). In a LISP network, edge routers don't need to maintain large internal routing tables. Instead, they query the MS for information on how to route packets to their destination.

LISP can be compared to a DNS server, which receives requests to resolve domain names, but in this case, LISP receives requests to resolve network node locations, facilitating dynamic routing management (Figure 6.3).

This approach has several advantages:

- **Reduced complexity:** Internal routers don't need to maintain large routing tables, reducing the load on these devices and simplifying their management.
- **Scalability:** By centralizing the management of location information, LISP makes it easier to manage extended networks with a large number of mobile nodes.
- **Flexibility:** LISP facilitates the mobility of devices on the network without requiring complex changes in routing configuration.

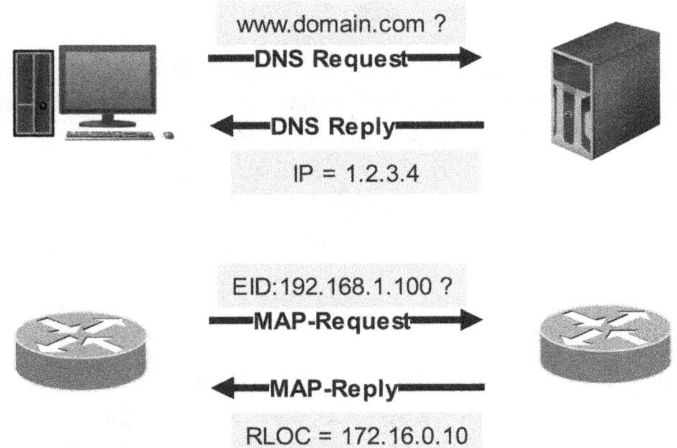

FIGURE 6.3
Comparison of LISP and DNS resolution processes.

6.4.4.2.3 LISP Terminology

To understand how LISP works, it is essential to master some of the key terminology used in this protocol:

- **EID:** The EID is an IP address that represents an element in the network. EIDs are used to identify devices regardless of their physical location.
- **RLOC:** The RLOC is an IP address assigned to a router where the EID is currently connected. The RLOC may change if the device moves, but the EID remains the same.
- **xTR (tunnel router):** This is the router that encapsulates and decapsulates LISP packets. xTRs are classified into Ingress xTR (I-xTR), which encapsulates outgoing packets, and Egress xTR (E-xTR), which decapsulates incoming packets.
- **MS:** A server that maintains a database of mappings between EIDs and corresponding RLOCs. The MS responds to xTR requests to provide the necessary routing information.
- **MR:** A device that receives mapping requests from an xTR and forwards them to the appropriate MS.

6.4.4.2.4 How LISP Works

To send data from PC1 to PC2, a number of steps are required to ensure that packets are transmitted through the various network zones. The essential steps are listed below (Figure 6.4):

- **Step 1:** PC1 prepares the data packet with its EID source address (172.16.10.2) and EID destination address (172.16.20.2) and then sends it to R1.

  Note that when a device connects to the network, its EID is stored on the MS, which associates this EID with the corresponding RLOC.
- **Step 2:** R1, receiving the packet, queries the MR (R3) to resolve the destination EID 172.16.20.2 in order to obtain its associated RLOC.

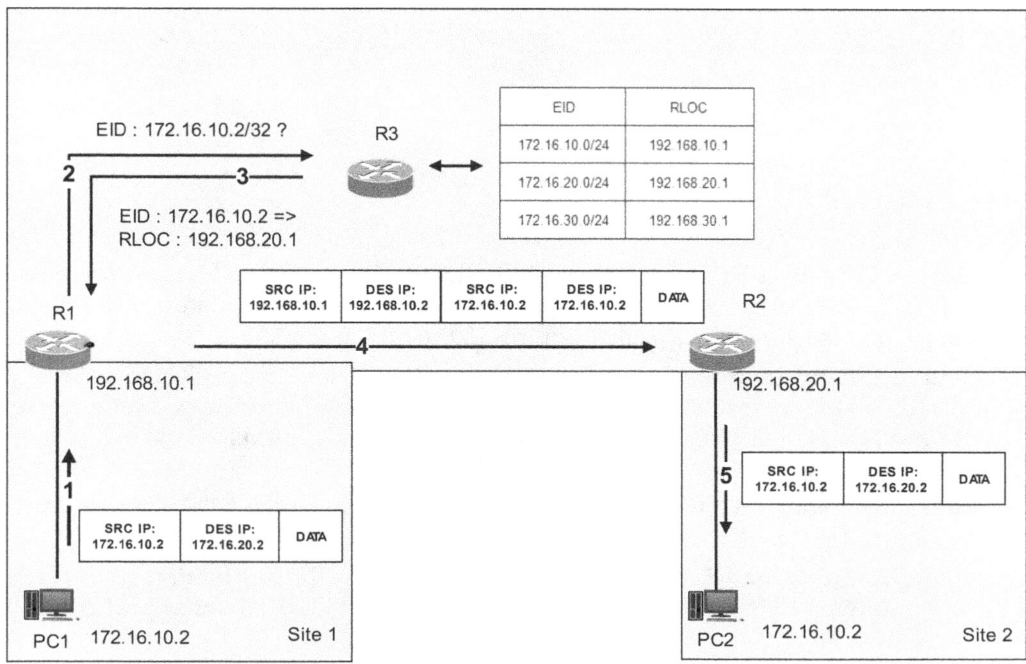

FIGURE 6.4
LISP communication process between two remote sites.

- **Step 3:** The MR (R3) returns to R1 the RLOC corresponding to EID 172.16.20.2, which in this case is 192.168.20.1. R1 stores this mapping in its cache for possible reuse.
- **Step 4:** R1 encapsulates the packet with RLOC IP addresses. The source IP address is 192.168.10.1, and the destination IP address is 192.168.20.1. R1 then forwards this encapsulated packet to R2.
- **Step 5:** R2 decompresses the packet, recovers the original EID (172.16.10.2) and sends it to PC2 at the EID destination address (172.16.20.2). This completes the communication.

LISP thus reduces the need for complex and extensive routing tables on each router, while offering a flexible and scalable solution for modern network management. The centralization and simplification are particularly advantageous in large-scale environments, where routing management can quickly become a major challenge.

6.4.4.2.5 LISP frame structure

A LISP frame is essentially an IP data frame encapsulated in another IP packet with additional headers (Figure 6.5). This encapsulation enables packets to be transported through tunnels established between routers (xTRs) in the LISP network. Here are the essential fields of a LISP frame:

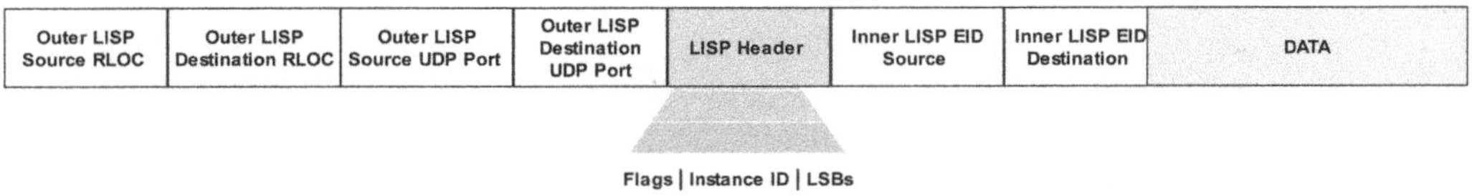

Outer LISP Source RLOC	Outer LISP Destination RLOC	Outer LISP Source UDP Port	Outer LISP Destination UDP Port	LISP Header	Inner LISP EID Source	Inner LISP EID Destination	DATA

Flags | Instance ID | LSBs

FIGURE 6.5
LISP frame structure.

- **Outer LISP source RLOC:** It is the source RLOC address. This address represents the LISP router from which the encapsulated packet (I-xTR) originates. It identifies the current location of the packet's origin in the LISP network.
- **Outer LISP destination RLOC:** This field contains the destination RLOC address, corresponding to the LISP destination router (E-xTR) where the packet will be decapsulated to reach its final destination. This address is used to route the packet through the underlying infrastructure.
- **Outer LISP source UDP port:** This field indicates the source UDP port used by the source LISP router.
- **Outer LISP destination UDP port:** This field contains the destination UDP port, corresponding to the destination LISP router. The default destination port is usually 4341.
- **LISP header:**
  - **Flags:** Various flags that modify LISP protocol behavior for this specific packet.
  - **Instance ID:** This 24-bit field is used to distinguish between several LISP instances running on the same router. It is particularly useful in multi-tenant environments where several logical networks may share the same physical infrastructure.
  - **Locator-Status-Bits:** These bits provide information on the status of locators in the network, such as their availability or accessibility status.
- **Inner LISP EID source:** It is the source EID address, representing the IP address of the original sender.
- **Inner LISP EID destination:** This field contains the EID destination address, which is the IP address of the target device for which the packet is intended.
- **DATA:** This is the packet payload, containing the actual data that is transmitted between the source and destination EIDs. These data can include TCP segments, UDP datagrams, or any other type of application data.

6.4.4.2.6 Data exchange between a LISP Network and a Non-LISP Network

In a network environment where LISP and non-LISP segments coexist, the exchange of data between these two types of the network requires specific mechanisms to ensure smooth communication. The LISP protocol introduces distinct concepts and infrastructure elements that enable this interaction, while maintaining the separation between identifiers (EIDs) and locators (RLOCs). To achieve this, it uses two types of routers: PETR and PITR (Figure 6.6).

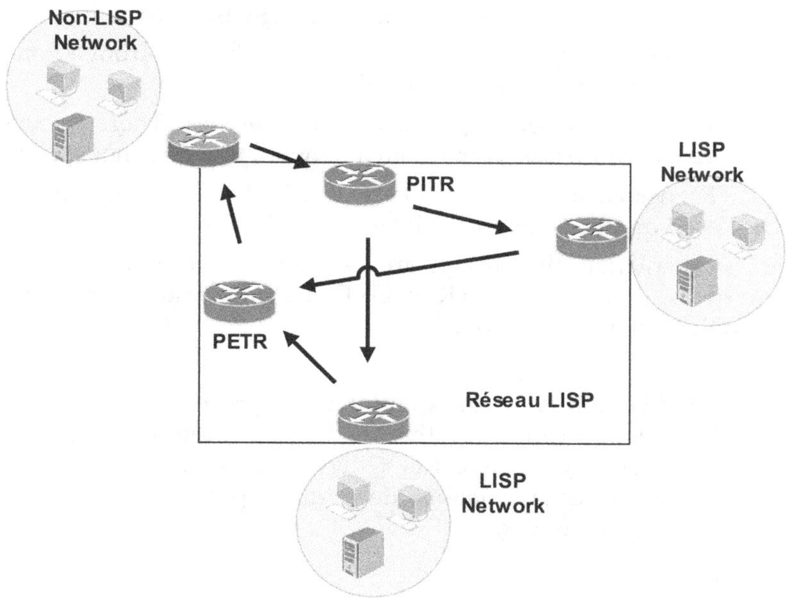

FIGURE 6.6
Interconnection and data exchange between LISP and non-LISP networks.

- **Proxy egress tunnel router (PETR):** A router that acts as a gateway between a LISP network and a non-LISP network for outgoing packets. The PETR receives packets from the LISP network, decapsulates them and forwards them to the non-LISP network.
- **Proxy ingress tunnel router (PITR):** A router that acts as a gateway between a non-LISP network and a LISP network for incoming packets. The PITR receives packets from the non-LISP network, encapsulates them and forwards them to the LISP network.

When packets need to be exchanged between a LISP network and a non-LISP network, the following elements come into play to ensure efficient communication:

- **Data exchange from a LISP network to a non-LISP network:**
  - When data need to be sent from a LISP network to a non-LISP network, the Egress Tunnel Router (E-xTR) or a PETR comes into play.
  - The E-xTR receives packets from the LISP network. It decapsulates them, that is, removes the LISP header and recovers the original packet.
  - Once decapsulated, packets are transferred to the non-LISP network, using RLOCs to determine the exit route. The PETR plays a crucial role, acting as a gateway that enables packets to reach their destination in the non-LISP network.

- **Data exchange from a Non-LISP network to a LISP network:**
  - In the opposite direction, when packets need to be sent from a non-LISP network to a LISP network, a PITR is used.
  - The PITR receives packets from the non-LISP network. These packets have no LISP header, because they come from a network that does not support LISP.
  - The PITR encapsulates these packets in a LISP header, assigning them an RLOC based on the destination EID in the LISP network.
  - After encapsulation, the packets are transmitted through the LISP network, where the corresponding I-xTR or E-xTR will decapsulate them and deliver them to their final destination.
- **Mapping table:**
  - The role of MS and MR is also essential in this process. When a PITR or PETR receives a packet, it can query the MR to obtain the necessary information on the corresponding EID and RLOC. This information enables the router to determine how to encapsulate or decapsulate packets for transfer between LISP and non-LISP networks.

6.4.4.2.7 Combined Use of LISP and VXLAN

In an SD-LAN architecture, LISP and VXLAN are combined to create an efficient network. VXLAN handles the encapsulation and transport of data in the forwarding plane, while LISP manages the control plane, mapping host identities to their physical locations. Together, they offer:

- **Simplified host mobility:** LISP enables a host to retain its IP address while on the move, while VXLAN ensures traffic segmentation and routing across the overlay.
- **Segmentation and isolation:** VXLAN guarantees precise segmentation, and LISP associates data flows with hosts in compliance with security policies.
- **Scalability:** LISP manages identities and VXLAN encapsulation, enabling the network to expand while maintaining strict segmentation and reduced complexity.

When a packet crosses an SD-LAN network, LISP identifies the source and destination, and VXLAN encapsulates the traffic in a tunnel through the Layer 3 overlay, maintaining security, segmentation, and efficiency, even as hosts move or the network evolves.

6.4.4.2.8 Conclusion

The LISP protocol, by separating identifiers from locators in routing, brings a new dimension to network management, particularly in complex, dynamic environments. Its ability to centralize and simplify routing table management makes it a valuable tool in NFV and SDN convergence, where agility, flexibility, and scalability are crucial requirements. LISP illustrates how innovation in routing protocols can support evolutions toward more intelligent and efficient network architectures.

6.4.5 NFV-SDN Integration for Real-Time Network Services

Real-time network functions, or "inline network functions", refer to tasks, services, or processes that are performed directly in the network data stream. These functions are embedded in the data transmission path, meaning they process and manipulate data packets as they pass through the network. These functions include firewall filtering systems, load balancing, intrusion detection systems (IDS), and data encryption/decryption.

In what follows, we'll explore the impact and added value of NFV and SDN technologies on these functions.

6.4.5.1 Load Balancing via NFV-SDN

The role of a load balancer service is to receive incoming packets and redirect them to the appropriate servers. Thanks to SDN technology, it is possible for an OpenFlow-enabled NFV machine (such as a switch or other network device) to be configured to function as a load balancer at a lower cost than acquiring hardware dedicated to this task.

A load balancer using OpenFlow offers a wide range of options for determining how to route traffic, which is generally simpler and faster.

If required, another compatible protocol can be used to provide additional functionality.

The advantage of using an SDN controller lies in its ability to analyze the load on each link leading to the destination servers, as well as load information on servers behind the firewall, among other parameters. This enables the SDN controller to make optimized decisions.

The centralized, global view offered by the SDN network can be enhanced by an SDN application capable of collecting a wider range of data, going beyond IP address and TCP port. This application can then support the SDN controller by taking these additional factors into account when routing transactions to specific servers.

6.4.5.2 Optimizing Firewalls with NFV-SDN

A firewall is a network element that receives incoming packets and forwards them, destroys them, or performs other actions, such as redirecting them to another port or destination for further analysis. Like load balancers, NFV firewalls using SDN and OpenFlow can exploit several available matching options to process packets.

Simple firewalls are particularly well-suited to an SDN-based solution, as they can provide fast, optimized filtration in cases where it is limited to the options offered by OpenFlow. Even if OpenFlow is limited by its inability to inspect packets deeply, these firewalls can serve as first-level or first-barrier filtration, significantly reducing the load on the enterprise's advanced firewalls.

6.4.5.3 SDN Enhances IDS

An IDS system is a passive security device that listens to outgoing and incoming traffic to identify suspicious traffic and potential attacks. An IDS looks for violations of application protocols and uses rules to analyze traffic statistics and patterns that may indicate an attack.

Typical solutions use a "virtual traffic replicator", configured to capture traffic from a particular source, such as an IP address, VLAN, or physical port and then copy and transfer it to an IDS for analysis.

OpenFlow is well-suited to this application, as it relies on extended flow selection criteria to perform certain actions.

As in the case of a firewall, an SDN application can be designed to support a VNF that acts as a traditional "Virtual Traffic Replicator", passively routing packets to the IDS system.

6.5 When Should NFV and SDN Be Combined?

NFV is particularly suitable for use in conjunction with SDN when there are a large number of physical network components to be virtualized. Indeed, if only a few VNFs are involved, it would be unwise to adopt the complex NFV reference architecture proposed by ETSI. On the other hand, SDN treats VNFs as just one resource among many, and effectively manages complex environments, whether in data centers, SD-LAN networks, or elsewhere. It's important to note that SDN is not limited to VNF management; its scope of application is much broader than that of NFV.

6.6 Conclusion

This chapter examined the transformative convergence of NFV and SDN, two critical technologies redefining modern network architectures. We examined how NFV enables efficient virtualization of network functions and improves data center management, while SDN offers centralized control and increased flexibility in the network.

By integrating NFV and SDN, organizations can achieve more agile, high-performance networks, adapted to the evolving demands of the digital age. Examples of synergy across various contexts have demonstrated the potential of these technologies to deliver robust and cost-effective network solutions.

As the technological landscape continues to evolve, NFV and SDN are positioning themselves as essential components for network operators and enterprises looking to optimize their infrastructure for the future. The adoption of these technologies is not only strategic, but also essential to remain competitive in an environment increasingly focused on network performance and innovation.

Lab 10: Isolating Traffic with VRF

Objectives

- Understand the principle of segmentation using VRFs.
- Configure Cisco equipment for segmentation via VRFs.

Case Study

This case study examines the application of computer network segmentation using VRFs. It highlights the benefits of this method in environments where all segments share the same IP address range, enabling efficient data flow isolation while simplifying network management.

Due to a shortage of IP addresses, ABC wants to use the same network address on each site for each customer.

Required Software

- **GNS3 or equivalent**

Network Topology

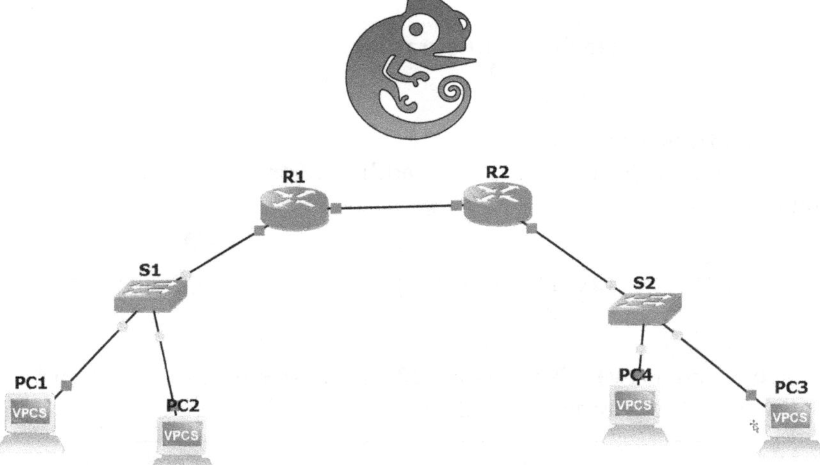

IP Address Table

Emulated Device	Device	Interface	IP Address/ Subnet Mask	VRF	Default Gateway
Cisco Router—C7200 (Dynamips, v15.2)	R1	G0/0	V10:172.16.1.1/24	vrf_1	–
Cisco Router—C7200 (Dynamips, v15.2)	R1	G0/0	V20:172.16.1.1/24	vrf_2	–
Cisco Router—C7200 (Dynamips, v15.2)	R1	G1/0	V10:192.168.10.1	vrf_1	–
Cisco Router—C7200 (Dynamips, v15.2)	R1	G1/0	V20:192.168.10.1	vrf_2	–
Cisco Router—C7200 (Dynamips, v15.2)	R2	G0/0	V10:172.16.1.2/24	vrf_1	–
Cisco Router—C7200 (Dynamips, v15.2)	R2	G0/0	V20:172.16.1.2/24	vrf_2	–
Cisco Router—C7200 (Dynamips, v15.2)	R2	G1/0	V10:192.168.20.1	vrf_1	–
Cisco Router—C7200 (Dynamips, v15.2)	R2	G1/0	V20:192.168.20.1	vrf_2	–
VPCS	PC1	eth0	192.168.10.2	vrf_1	192.168.10.1
VPCS	PC2	eth0	192.168.10.2	vrf_2	192.168.10.1
VPCS	PC3	eth0	192.168.20.2	vrf_1	192.168.20.1
VPCS	PC4	eth0	192.168.20.2	vrf_2	192.168.20.1
Ethernet Switch	S1	–	–	–	–
	S2	–	–	–	–

Part A: Establishing Basic Device Configuration

1. Create the network topology.
2. Assign IP addresses to PC interfaces.
   Use the device's CLI to assign an IP address. For example, on PC1, use the following command:

```
PC1> ip 192.168.10.2/24 192.168.10.1
```

3. On switch S1, create **VLAN10, VLAN20,** and **trunk mode (dot1q)** and configure the ports using the parameters in the following table:

Element	Port	Configuration
R1: G1/0	0	Dot1q
PC1:eth0	1	Vlan10
PC2:eth0	2	Vlan20

4. Apply the same configuration for switch **S2**.

Part B: Network Segmentation Using VRFs

1. Create and configure VRFs on the Cisco routers.

```
R1(config)# vrf definition vrf_1
R1(config-vrf)# rd 100:1
R1(config-vrf)#address-family ipv4
R1(config)#
R1(config)# vrf definition vrf_2
R1(config-vrf)# rd 100:2
R1(config-vrf)#address-family ipv4
```

2. On R1, configure the interfaces and link them to the VRFs.

```
! Enable the physical interface G1/0
R1(config)# interface GigabitEthernet1/0
R1(config-if)# no shutdown
R1(config-if)# exit

! Configure subinterface G1/0.10 for VLAN 10, assign it to VRF vrf_1
R1(config)# interface GigabitEthernet1/0.10
R1(config-subif)# encapsulation dot1Q 10
R1(config-subif)# vrf forwarding vrf_1
R1(config-subif)# ip address 192.168.10.1 255.255.255.0
R1(config-subif)# exit

! Configure subinterface G1/0.20 for VLAN 20, assign it to VRF vrf_2
R1(config)# interface GigabitEthernet1/0.20
R1(config-subif)# encapsulation dot1Q 20
R1(config-subif)# vrf forwarding vrf_2
R1(config-subif)# ip address 192.168.10.1 255.255.255.0
R1(config-subif)# exit

! Enable the physical interface G0/0
R1(config)# interface GigabitEthernet0/0
R1(config-if)# no shutdown
R1(config-if)# exit

! Configure subinterface G0/0.10 for VLAN 10, assign it to VRF vrf_1
R1(config)# interface GigabitEthernet0/0.10
R1(config-subif)# encapsulation dot1Q 10
R1(config-subif)# vrf forwarding vrf_1
R1(config-subif)# ip address 172.16.1.1 255.255.255.0
R1(config-subif)# exit

! Configure subinterface G0/0.20 for VLAN 20, assign it to VRF vrf_2
R1(config)# interface GigabitEthernet0/0.20
R1(config-subif)# encapsulation dot1Q 20
R1(config-subif)# vrf forwarding vrf_2
R1(config-subif)# ip address 172.16.1.1 255.255.255.0
R1(config-subif)# exit
```

3. Display the configuration parameters of R1.
   a. Use the "show ip interface brief" command to display the interface statuses:

```
R1#sh ip int br
Interface IP-Address OK? Method Status Prot ocol
Ethernet0/0 unassigned YES unset administratively down down
GigabitEthernet0/0 unassigned YES unset up up
GigabitEthernet0/0.10 172.16.1.1 YES manual up up
GigabitEthernet0/0.20 172.16.1.1 YES manual up up
GigabitEthernet1/0 unassigned YES unset up up
GigabitEthernet1/0.10 192.168.10.1 YES manual up up
GigabitEthernet1/0.20 192.168.10.1 YES manual up up
```

   b. Use the "show ip vrf" command to display the configured VRFs:

```
R1#sh ip vrf
  Name Default RD Interfaces
  vrf_1 100:1 Gi1/0.10 Gi0/0.10

  vrf_2 100:2 Gi1/0.20 Gi0/0.20
```

4. On R2, configure the interfaces and associate them with **VRFs** according to the addressing table.
5. Configure **OSPF** routing on router R1.

```
R1(config)#router ospf 10 vrf vrf_1
R1(config-router)#network 192.168.10.0 0.0.0.255 area 0
R1(config-router)#network 172.16.1.0 0.0.0.255 area 0
R1(config-router)#exit
R1(config)#router ospf 20 vrf vrf_2
R1(config-router)#network 192.168.10.0 0.0.0.255 area 0
R1(config-router)#network 172.16.1.0 0.0.0.255 area 0
```

6. Enable **OSPF** routing on router R2.

```
R1(config)#router ospf 10 vrf vrf_1
R1(config-router)#network 192.168.20.0 0.0.0.255 area 0
R1(config-router)#network 172.16.1.0 0.0.0.255 area 0
R1(config-router)#exit
R1(config)#router ospf 20 vrf vrf_2
R1(config-router)#network 192.168.20.0 0.0.0.255 area 0
R1(config-router)#network 172.16.1.0 0.0.0.255 area 0
```

7. On R1, display the **VRF** routing table.

```
R1#sh ip route vrf vrf_1

Routing Table: vrf_1
Codes: L - local, C - connected, S - static, R - RIP, M - mobile, B
  - BGP
       D - EIGRP, EX - EIGRP external, O - OSPF, IA - OSPF inter
  area
       N1 - OSPF NSSA external type 1, N2 - OSPF NSSA external type 2
       E1 - OSPF external type 1, E2 - OSPF external type 2
       i - IS-IS, su - IS-IS summary, L1 - IS-IS level-1, L2 - IS-IS
  level-2
       ia - IS-IS inter area, * - candidate default, U - per-user
  static route
       o - ODR, P - periodic downloaded static route, H - NHRP,
  l - LISP
       + - replicated route, % - next hop override

Gateway of last resort is not set

      172.16.0.0/16 is variably subnetted, 2 subnets, 2 masks
C 172.16.1.0/24 is directly connected, GigabitEthernet0/0.10
L 172.16.1.1/32 is directly connected, GigabitEthernet0/0.10
      192.168.10.0/24 is variably subnetted, 2 subnets, 2 masks
C 192.168.10.0/24 is directly connected, GigabitEthernet1/0.10
L 192.168.10.1/32 is directly connected, GigabitEthernet1/0.10
O 192.168.20.0/24 [110/2] via 172.16.1.2, 00:03:03,
  GigabitEthernet0/0.10
```

```
R1#sh ip route vrf vrf_2

Routing Table: vrf_2
Codes: L - local, C - connected, S - static, R - RIP, M - mobile,
  B - BGP
       D - EIGRP, EX - EIGRP external, O - OSPF, IA - OSPF inter area
       N1 - OSPF NSSA external type 1, N2 - OSPF NSSA external type 2
       E1 - OSPF external type 1, E2 - OSPF external type 2
       i - IS-IS, su - IS-IS summary, L1 - IS-IS level-1, L2 - IS-IS
  level-2
       ia - IS-IS inter area, * - candidate default, U - per-user
  static route
       o - ODR, P - periodic downloaded static route, H - NHRP, l
  - LISP
       + - replicated route, % - next hop override

Gateway of last resort is not set

      172.16.0.0/16 is variably subnetted, 2 subnets, 2 masks
C 172.16.1.0/24 is directly connected, GigabitEthernet0/0.20
L 172.16.1.1/32 is directly connected, GigabitEthernet0/0.20
      192.168.10.0/24 is variably subnetted, 2 subnets, 2 masks
C 192.168.10.0/24 is directly connected, GigabitEthernet1/0.20
L 192.168.10.1/32 is directly connected, GigabitEthernet1/0.20
```

Part C: Testing and Verification of the Configuration

1. On PC1, perform a **ping** test to verify connectivity with PC3.
2. On PC2, perform a **ping** test to verify connectivity with PC4.

Lab 11: Inter-VRF Routing with Controlled Isolation on Cisco Devices

Objectives

- Understand the concept of segmentation using VRFs.
- Understand inter-segment routing with VRFs.
- Configure Cisco equipment for inter-segment VRF routing.

Case Study

This case study explores the use of VRF-based network segmentation to fulfill specific routing requirements between distinct VRFs. It highlights the mechanisms for defining precise routing policies while maintaining the isolation of network segments, ensuring flexible and secure management of inter-VRF traffic flows.

In line with its security strategy, ABC wants the segments containing PC1 and PC2 to be able to communicate, while maintaining isolation from the other segments represented by PC3.

Required Software

- **GNS3 or equivalent**

Network Topology

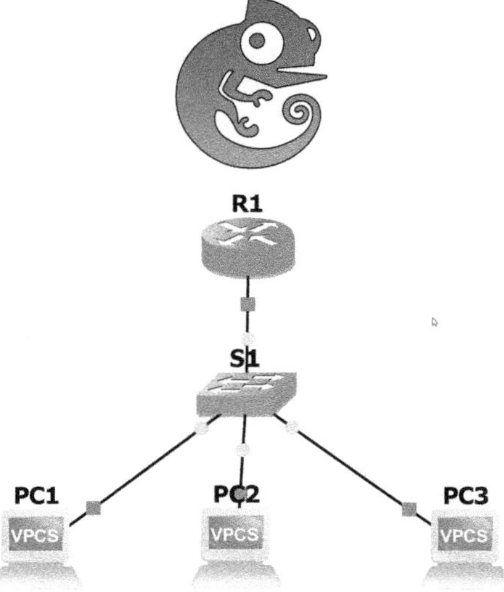

IP Address Table

Emulated Device	Device	Interface	IP Address/Subnet Mask	VRF	Default Gateway
Cisco Router—C7200 (Dynamips, v15.2)	R1	G0/0	V10:192.168.10.1/24	vrf_1	–
Cisco Router—C7200 (Dynamips, v15.2)	R1	G0/0	V20:192.168.20.1/24	vrf_2	–
Cisco Router—C7200 (Dynamips, v15.2)	R1	G0/0	V30:192.168.30.1/24	vrf_3	–
VPCS	PC1	eth0	192.168.10.2	vrf_1	192.168.10.1
VPCS	PC2	eth0	192.168.20.2	vrf_2	192.168.20.1
VPCS	PC3	eth0	192.168.30.2	vrf_3	192.168.30.1
Ethernet Switch	S1	–	–	–	–

Part A: Establishing Basic Device Configuration

1. Create the network topology.
2. Assign IP addresses to PC interfaces.
3. On switch S1, create VLAN10, VLAN20, VLAN30, and trunk mode (dot1q) and configure the ports based on the parameters in the following table:

Element	Port	Configuration
R1: G0/0	0	Dot1q
PC1:eth0	1	Vlan10
PC2:eth0	2	Vlan20
PC3:eth0	3	Vlan30

Part B: Configuring Routing between VRF Segments

1. Create and configure the **VRFs**: vrf_1, vrf_2, and vrf_3 on the Cisco routers.

```
R1(config)# vrf definition vrf_1
R1(config-vrf)# rd 100:1
R1(config-vrf)#address-family ipv4
R1(config)#
R1(config)# vrf definition vrf_2
R1(config-vrf)# rd 100:2
R1(config-vrf)#address-family ipv4
R1(config)# vrf definition vrf_3
R1(config-vrf)# rd 100:3
R1(config-vrf)#address-family ipv4
```

2. On R1, configure the interfaces and associate them with **VRFs** according to the addressing table.
3. Display R1 configuration parameters.
   a. Use the "show ip interface brief" command:

```
R1#sh ip int brief
Interface IP-Address OK? Method Status Protocol
Ethernet0/0 unassigned YES unset administratively down down
GigabitEthernet0/0 unassigned YES unset up up
GigabitEthernet0/0.10 192.168.10.1 YES manual up up
GigabitEthernet0/0.20 192.168.20.1 YES manual up up
GigabitEthernet0/0.30 192.168.30.1 YES manual up up
GigabitEthernet1/0 unassigned YES unset administratively down down
```

   b. Use the "show ip vrf" command:

```
R1#sh ip vrf
  Name Default RD Interfaces
  vrf_1 100:1 Gi0/0.10
  vrf_2 100:2 Gi0/0.20
  vrf_3 100:3 Gi0/0.30
```

4. Allow import and export of routes between vrf_1 and vrf_2

```
R1(config)#vrf definition vrf_1
R1(config-vrf)#address-family ipv4
R1(config-vrf-af)#route-target export 100:1
R1(config-vrf-af)#route-target import 100:2
R1(config)#
R1(config)#vrf definition vrf_2
R1(config-vrf)#route-target export 100:2
R1(config-vrf)#route-target import 100:1
```

5. Enable **BGP** routing between vrf_1 and vrf_2

```
R1(config)#router bgp 10
R1(config-router)#address-family ipv4 vrf vrf_1
R1(config-router-af)#redistribute connected
R1(config-router-af)#exit
R1(config-router)#address-family ipv4 vrf vrf_2
R1(config-router-af)#redistribute connected
R1(config-router-af)#exit
```

6. On R1, display the **VRF** routing table

```
R1#sh ip route vrf vrf_1
Routing Table: vrf_1
Codes: L - local, C - connected, S - static, R - RIP, M - mobile, B
  - BGP
       D - EIGRP, EX - EIGRP external, O - OSPF, IA - OSPF inter area
       N1 - OSPF NSSA external type 1, N2 - OSPF NSSA external type 2
       E1 - OSPF external type 1, E2 - OSPF external type 2
       i - IS-IS, su - IS-IS summary, L1 - IS-IS level-1, L2 - IS-IS
  level-2
       ia - IS-IS inter area, * - candidate default, U - per-user
  static route
       o - ODR, P - periodic downloaded static route, H - NHRP, l
  - LISP
       + - replicated route, % - next hop override

Gateway of last resort is not set

      192.168.10.0/24 is variably subnetted, 2 subnets, 2 masks
C 192.168.10.0/24 is directly connected, GigabitEthernet0/0.10
L 192.168.10.1/32 is directly connected, GigabitEthernet0/0.10
      192.168.20.0/24 is variably subnetted, 2 subnets, 2 masks
B 192.168.20.0/24
           is directly connected (vrf_2), 00:00:49,
  GigabitEthernet0/0.20
L 192.168.20.1/32 is directly connected, GigabitEthernet0/0.20
```

```
R1#sh ip route vrf vrf_2
Routing Table: vrf_2
Codes: L - local, C - connected, S - static, R - RIP, M - mobile, B
  - BGP
       D - EIGRP, EX - EIGRP external, O - OSPF, IA - OSPF inter area
       N1 - OSPF NSSA external type 1, N2 - OSPF NSSA external type 2
       E1 - OSPF external type 1, E2 - OSPF external type 2
       i - IS-IS, su - IS-IS summary, L1 - IS-IS level-1, L2 - IS-IS
  level-2
       ia - IS-IS inter area, * - candidate default, U - per-user
  static route
       o - ODR, P - periodic downloaded static route, H - NHRP, l
  - LISP
       + - replicated route, % - next hop override

Gateway of last resort is not set

      192.168.10.0/24 is variably subnetted, 2 subnets, 2 masks
B 192.168.10.0/24
           is directly connected (vrf_1), 00:01:00,
  GigabitEthernet0/0.10
L 192.168.10.1/32 is directly connected, GigabitEthernet0/0.10
      192.168.20.0/24 is variably subnetted, 2 subnets, 2 masks
C 192.168.20.0/24 is directly connected, GigabitEthernet0/0.20
L 192.168.20.1/32 is directly connected, GigabitEthernet0/0.20
```

Part C: Testing and Verification of the Configuration

1. On PC1, verify connectivity with PC2 using the **ping** command.
2. On PC1, ensure that **ping** requests to PC3 fail, validating the isolation.

Lab 12: Enabling Secure Shared Resource Access via VRF-to-Global Routing

Objectives

- Understand the concept of segmentation using VRFs.
- Understand inter-segment routing with VRFs.
- Configure route exchange between the global routing table and VRFs.

Case Study

This case study explores the application of VRF segmentation in environments that require access to shared resources, such as data center servers. It explores how to ensure conditional routing between VRFs and the global routing table while maintaining strict network segment isolation, guaranteeing secure and optimized access to shared resources.

ABC wants to guarantee access to a web server for all segments of the company.

Required Software

- **GNS3 or equivalent**

Network Topology

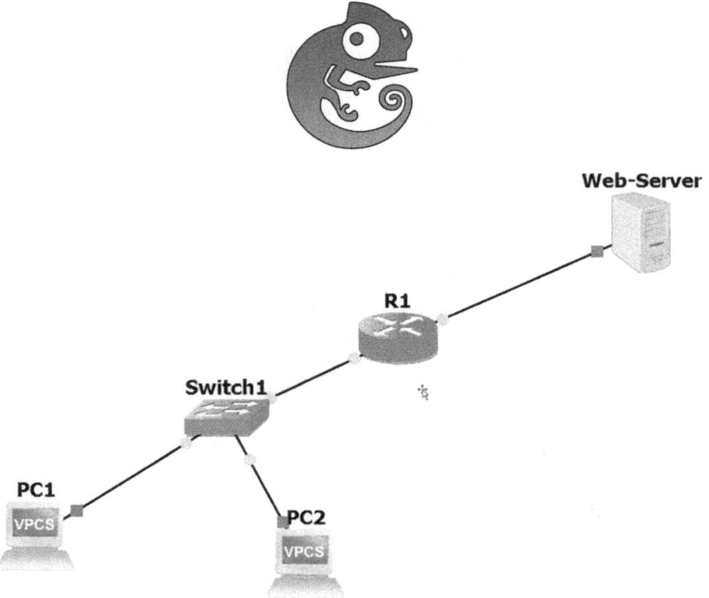

IP Address Table

Emulated Device	Device	Interface	IP Address/Subnet Mask	VRF	Default Gateway
Cisco Router—C7200 (Dynamips, v15.2)	R1	G0/0	V10:192.168.10.1/24	vrf_1	–
Cisco Router—C7200 (Dynamips, v15.2)	R1	G0/0	V20:192.168.20.1/24	vrf_2	–
Cisco Router—C7200 (Dynamips, v15.2)	R1	G1/0	172.16.0.1/24		–
VPCS	PC1	eth0	192.168.10.2/24	vrf_1	192.168.10.1
VPCS	PC2	eth0	192.168.20.2/24	vrf_2	192.168.20.1
Docker Container—Toolbox	Web-Server	eth0	172.16.0.2/24		172.16.0.1
Ethernet Switch	S1	–	–	–	–

Part A: Establishing Basic Device Configuration

1. Create the network topology.
2. Assign IP addresses to PC interfaces and Web-Server.
3. On switch S1, create VLAN10, VLAN20, and trunk mode (dot1q) and configure the ports using the parameters in the following table:

Element	Port	Configuration
R1: G0/0	0	Dot1q
PC1:eth0	1	Vlan10
PC2:eth0	2	Vlan20

4. Set the IP address of the G1/0 interface on R1 and then ensure communication between R1 and Web-Server.

Part B: VRF Segment Configuration

1. Create and configure VRFs: vrf_1 and vrf_2 on R1.
2. Configure the interfaces and assign them to the **VRFs** according to the addressing table.
3. Display R1 configuration parameters to ensure correct configuration.

Part C: Importing Routes from the Global Routing Table to VRFs

1. Create an access list to authorize routes for import:

```
R1(config)# access-list 10 permit 172.16.0.0 0.0.0.255
```

2. Create a **"glob-to-vlan" route-map** and associate it with access list **10**

```
R1(config)# route-map glob-to-vlan permit 1
R1(config-route-map)match ip address 10
```

3. Allow import of routes from global table to VRFs

```
R1(config)#vrf definition vrf_1
R1(config-vrf)#address-family ipv4
R1(config-vrf-af)# import ipv4 unicast map glob-to-vlan
R1(config-vrf)#vrf definition vrf_2
R1(config-vrf)#address-family ipv4
R1(config-vrf-af)# import ipv4 unicast map glob-to-vlan
```

4. Enable **BGP** routing between the global table and VRFs

```
R1(config)#router bgp 10
R1(config-router)#address-family ipv4
R1(config-router-af)#redistribute connected
R1(config-router-af)#exit
```

5. Add a static route on the global routing table to vrf_1 and vrf_2.

```
R1(config)#ip route 192.168.10.0 255.255.255.0 g0/0.10
R1(config)#ip route 192.168.20.0 255.255.255.0 g0/0.20
```

6. On R1, display the **VRF** routing table

```
R1#sh ip route
...
      172.16.0.0/16 is variably subnetted, 2 subnets, 2 masks
C 172.16.0.0/24 is directly connected, GigabitEthernet1/0
L 172.16.0.1/32 is directly connected, GigabitEthernet1/0
S 192.168.10.0/24 is directly connected, GigabitEthernet0/0.10
S 192.168.20.0/24 is directly connected, GigabitEthernet0/0.20
```

```
R1#sh ip route vrf vrf_1
Routing Table: vrf_1
...
      172.16.0.0/16 is variably subnetted, 2 subnets, 2 masks
B 172.16.0.0/24 is directly connected, 00:04:55, GigabitEthernet1/0
L 172.16.0.1/32 is directly connected, GigabitEthernet1/0
      192.168.10.0/24 is variably subnetted, 2 subnets, 2 masks
C 192.168.10.0/24 is directly connected, GigabitEthernet0/0.10
L 192.168.10.1/32 is directly connected, GigabitEthernet0/0.10
```

```
R1#sh ip route vrf vrf_2
...
      172.16.0.0/16 is variably subnetted, 2 subnets, 2 masks
B 172.16.0.0/24 is directly connected, 00:05:35, GigabitEthernet1/0
L 172.16.0.1/32 is directly connected, GigabitEthernet1/0
      192.168.20.0/24 is variably subnetted, 2 subnets, 2 masks
C 192.168.20.0/24 is directly connected, GigabitEthernet0/0.20
L 192.168.20.1/32 is directly connected, GigabitEthernet0/0.20
```

Note: If BGP routes are not displayed, simply wait a moment for updates.

Part D: Testing and Verification of the Configuration

1. On PC1, verify connectivity with the Web-Server using the **ping** command.
2. On PC2, verify connectivity with the Web-Server using the **ping** command.
3. On PC1, ensure that **ping** requests to PC2 fail, validating the isolation.

Lab 13: Deploying LISP Architecture and Mobility in Cisco Networks

Objectives

- Understand the function of the LISP protocol.
- Identify the elements of an architecture using the LISP protocol.
- Set up routing with the IS-IS protocol.
- Deploy a Cisco architecture using the LISP protocol.
- Enable user mobility using the LISP protocol.
- Differentiate between Underlay and Overlay networks.

Case Study

This case study examines the role of LISP in modern network architectures, focusing on distinguishing the key elements of these infrastructures. It also covers the configuration of routing with the IS-IS protocol and the implementation of a Cisco architecture using LISP. Finally, the study examines the differences between Underlay and Overlay networks, providing a better understanding of the segmentation and management of data flows in SDN networks.

ABC wants to ensure the mobility of network elements (user PCs, servers, etc.), while retaining their IP addresses to provide centralized access management.

Required Software

- **GNS3 or equivalent**

Network Topology

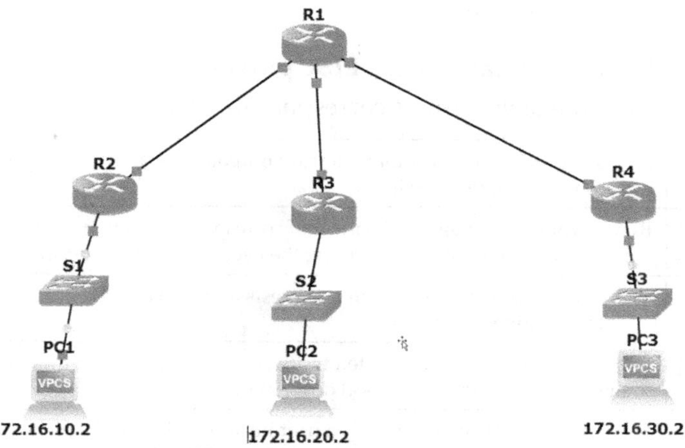

IP Address Table

Emulated Device	Device	Interface	IP Address/Subnet Mask	Default Gateway
Cisco CSR1000v (IOS XE v17.3.1a, QEMU)	R1	G1->R2	10.10.0.1/24	-
		G2->R3	10.20.0.1/24	
		G3->R4	10.30.0.1/24	
	R2	G1->R1	10.10.0.2/24	
		G2->S1	G2.10 : 172.16.10.1 G2.20 : 172.16.20.1 G2.30 : 172.16.30.1	
	R3	G1->R1	10.20.0.2/24	
		G2->S2	G2.10 : 172.16.10.1 G2.20 : 172.16.20.1 G2.30 : 172.16.30.1	
	R4	G1->R1	10.30.0.2/24	
		G2->S1	G2.10 : 172.16.10.1 G2.20 : 172.16.20.1 G2.30 : 172.16.30.1	
VPCS	PC1	eth0	172.16.10.2 (VLAN10)	172.16.10.1
	PC2	eth0	172.16.20.2 (VLAN20)	172.16.20.1
	PC3	eth0	172.16.30.2 (VLAN30)	172.16.30.1
Ethernet Switch	S1	-		
	S2			
	S3			

Part A: Review LISP Protocol Theory

1. Recall the role and advantages of the **LISP** protocol.
2. Link each item in the table with its corresponding definition:

1. EID	A. It's a router that encapsulates a site's outgoing traffic by adding a LISP header before sending it to a remote site.
2. RLOC	B. A server that manages a database of correspondences between EIDs and RLOCs. It responds to requests by providing the necessary routing information.
3. xTR	C. A device that receives mapping requests and forwards them to the appropriate MS to obtain routing information.
4. MS	D. A router receives encapsulated traffic, decapsulates it by removing the LISP header, and then delivers it to its local destination.
5. MR	E. An IP address used to identify a user host regardless of its physical location.
6. ITR	F. Equipment responsible for LISP packet encapsulation and decapsulation
7. ETR	G. An IP address associated with a router to which the EID is connected

3. The following exercise refers to the network topology presented in this Lab, where PC1 is connected to R2 (acting as RLOC1), and PC2 is connected to R3 (acting as RLOC2), with R1 serving as both the MS and MR to facilitate communication via LISP.

   Reorder the steps that allow **PC1,** connected to **RLOC1 (R2),** to communicate with **PC2** connected to **RLOC2 (R3)** via LISP, with R1 playing the role of **MS** and **MR**:

   - R1 (MR) receives the request and consults its database to find the EID-to-RLOC mapping for PC2, returning RLOC2 as a response to RLOC1.
   - RLOC1 (R2) intercepts this packet and checks its local EID-to-RLOC mapping for PC2's EID.
   - PC1 sends a packet to PC2 using PC2's EID as the destination address.
   - If the EID-to-RLOC mapping for PC2's EID is not in its cache, RLOC1 sends a Map-Request to R1 (MS/MR) to resolve PC2's EID into a corresponding RLOC.
   - The packet is routed through the network to RLOC2 (R3), which decapsulates the packet and forwards it to PC2 using its EID.
   - PC2 receives the packet, and communication is established between PC1 and PC2 via their RLOC1 and RLOC2 routers.
   - RLOC1 updates its cache with the EID-to-RLOC mapping for PC2 and encapsulates the packet destined for PC2 with RLOC2 as the new destination address.

Part B: Setting Up Basic Device Configuration

1. Create the network topology.
2. Assign IP addresses to PC interfaces.
3. On switch S1, create VLAN10, VLAN20, VLAN30, and Trunk mode (dot1q) and configure the ports based on the parameters in the following table:

Element	Port	Configuration
R1 : G2	0	802.1Q
PC1:eth0	1	Vlan10
PC2:eth0	2	Vlan20
PC3:eth0	3	Vlan30

4. Make the same configuration on switches S2 and S3. Connect the PCs to the appropriate port.
5. On routers, configure interface IP addresses by referring to the addressing table.
6. Set up a local loopback address on each router:

```
R1(config)#int loopback0
R1(config-if)#ip add 1.1.1.1 255.255.555.255
```

```
R2(config)#int loopback0
R2(config-if)#ip add 2.2.2.2 255.255.555.255
```

```
R3(config)#int loopback0
R3(config-if)#ip add 3.3.3.3 255.255.555.255
```

```
R4(config)#int loopback0
R4(config-if)#ip add 4.4.4.4 255.255.555.255
```

Part C: Configuring IS-IS Routing between Routers

1. On R1, activate the **IS-IS** routing protocol and define its parameters.

```
R1(config)#router isis
R1(config-router)#net 49.0001.0000.0000.0001.00
```

> The explanation for the value "49.0001.0000.0000.0001.00" is as follows:
> 49: This prefix is reserved for private networks.
> 0001: This is the area ID, which identifies the area in which the router is located.
> 0000.0000.0001: This is the unique System ID for the router within this zone. It must be unique for each ISIS router.
> 00: This is the Network Selector, often set to 00 by default, as it generally represents a level 1 network.

```
R1(config-router)#is-type level-1
```

An IS-IS level 1 router only has link-state information for the topology within its own area (intra-area). When it needs to route packets to other areas, it sends these packets to a level 2 router, which is responsible for inter-area routing.
We'll assume that all routers are in the same area.

```
R1(config)#interface Loopback 0
R1(config-if)#ip router isis
R1(config)#interface G1
R1(config-if)#ip router isis
R1(config)#interface G2
R1(config-if)#ip router isis
R1(config)#interface G3
R1(config-if)#ip router isis
```

2. On R2, activate the **IS-IS** routing protocol and define its parameters.

```
R2(config)#router isis
R2(config-router)#net 49.0001.0000.0000.0002.00
R2(config-router)#is-type level-1
R2(config)#interface Loopback 0
R2(config-if)#ip router isis
R2(config)#interface G1
R2(config-if)#ip router isis
```

Note: It is important not to add the subnets of the G2 interface to the IS-IS protocol.

3. On R3, activate the **IS-IS** routing protocol and define its parameters.

```
R3(config)#router isis
R3(config-router)#net 49.0001.0000.0000.0003.00
R3(config-router)#is-type level-1
R3(config)#interface Loopback 0
R3(config-if)#ip router isis
R3(config)#interface G1
R3(config-if)#ip router isis
```

4. On R4, activate the **IS-IS** routing protocol and define its parameters.

```
R4(config)#router isis
R4(config-router)#net 49.0001.0000.0000.0004.00
R4(config-router)#is-type level-1

R4(config)#interface Loopback 0
R4(config-if)#ip router isis
R4(config)#interface G1
R4(config-if)#ip router isis
```

5. Verify that the routing tables are correctly populated and make sure you can **ping** between routers.

Part D: Configuring the LISP Protocol on Routers

Step 1: MS/MR configuration

1. Configure R1 as **MS/MR**.

```
R1(config)# router lisp
ipv4 service
  map-server
  map-resolver
  exit-service-ipv4
```

2. On R1, create a site named **"ABC_site"**, define the word **"cisco"** as the authentication key, and specify the networks authorized to register.

```
R1(config)# router lisp
 ABC_site
  authentication-key cisco
  eid-record 172.16.10.0/24 accept-more-specifics
  eid-record 172.16.20.0/24 accept-more-specifics
  eid-record 172.16.30.0/24 accept-more-specifics
  exit-site
```

Step 2: RLOC configuration

1. On R2, create a "locator-set" named **"site1"** and define the interface to be used for the **LISP** protocol.

```
R2(config)# router lisp
locator-set site1
  IPv4-interface Loopback0 priority 1 weight 1
  exit-locator-set
```

2. Configure R2 as both an **"ITR"** and **"ETR"** router (i.e., an **"XTR"** router) and connect it to the **MS/MR** router.

```
R2(config)# router lisp
instance-id 0
ipv4 service
 eid-table default
 itr
 itr map-resolver 1.1.1.1
 etr
 etr map-server 1.1.1.1 key cisco
 exit-service-ipv4
 exit-instance-id
```

3. On R2, set EID networks (**V10, V20,** and **V30**) to be automatically discovered and registered on the **MS/MR**.

```
R2(config)# router lisp
instance-id 0
  loc-reach-algorithm rloc-probing
  dynamic-eid V10
   database-mapping 172.16.10.0/24 locator-set site1
   exit-dynamic-eid
  dynamic-eid V20
   database-mapping 172.16.20.0/24 locator-set site1
   exit-dynamic-eid
  dynamic-eid V30
   database-mapping 172.16.30.0/24 locator-set site1
   exit-dynamic-eid
```

4. On R2, associate each **G2** sub-interface with its **"dynamic-eid"** value.

```
R2(config)# int G2.10
lisp mobility V10
R2(config)# int G2.20
lisp mobility V20
R2(config)# int G2.30
lisp mobility V30
```

5. Repeat step **2** on routers R3 and R4, keeping the same parameters for all commands.

Part E: Testing and Verification of the Configuration

1. On PC1, **ping** 172.16.10.1.
2. On R1, type the command "sh lisp site" and check that PC1 has been registered.

```
R1#sh lisp site
LISP Site Registration Information
* = Some locators are down or unreachable
# = Some registrations are sourced by reliable transport

Site Name    Last      Up     Who Last        Inst          EID Prefix
          Register   Registered            ID
ABC_site    never         no               --           172.16.10.0/24
            00:01:06      yes#     2.2.2.2:35620         172.16.10.2/32
            never         no               --           172.16.20.0/24
            never         no               --           172.16.30.0/24
R1#
```

3. On PC2, **ping** 172.16.20.1 and check that PC2 has been registered.
4. On PC1, check that you can **ping** PC2 and PC3.
5. Move PC1 to R3 and PC2 to R2, then check that you can still **ping** between the two PCs.

Analysis of Results: Case Studies and Implications of Network Architecture

The corporate network can be divided into two distinct networks:

- **Network 1:** Consisting of R1, R2, R3, and R4, with its own addressing plan (private or possibly public) and using a standard routing protocol that completely ignores the existence of Network 2 (network addresses 172.16.10.0/24, 172.16.20.0/24, and 172.16.30.0/24). This network is called the **Underlay** network.

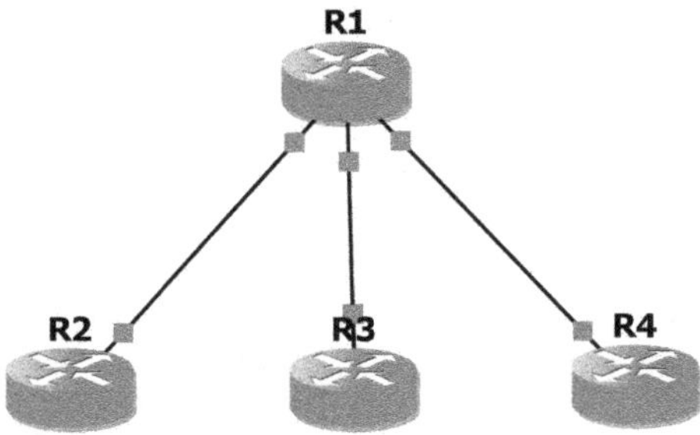

- **Network 2:** Comprising switches S1, S2, and S3, plus end devices. This network can be simplified as follows:

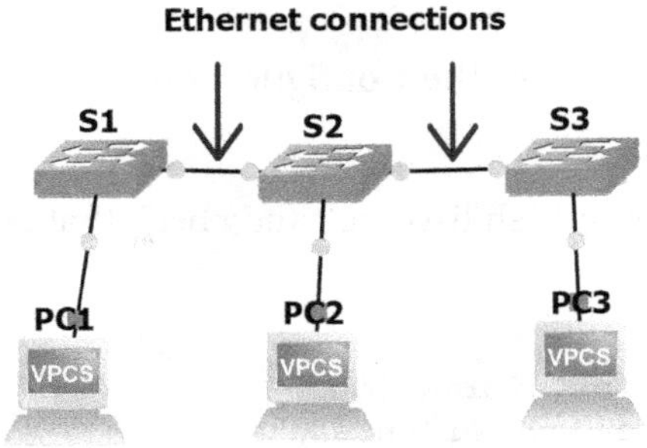

A routing mechanism can be set up if the network addresses are different. It is also possible to keep the same network address by integrating tunnels such as VXLAN. This network is known as an **overlay** network.

Please note that PC1, PC2, and PC3 may be located at sites separated by great distances. This architecture is used in the following cases, among others:

- When a server needs to be moved to another data center while retaining its IP address.
- When users move within a campus network and need to retain their IP address in order to maintain access to resources.

Lab 14: Integrating LISP and Non-LISP Networks in Cisco Architectures

Objectives

- Understand the architecture of integrating LISP and non-LISP networks.
- Identify the components of such architecture.
- Deploy a Cisco network with this architecture.

Case Study

This case study examines the integration of a network architecture combining LISP and non-LISP environments, analyzing their interactions and the elements specific to each part. It explores the various components of such an architecture and presents the steps involved in configuring a Cisco network that integrates both LISP and non-LISP segments, offering a flexible and scalable connectivity solution.

ABC wants to ensure its users have LISP network connectivity to traditional external networks, whether for shared resources or Internet access.

Required Software

- **GNS3 or equivalent**

Network Topology

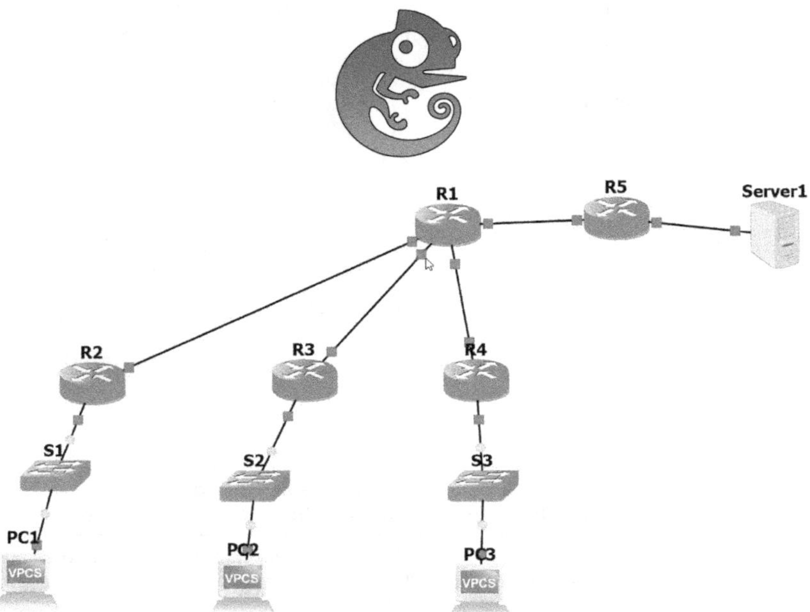

IP Address Table

Emulated Device	Device	interface	IP Address/Subnet Mask	Default Gateway
Cisco CSR1000v (IOS XE v17.3.1a, QEMU)	R1	G1->R2	10.10.0.1/24	–
Cisco CSR1000v (IOS XE v17.3.1a, QEMU)	R1	G2->R3	10.20.0.1/24	–
Cisco CSR1000v (IOS XE v17.3.1a, QEMU)	R1	G3->R4	10.30.0.1/24	–
Cisco CSR1000v (IOS XE v17.3.1a, QEMU)	R1	G4->R5	10.40.0.1/24	–
Cisco CSR1000v (IOS XE v17.3.1a, QEMU)	R2	G1->R1	10.10.0.2/24	–
Cisco CSR1000v (IOS XE v17.3.1a, QEMU)	R2	G2->S1	G2.10: 172.16.10.1 G2.20: 172.16.20.1 G2.30: 172.16.30.1	–
Cisco CSR1000v (IOS XE v17.3.1a, QEMU)	R3	G1->R1	10.20.0.2/24	–
Cisco CSR1000v (IOS XE v17.3.1a, QEMU)	R3	G2->S2	G2.10: 172.16.10.1 G2.20: 172.16.20.1 G2.30: 172.16.30.1	–
Cisco CSR1000v (IOS XE v17.3.1a, QEMU)	R4	G1->R1	10.30.0.2/24	–
Cisco CSR1000v (IOS XE v17.3.1a, QEMU)	R4	G2->S1	G2.10: 172.16.10.1 G2.20: 172.16.20.1 G2.30: 172.16.30.1	–
Cisco CSR1000v (IOS XE v17.3.1a, QEMU)	R5	G1-> R1	10.40.0.2/24	
Cisco CSR1000v (IOS XE v17.3.1a, QEMU)	R5	G2->Server1	40.0.0.1/30	
VPCS	PC1	eth0	172.16.10.2 (VLAN10)	172.16.10.1
VPCS	PC2	eth0	172.16.20.2 (VLAN20)	172.16.20.1
VPCS	PC3	eth0	172.16.30.2 (VLAN30)	172.16.30.1
Docker Container—Toolbox	Server1	eth0	40.0.0.2/30	40.0.0.1/30
Ethernet Switch	S1			
Ethernet Switch	S2			
Ethernet Switch	S3			

Part A: Theoretical Background on LISP and Non-LISP Networks

1. Give two cases where it would be necessary to ensure communication between a LISP network and a non-LISP network.
2. Link each item in the table with its corresponding definition:

1. PETR	A. It's a router that combines the functions of PITR and PETR to enable bidirectional communication between LISP and non-LISP networks.
2. PITR	B. A router that decapsulates packets from LISP networks and sends them to non-LISP networks.
3. PxTR	C. A router that encapsulates packets from non-LISP networks and sends them to LISP networks.

3. The following exercise refers to the network topology presented in this Lab, where PC1 is connected to R2 (acting as an ITR), and Server1 resides on a non-LISP network accessible through R5, which acts as a Proxy xTR (PxTR), with R1 serving as both the Mapping Server and Mapping Resolver (MS/MR).

   Re-arrange the steps that allow **PC1,** connected to **R2**, to communicate with **Server1**, a server on a **non-LISP network:**

   - R1 (MS/MR) returns mapping information, indicating that server1 is accessible via R5 (PxTR).
   - R2 sends the encapsulated packet to R5 (PxTR), using the latter's address as the destination.
   - PC1 sends a packet to server1, and R2 (RLOC1) encapsulates this packet using server1's destination address.
   - R2 decapsulates the response and transmits it to PC1.
   - Server1 receives the packet and sends a response to the PC via R5 (PxTR).
   - R2 interrogates R1 (MS/MR) to obtain the mapping corresponding to server1's address.
   - R5 (PxTR) encapsulates the response and sends it back to R2 (RLOC1) via the LISP architecture.
   - R5 (PxTR) receives the packet, decapsulates it and forwards it to server1 on the non-LISP network.

Part B: Setting Up Basic Device Configuration

Note: Leverage the pre-configured file from **Lab 13** and incorporate the new elements into it for this case study.

1. Assign an IP address to Server1.
2. Configure the R5 router interfaces. Verify the **ping** between R5 and Server1.
3. Configure the **"loopback0"** interface with an IP address.

```
R5(config)#int loopback0
R5(config-if)#ip add 5.5.5.5 255.255.555.255
```

4. Configure the **IS-IS** routing protocol on R5.

```
R5(config)#router isis
R5(config-router)#net 49.0001.0000.0000.0005.00
R5(config-router)#is-type level-1

R5(config)#interface Loopback 0
R5(config-if)#ip router isis
R5(config)#interface G1
R5(config-if)#ip router isis
```

5. Ensure the routing tables are correctly populated and ensure connectivity with **ping** tests between routers.

Part D: Configuring the LISP Protocol on Routers

Step 1: Setting up R5 as a PxTR router

1. On R5, set the basic parameters to use **LISP** and then configure it as a **PxTR**.

```
R5(config)# router lisp
lisp router
 locator-set default
  IPv4-interface Loopback0 priority 1 weight 1
  exit-locator-set
instance-id 0
  ipv4 service
   eid-table default
   map-cache 0.0.0.0/0 map-request
   itr map-resolver 1.1.1.1
   etr map-server 1.1.1.1 key cisco
   etr
   proxy-etr
   proxy-itr 5.5.5.5
   exit-service-ipv4
  exit-instance-id
exit-router-lisp
```

Step 2: Configuring routers to use PxTR

1. Configure **R2** to use **PxTR**.

```
R2(config)# router lisp
instance-id 0
ipv4 service
use-petr 5.5.5.5
```

2. Apply step **2** on routers R3 and R4, keeping the same parameters for all commands.

Step 3: Define a default route to the PxTR router

Define a default route to **the PxTR** on R1.

```
R1(config)# ip route 0.0.0.0 0.0.0.0 10.40.0.2
```

Part E: Testing and Verification of the Configuration.

1. On PC1, perform a **ping** test to 172.16.10.1.
2. On PC1, validate connectivity to Server1 with a **ping** test.

Note

1 See reference number 8.

7

Understanding and Deploying SDN Overlay Networks

This chapter examines software-defined networking (SDN) overlay networks, a critical technology in the evolution of modern network infrastructure. These networks, which create virtual network layers independent of the underlying physical infrastructure, play a vital role in enhancing the flexibility, scalability, and efficiency of network services. We will examine the various applications of these networks in different contexts and the technologies and methods used to implement them, including tunneling processes and overlay protocols. This chapter focuses on virtual extensible local area network (VXLAN), a widely used overlay protocol, examining its functionality, applications in data centers, and integration with SDN architectures to optimize network management. Additionally, we discuss VXLAN management methods, comparing static and dynamic approaches, and addressing the technical challenges associated with these networks. This chapter seeks to provide a comprehensive understanding of the design, deployment, and management of SDN overlay networks in the context of advanced networking technologies.

This chapter covers the following topics:

1. Introduction
2. Diversified applications of overlay networks
3. Overlay network technologies and methods
4. Overlay VXLAN networks
6. VXLAN and SDN: Technical complementarity
7. VXLAN management methods: Static versus dynamic
8. Technical challenges of VXLAN networks
9. Conclusion

7.1 Introduction

An overlay network is a virtual network constructed on top of an existing network infrastructure. The nodes of this virtual network are connected by virtual links that correspond to paths in the underlying network, often the Internet or another communications network.

The primary goal of this technology is to enable the creation of virtual networks and services independent of the underlying physical infrastructure, while ensuring efficient and secure communication between endpoints across various networks. An overlay network decouples network services from the underlay infrastructure by encapsulating network

 DOI: 10.1201/9781003679394-7

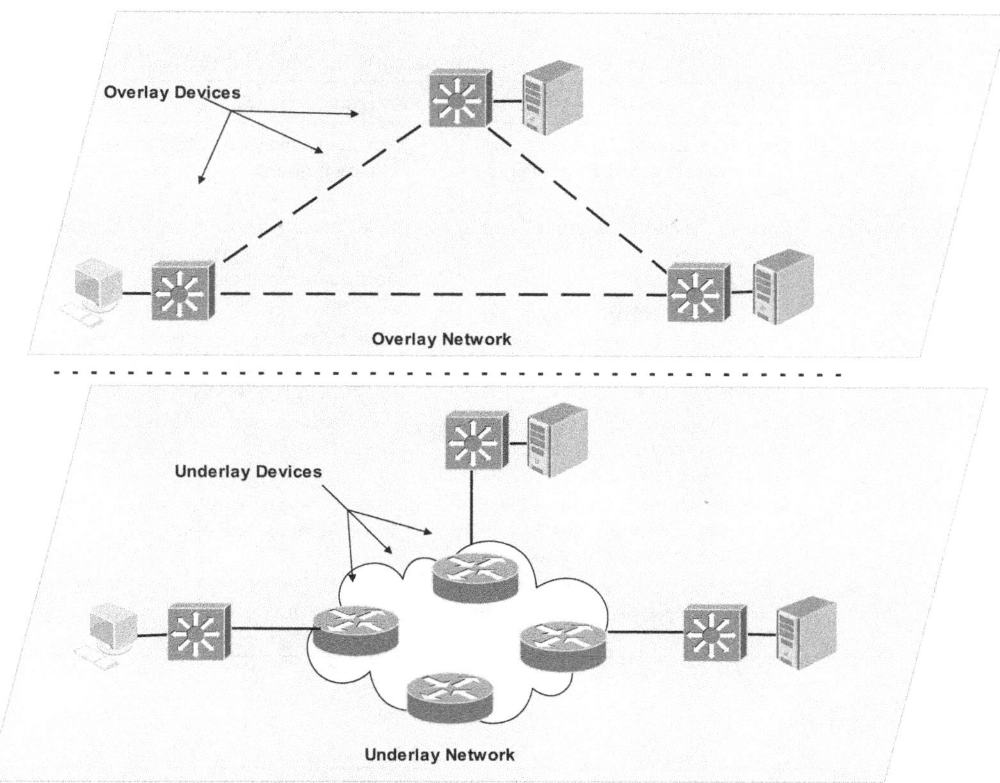

FIGURE 7.1
Overlay and underlay network structures.

packets within transport packets. Once the encapsulated packet has been transferred to the appropriate endpoint, it is then de-encapsulated and routed to the destination.

An overlay network can be a Layer 2 LAN with VLANs or a more complex Layer 3 network such as an SD-LAN or SD-WAN (Figure 7.1).

Overlay networks offer several advantages over traditional networks, including (Table 7.1):

- **Greater flexibility:** They can be easily created, modified, and deleted, enabling network administrators to respond quickly to changing business needs.
- **Enhanced scalability:** They can be easily extended to support a greater number of elements and applications.
- **Better resource management:** They enable more efficient management of network resources such as bandwidth and storage.
- **Enhanced security:** They can be used to create isolated virtual networks, improving application and data security.

TABLE 7.1

Comparison of Underlay and Overlay Networks: Transmission, Encapsulation, and Scalability

Element	Underlay Network	Overlay Network
Data transmission	Data are transmitted via network equipment such as routers and switches.	Data are transmitted over virtual links between nodes.
Encapsulation and packet overloading	Packets are encapsulated at layers 2 and 3 of the OSI model.	Packet encapsulation must be based on the source and destination, which leads to additional overhead.
Packet control	Hardware-oriented	Software-oriented
Time to market	Deploying new services involves a large number of configurations, which is a pain.	When deploying new services, only the virtual network topology needs to be modified, enabling rapid service deployment.
Multi-path routing	Due to low scalability, multi-path routing is required, increasing network overhead and complexity.	Multi-path routing within a virtual network is supported.
Scalability	Scalability is difficult. Once the underlying network has been built, it's difficult to add new elements.	They can be easily upgraded to accommodate more elements and applications
Protocols	Ethernet switching, VLANs, and routing protocols (OSPF, IS-IS, and BGP)	VXLAN, NVGRE, SST, GRE, EVPN, and so forth.

7.2 Diversified Applications of Overlay Networks

Overlay networks, by creating a virtual network layer atop the existing physical infrastructure, are applied in diverse areas beyond traditional applications like VPNs and P2P networks. This section explores the scope of these applications, highlighting their crucial role in data centers, cloud computing, mobile and IoT networks, as well as multicast networks.

- **VPN networks:** VPNs are among the most common applications for overlay networks. They enable companies to connect remote sites or mobile users (telecommuters) securely to their corporate network. Using encapsulation and tunneling technologies, VPNs create an encrypted "tunnel" across a public network, often the Internet, ensuring that transmitted data remain confidential and protected from interception.
- **Peer-to-Peer (P2P) networks:** In P2P networks, overlay networks enable users to form a network by connecting their computers directly to each other, without passing through a central server. This is used not only for file sharing, but also for streaming and communication applications. Overlay networks facilitate discovery and connectivity between peers, improving network efficiency and resilience.
- **Data centers and cloud computing:** Modern data centers and cloud computing environments leverage overlay networks extensively. In these environments, overlay networks enable virtual segmentation and isolation of individual machines,

NFVs, or applications without requiring physical changes to the network infrastructure.

- **Mobile and IoT networks:** With the explosion in the number of devices connected via mobile and IoT technologies, managing connectivity and security is becoming a major challenge. Overlay networks can simplify the management of these devices by enabling a virtual network configuration that can be easily modified and adapted without disrupting the underlying infrastructure. This is crucial to support dynamic scalability and security policy management in IoT networks.
- **Multicast networks:** Overlay networks also simplify the implementation of multicast solutions, particularly in wide-area networks where native multicast support is not available. Indeed, overlay protocols such as generic routing encapsulation (GRE) can be used to encapsulate multicast traffic in unicast packets, enabling multicast between sites across networks that do not natively support this function.

7.3 Overlay Network Technologies and Methods

Overlay networks use a variety of technologies and methods to ensure efficient and secure data transmission. This section explores the essential tunneling processes and the main overlay protocols used to facilitate network virtualization and optimization.

7.3.1 Tunneling Process

Tunneling is a core mechanism for implementing overlay networks. This process involves encapsulating data packets within a transport protocol to enable transmission across the underlay network (Figure 7.2).

- **Encapsulation:** The original data are encapsulated with a header specific to the overlay protocol, isolating user data from the underlay network.
- **Transmission:** Encapsulated packets are then transmitted through the underlay network, treated as ordinary packets by the core network.
- **De-encapsulation:** On receipt, the overlay network termination device removes the encapsulation header to extract and route the original data to its final destination.

This method not only ensures data confidentiality and integrity but also facilitates the coexistence of multiple virtual networks on the same physical infrastructure.

7.3.2 Overlay Protocols

Overlay protocols define the rules and formats of communication in overlay networks. Here are some of the most commonly used protocols, each with specific features tailored to different network requirements:

- **VXLAN:** Uses an encapsulation scheme to extend LAN networks over a WAN. VXLAN can encapsulate Ethernet frames in UDP packets, enabling up to 16 million isolated logical networks using the same address space.

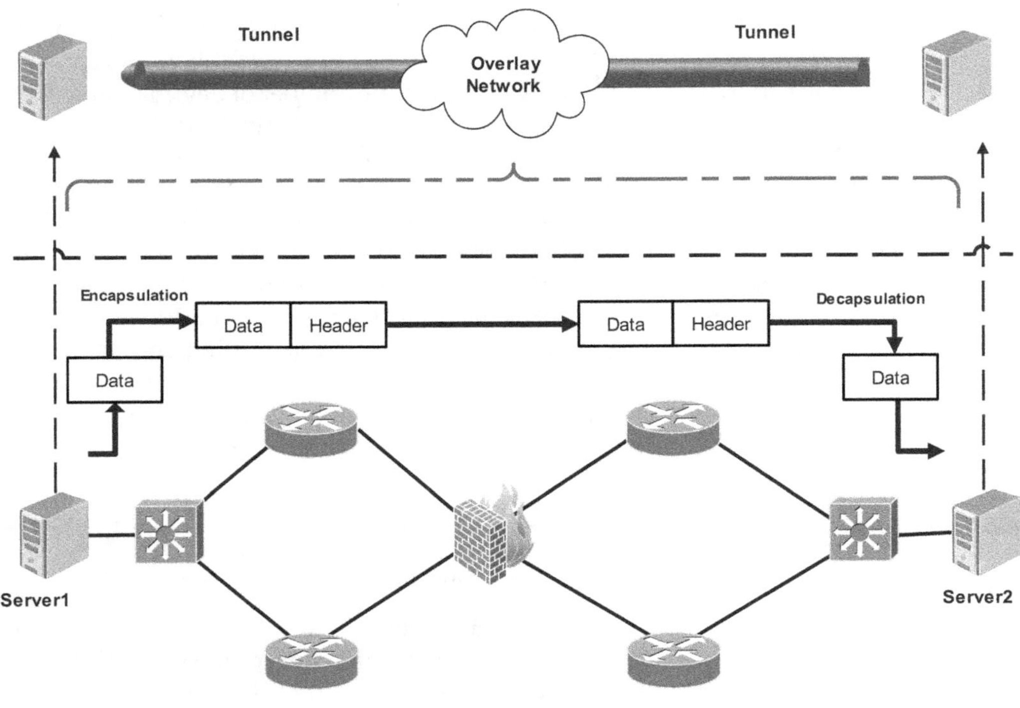

FIGURE 7.2
Tunneling in overlay network architecture.

- **Network Virtualization using GRE (NVGRE):** Similar to VXLAN, NVGRE uses GRE for encapsulation, enabling multiple virtual networks to be segmented on the same physical infrastructure. NVGRE also supports a large number of virtual network segments.
- **Stateless Transport Tunneling (STT):** Provides an efficient method of encapsulating virtual network traffic using TCP as the transport protocol, optimizing traffic management in cloud computing environments.

Each protocol has its advantages, for example, VXLAN is widely supported by modern data center equipment and offers large scale, while STT is optimized for use with hypervisors that already handle TCP traffic.

7.4 VXLAN Network Overlay

7.4.1 Introducing VXLAN

VXLAN is a network virtualization protocol that extends LANs across long distances and heterogeneous networks, including the Internet. By encapsulating Layer 2 Ethernet frames in Layer 3 UDP packets, VXLAN facilitates the creation of isolated logical networks within the same physical infrastructure. This technology is deployed in various environments, including data centers and SD-LANs, to enhance traffic isolation and simplify the management of complex networks.

VXLAN overcomes the IEEE 802.1Q limitation of 4096 VLANs, providing greater scalability and isolation, particularly in cloud environments. This technology also improves IP address space utilization.

7.4.2 VXLAN Architecture

The VXLAN architecture is based on key components that interact to provide network virtualization functionality (Figure 7.3):

- **VXLAN Tunnel Endpoint (VTEP):** VTEPs are entities that encapsulate or decapsulate Ethernet frames in or from VXLAN packets. Each VTEP has two interfaces: one for the LAN and one for the VXLAN tunnel.
- **Segmentation:** Each VXLAN segment is identified by a 24-bit VXLAN Network Identifier (VNI), enabling up to 16 million isolated networks in a VXLAN environment.
- **Discovery and management:** Each VTEP maintains a MAC-VTEP mapping table, sometimes called a MAC VTEP table or a bridging table for VXLAN. This table is used to store associations between the MAC addresses of end machines (such as site PCs) and the corresponding VTEP identifier. When a VTEP receives a packet destined for a MAC address it doesn't know, it can use this table to determine which other VTEP to send the packet to

VTEPs use the Internet Group Management Protocol (IGMP) to manage broadcasting and communication within the VXLAN network. IGMP helps to ensure that only VTEPs interested in a certain traffic receive it, thus optimizing the use of bandwidth and network resources.

Multiple VLANs can be associated with a single VNI. This can offer several advantages:

- **Simplified network management:** Grouping multiple VLANs into a single VNI can simplify network management by reducing the number of VNIs to configure and manage. This is particularly useful in environments where network policies between different VLANs are similar or identical.
- **Optimized resource utilization:** Reducing the number of VXLAN tunnels required optimizes the use of network resources, such as the IP addresses and

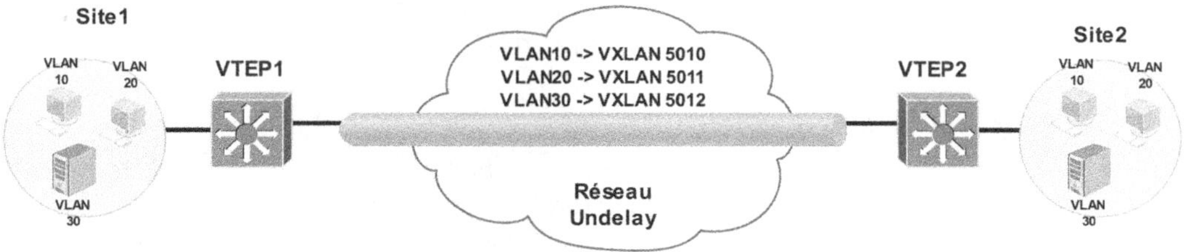

FIGURE 7.3
VXLAN architecture.

UDP ports used to transport VXLAN data. This optimization can also improve performance by reducing header overhead due to encapsulation.

- **Improved network flexibility:** This allows for greater flexibility in distributing workloads and in moving virtual machines or containers between different network segments, without requiring complex changes to the underlay network structure.

The decision to allocate one VNI per VLAN, or to group several VLANs under a single VNI, must be taken in light of specific network security, management, and scalability requirements. If security and isolation are priorities, it is advisable to opt for a separate VNI for each VLAN. On the other hand, if simpler management and greater scalability are required, it may make sense to group VLANs under a single VNI.

7.4.3 Data Transfer

Based on Figure 7.3, when PC1 located in site1 wishes to send data to PC2 in site2, the following process is implemented:

- **Initiating communication:** PC1 starts by sending an ARP request to find out PC2's MAC address, assuming it already knows its IP address.
- **ARP request management by VTEP1:**
  - VTEP1, which is the endpoint of the VXLAN tunnel in site 1, intercepts this ARP request. VTEP1 acts as an ARP proxy for addresses on other sites.
  - If PC2's MAC address is already in VTEP1's MAC table, VTEP can reply directly to PC1 with this MAC address, pretending to be PC2. This response is sent to PC1, which can then use the MAC address to communicate.
  - If PC2's MAC address is not known, VTEP1 sends an encapsulated ARP request to all VTEPs in the same VNI. Each VTEP receives this request and broadcasts it to its local hosts, and, if PC2 is present, VTEP2 receives PC2's ARP response, encapsulates it, and sends it back to VTEP1, which then updates its MAC table with this new information.
- **Data encapsulation:**
  - After receiving PC2's MAC address, PC1 prepares an Ethernet packet, using this MAC address as its destination.
  - If traffic has to cross a specific VLAN, the Ethernet packet is tagged according to the 802.1Q standard.
  - The Ethernet packet, possibly tagged, is then encapsulated in a VXLAN packet by VTEP1. The VXLAN header contains the VNI corresponding to the targeted VLAN.
- **VTEP2 reception and de-encapsulation:**
  - VTEP2 receives the VXLAN packet, extracts it from the tunnel, and decapsulates the VXLAN header to recover the Ethernet packet.
  - It checks the dot1q header to ensure that the packet belongs to a VLAN it manages, removes the dot1q header, checks the destination of the Ethernet packet, and forwards the final packet to PC2.

This process illustrates the synergy between Ethernet, 802.1Q, and VXLAN in facilitating secure and efficient data transfer across wide-area networks, while maintaining the segmentation required by VLAN configurations.

7.4.4 VXLAN Frame Format

The following figure illustrates the general frame format used by the VXLAN protocol, which is used for network virtualization in cloud and datacenter environments (Figure 7.4).

Here is an in-depth explanation of each part of the illustrated frame:

- **Outer Ethernet header:** Includes source and destination MAC addresses, used to transport the VXLAN frame across the underlying network to the destination VTEP.
- **External IP header:** Contains the source and destination IP addresses, typically the addresses of the VTEPs. This header is used to route encapsulated VXLAN frames across the IP network.
- **UDP header:** The VXLAN protocol uses UDP to encapsulate the original Ethernet frames. Using UDP enables efficient encapsulation and transport with a simple header and minimal state management.
- **VXLAN header:** This header mainly contains the VNI, which is essential for uniquely identifying virtual network segments within a VXLAN environment. The VNI ensures that frames are isolated and delivered to the correct broadcast domain.
- **Original L2 frame:** This is the original Ethernet frame encapsulated in the VXLAN packet. It contains MAC addresses, VLANs, and other information specific to the Ethernet frame.
- **Frame Check Sequence:** An error-checking field to guarantee the integrity of transmitted data.

7.4.5 VXLANs and Their Application to Data Centers

VXLANs offer an effective solution to the challenges posed by network management in modern data centers. These challenges include the massive increase in the number of networks and nodes and the need for dynamic, automated deployment. Here, we explore how VXLANs meet these requirements, improving the efficiency and agility of data center network infrastructures.

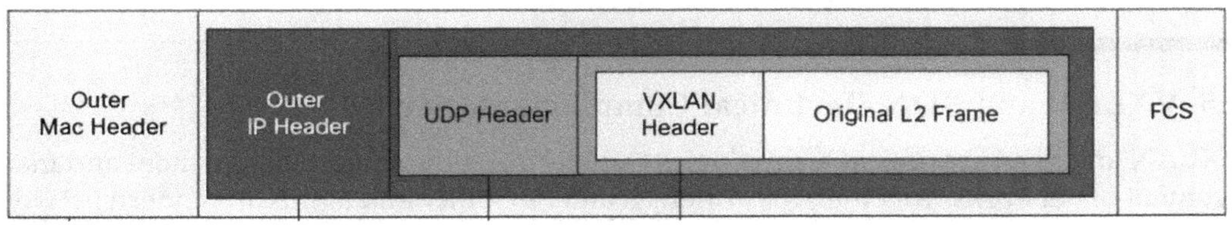

FIGURE 7.4
VXLAN frame format.

- **Increasing the number of networks and nodes:** VXLANs overcome the limitations of traditional VLANs, which are limited to 4096 unique identifiers, by offering up to 16 million VNIs. This enables the network to be efficiently segmented into thousands of isolated sub-networks within a single physical environment, making it easier to manage large numbers of virtual machines on thousands of physical servers.
- **Dynamic management of virtual machines:** Modern data centers require the flexibility to move, replicate, and resiliently manage VMs. VXLANs support these operations by dissociating the VM's IP address from its physical location. This means that VMs can move freely between servers or even data centers without requiring network reconfiguration, which is crucial for business continuity and fault management.
- **Automated tenant deployment:** A *tenant* represents an entity or group of users with distinct access rights within a shared infrastructure. Dynamic, automated tenant deployment is essential in cloud and multi-tenant environments. VXLANs facilitate this automation by enabling network administrators to rapidly create new network segments without manual intervention at the physical infrastructure level. Each tenant can be assigned to a separate VNI, simplifying administration and enhancing security.
- **VM isolation and security:** Isolation between VMs is another key VXLAN feature, allowing each tenant to operate in its own virtual broadcast domain. This is particularly important for data security, as it prevents VMs from seeing or interfering with the traffic of other VMs, even if their data resides on the same physical server. This isolation is reinforced by the use of security policies that can be applied specifically to each VNI, ensuring that communications between virtual machines remain private and secure within their own network segment.

Hypervisors play a key role in the implementation of overlay networks in data centers:

- **Encapsulation and routing:** Hypervisors can encapsulate packets sent by virtual machines (VMs) in protocols such as VXLAN or NVGRE, enabling these packets to traverse the underlying physical network while maintaining isolation between different virtual networks.
- **Centralized management:** Hypervisors are often managed by centralized network controllers, which configure network policies and distribute rules across the hypervisors, simplifying the management of complex virtual networks.

7.5 VXLAN and SDN: Technical Complementarity

VXLAN and SDN are critical technologies transforming the design, deployment and management of networks. Together, they offer greater flexibility and agility in modern network environments, particularly in data centers and cloud architectures.

7.5.1 Interaction between VXLAN and SDN

VXLAN technology enables networks to be significantly extended, overcoming the address space limitations of traditional VLANs. However, managing these extended networks can become complex without proper orchestration. By integrating SDN, network administrators can centrally manage and configure VXLAN networks through an SDN controller. This controller is capable of dynamically adjusting routing rules and network policies according to fluctuating conditions and business requirements.

For example, when a cloud application requires more bandwidth or needs to be deployed rapidly across multiple servers, the SDN controller can automatically adjust VXLAN configurations to meet these requirements without manual intervention.

This approach significantly reduces operational complexity and enhances network performance by enabling rapid, non-disruptive changes.

7.5.2 Synergy of VXLAN, NFV, and SDN Technologies for Optimized Data Center Management

In a data center using both VXLAN and SDN technologies, when two VMs located on the same server need to communicate, the hypervisor directs traffic via the virtual interfaces configured by the SDN controller. If the VMs are located in two different networks, they can use a virtual router to communicate. When VMs are on different servers, VXLAN encapsulates and transports traffic across the underlying network, using VXLAN tunnels set up by the SDN controller.

What's more, in these data centers, routers, switches, VTEPs, and so forth, facilitating communication between VMs is often implemented as network functions virtualization (NFV). This enables more flexible configuration and management by the SDN controller. Thus, the integration of VXLAN, NFV, and SDN technologies not only simplifies the implementation of network policies but also improves the overall operational efficiency of the data center.

7.5.3 Spine/Leaf Architecture

The "Spine/Leaf" architecture, also known as the "Closed network", is particularly well-suited to modern data center environments using technologies such as VXLAN. In a Spine/Leaf architecture, each *leaf* switch is connected to each *spine* switch, but there are no direct connections between the *leaf* switches themselves, nor between the *spine* switches. This topology prevents the formation of data loops in the network. The absence of horizontal connections between leaf switches and between spine switches means that there are no loop paths through which data could flow redundantly. This eliminates scenarios where Spanning Tree Protocol would normally be required to prevent the formation of loops (Figure 7.5).

This configuration offers several significant advantages:

- **Scalability:** Spine/Leaf architecture enables easy network expansion by simply adding more leaf or spine switches. This modularity facilitates data center growth without major disruption to existing service.
- **Reduced latency:** Thanks to the high-connectivity design of this architecture, each leaf switch is at a constant hop distance from any other leaf switch across

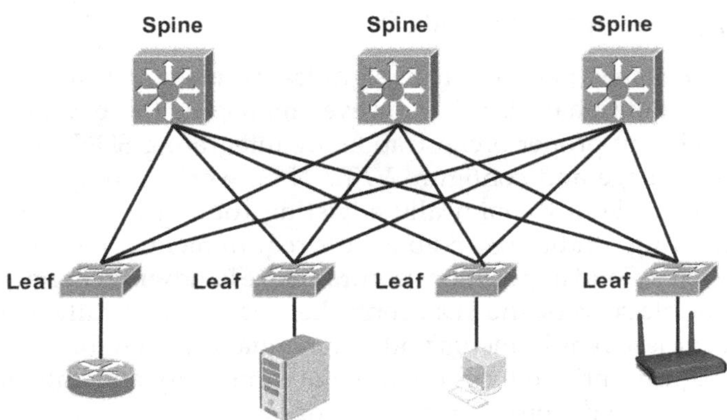

FIGURE 7.5
Spine/leaf architecture.

the spine switches. This minimizes network latency, as data packets have short, predictable paths.

- **Fault tolerance:** The Spine/Leaf architecture offers enhanced redundancy. If a spine switch fails, traffic can be rerouted to other spines without any significant impact on network performance, guaranteeing high availability.
- **Load balancing:** Multiple connectivity paths between leaf and spine switches enable efficient traffic distribution, reducing bottlenecks and optimizing bandwidth utilization.

Spine/Leaf architecture, very common in data center VXLAN deployments, is a popular choice for modern infrastructures due to its significant advantages in terms of network performance, scalability, and flexibility. Although not a mandatory requirement for using VXLAN, this architecture is often preferred to optimize network capabilities.

The Spine/Leaf architecture is not exclusive to SDN networks. It can also be implemented in traditional networks, where configuration and management are carried out via command-line interfaces or standard network management tools. In these cases, the architecture helps improve network performance, reliability, and scalability.

7.6 VXLAN Management Methods: Static versus Dynamic

7.6.1 VXLAN Static

7.6.1.1 Presentation

Static VXLANs (also known as controllerless VXLANs) refer to VXLAN configurations where VLAN-to-VNI mappings and VTEP addresses are manually configured by a network administrator. Unlike dynamic VXLANs, where these parameters are automatically discovered and managed by network controllers or protocols, static VXLANs rely on predefined, less flexible configurations but are often simpler and more stable for small to medium-sized environments.

The characteristics of static VXLANs are as follows:

- **Manual configuration:** VTEP IP addresses and mappings between VLANs and VNIs must be explicitly configured on each VTEP device. This requires a good prior knowledge of the network and its traffic requirements.
- **No automatic discovery:** There is no mechanism for automatic discovery of VTEPs or dynamic propagation of VLAN information. Any change in the network requires manual reconfiguration.
- **Simplicity and predictability:** The static model is often appreciated for its simplicity and predictability. Administrators can easily understand and audit the network configuration, which reduces the risk of unforeseen errors due to dynamic adjustments.
- **Less reliance on additional software:** Unlike dynamic configurations, which may require additional software or hardware for VXLAN management (such as SDN controllers), static VXLANs can be set up with standard network equipment without additional software.

Static VXLANs are often used in scenarios where the network topology is stable, where security requirements demand strict control over traffic flows, or in environments where dynamic management does not bring significant benefits in terms of cost or performance. They are also preferred in contexts where simplicity of deployment and management is a priority.

7.6.1.2 Multicast in VXLAN

Multicast is essential in VXLAN networks for efficiently managing BUM (Broadcast, Unknown Unicast, Multicast) traffic. These frames, which cannot be sent directly to a single recipient, require efficient broadcasting, especially in large networks with many devices and VTEPs. Using multicast allows a broadcast or multicast packet to be sent only once per network link, reducing unnecessary traffic as only interested VTEPs receive the packet.

There are several methods and protocols that can be used to manage multicast traffic in VXLAN environments. Here are some of them for multicast management in VXLANs:

- Protocol Independent Multicast **(PIM) protocol:** PIM is a multicast routing mechanism that manages the distribution of multicast data across an IP network. Independent of the underlying routing protocol, such as OSPF or BGP, it facilitates the unicast routing required for multicast.
- **BGP EVPN (Ethernet VPN):** BGP EVPN has become a popular choice for multicast management in VXLANs, not least because it supports both Layer 2 and Layer 3 services. BGP EVPN uses centralized control mechanisms to manage multicast memberships and routing tables, offering a dynamic and scalable alternative to PIM.
- **IGMP and MLD:** These protocols are used to manage host subscriptions to specific multicast streams in IPv4 (IGMP) and IPv6 (MLD) networks. In a VXLAN environment, IGMP and MLD can be used to inform VTEPs of required multicast groups, helping to control the distribution of multicast traffic.

- **Static multicast routing:** In some cases, especially in smaller or less dynamic environments, multicast routing can be handled statically, without the use of dynamic protocols. Although less flexible, this method may be sufficient for networks with well-defined and stable multicast requirements.

7.6.1.3 PIM Operating Modes

PIM operates in two main modes: dense mode and sparse mode. Each mode is adapted to different types of networks and multicast traffic distribution.

- **PIM Sparse-Mode**
  - **Features:** In Sparse-mode, multicast streams are not transmitted to all network segments by default. Instead, routers must explicitly "register" for the specific streams they need, using a process called "Join". This process is managed by one or more routers designated as central "Rendezvous Points (RP)", which act as hubs for multicast group information.
  - **Application:** Sparse-mode is designed for networks where multicast groups have few devices dispersed widely over a large network, reducing the amount of data sent unnecessarily over the network, saving bandwidth and reducing the load on routers.
- **PIM Dense Mode (DM):**
  - **Features:** In Dense Mode, multicast streams are initially broadcast to all network segments. This mode is based on the "flood and prune" principle, where streams are first sent to all routers, then those that have no members interested in the multicast stream send "prune" messages to stop the reception of unnecessary traffic.
  - **Application:** PIM Dense Mode is often used in networks where multicast groups have many receivers distributed in almost all branches of the network, making the initial flooding less costly in terms of bandwidth.
- **PIM Source Specific Multicast:**
  - **Features:** PIM Source Specific Multicast (SSM) is an optimization of Sparse Mode for cases where receivers are interested in streams from specific sources. In this mode, receivers must indicate not only the multicast group they wish to join, but also the specific IP address of the group's source.
  - **Use:** This mode is particularly effective for video and other streaming media applications where subscribers know the source address and wish to receive only content from that source, thus optimizing network resources.
- **PIM Bidirectional Mode:**
  - **Features:** In bidirectional mode, multicast traffic is sent and received on the same shared tree structure, without the need for specific source trees. This simplifies multicast tree management and reduces router overhead.
  - **Use:** This mode is used in scenarios where multicast traffic sources and receivers are active simultaneously and frequently, such as in interactive collaboration or teleconferencing environments.

7.6.2 VXLAN Dynamic

7.6.2.1 Presentation

Unlike static VXLANs, dynamic VXLANs use network control protocols to automate the discovery of VTEPs and the distribution of routing information. This considerably reduces configuration complexity and the risk of manual errors.

7.6.2.2 Dynamic VXLAN Control Protocols

For dynamic VXLANs, several control protocols are used to automate and optimize network configuration, discovery, and management. Here are the main control protocols used in these contexts:

- **BGP EVPN:** This is currently the most widespread control protocol for dynamic VXLAN networks. It enables automatic VTEP discovery and route distribution for both unicast and multicast traffic. BGP EVPN supports layer 2 and layer 3 services and facilitates efficient management of network policies in large-scale environments.
- **LISP:** LISP can be used for address encapsulation and management in VXLAN environments, offering an alternative method of separating location and host identities, facilitating more dynamic address management.
- **OSPF:** Although not specifically used to control VXLANs themselves, OSPF can be used in the Underlay infrastructure to manage internal routes and optimize routing between different VTEPs across the physical network.
- **IS-IS:** Like OSPF, IS-IS can be used to optimize communication and routing within the Underlay network that supports VXLAN tunnels, helping to distribute routing information efficiently.

These protocols each contribute to different aspects of dynamic VXLAN management, from automatic VTEP discovery to routing optimization and multicast traffic management. However, BGP EVPN remains the most common choice for integrated, comprehensive management of dynamic VXLAN environments.

7.6.2.3 Choice between Static and Dynamic

The choice between static and dynamic VXLANs depends largely on the size and complexity of the network environment and the resources available for network management. Static VXLANs may be appropriate for smaller networks or situations where strict control is required. On the other hand, for large cloud infrastructures or data centers, dynamic VXLANs are preferable because of their simplified management and adaptability.

The performance of dynamic VXLANs is generally superior due to the better resource management and routing optimization achieved by control protocols such as BGP EVPN. However, it also requires in-depth technical expertise to configure and maintain these protocols correctly.

7.7 Technical Challenges of VXLAN Networks

Despite VXLAN's advantages in virtualization and flexibility, several technical challenges persist:

- **Security:** While VXLAN provides network isolation, securing data transmitted between VTEPs requires additional measures, such as IPsec encryption.
- **Performance:** Encapsulation and decapsulation require processing resources, which can affect network performance. Hardware and software solutions are used to speed up these operations.
- **Compatibility and integration:** While VXLAN is designed for compatibility with diverse network infrastructures and virtualization platforms, its integration into complex environments can pose challenges.

7.8 Conclusion

This chapter has thoroughly examined SDN Overlay networks, detailing their design, deployment, and management. The analysis of VXLANs has demonstrated how these technologies enable the creation of efficient and flexible virtual networks, adept at meeting the dynamic demands of modern data centers. We saw that the interaction between VXLANs and SDN architectures offers significant advantages, including improved scalability, optimized management of network resources, and greater agility in deploying services.

While the technical challenges of these technologies are significant, their substantial benefits outweigh them. Dynamic management of VXLANs, supported by advanced control protocols, represents considerable potential for automating and improving network performance.

In conclusion, SDN overlay networks, particularly VXLAN-based solutions, are vital components of future network infrastructure. They offer a robust platform for innovation in network data and service management, advocating further integration of virtualization and automation. Understanding and mastering these technologies will be crucial for network architects and IT professionals seeking to optimize network performance and meet the evolving needs of modern businesses.

Lab 15: Deploying Static VXLAN Over Underlay Networks with Multicast Control

Objectives

- Understand the architecture of integrating underlay and overlay networks.
- Grasp the theoretical foundations of VXLANs.
- Identify the key components of this architecture.
- Deploy a Cisco network for static VXLAN implementation with multicast flow control.

Case Study

This case study examines the integration of underlay and overlay networks into a network architecture, with particular emphasis on the theoretical principles of VXLAN. It identifies the building blocks of this architecture and guides the configuration of a Cisco network to implement static VXLANs, with multicast flow management, offering a solution for flexible and scalable network segmentation.

Company ABC aims to segment groups of servers, with each segment maintaining a distinct network strategy. The segments may extend across multiple remote physical locations while maintaining the same network addressing for the servers. The number of segments reaches into the thousands. The company has therefore opted to use VXLAN technology.

Required Software

- GNS3 or equivalent

Network Topology

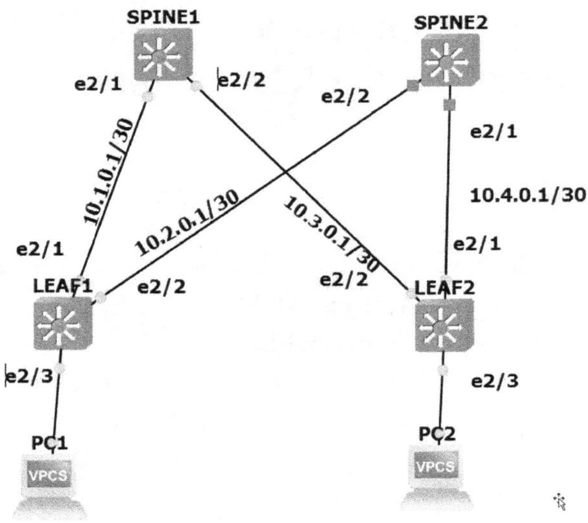

IP Address Table

Emulated Device	Device	Interface	IP Address/Subnet Mask	Default Gateway
Cisco NX-OSv Virtual Switch (v7.3.0 D1.1)	SPINE1	e2/1	10.1.0.1/30	–
Cisco NX-OSv Virtual Switch (v7.3.0 D1.1)	SPINE1	e2/2	10.3.0.1/30	–
Cisco NX-OSv Virtual Switch (v7.3.0 D1.1)	SPINE2	e2/1	10.4.0.1/30	–
Cisco NX-OSv Virtual Switch (v7.3.0 D1.1)	SPINE2	e2/2	10.2.0.1/30	–
Cisco NX-OSv Virtual Switch (v7.3.0 D1.1)	LEAF1	e2/1	10.1.0.2/30	–
Cisco NX-OSv Virtual Switch (v7.3.0 D1.1)	LEAF1	e2/2	10.2.0.2/30	–
Cisco NX-OSv Virtual Switch (v7.3.0 D1.1)	LEAF2	e2/1	10.4.0.2/30	–
Cisco NX-OSv Virtual Switch (v7.3.0 D1.1)	LEAF2	e2/2	10.3.0.2/30	–
VPCS	PC1	eth0	172.16.10.2 (VLAN10)	172.16.10.1
VPCS	PC3	eth0	172.16.10.3 (VLAN10)	172.16.10.1

Note: If you lack sufficient CPU or RAM resources, you can use a single SPINE.

Part A: Theoretical Background on VXLAN

1. Recall the concept and advantages of VXLANs.
2. Match each item in the table with its appropriate definition:

A. VTEP	1. Designates a configuration where tunnels and mappings between VTEPs and VNIs are defined manually, without the use of dynamic discovery or management protocols.
B. VNI	2. Refers to a configuration where VXLAN tunnels are automatically managed by control protocols such as BGP EVPN, facilitating the discovery of VTEPs and the distribution of routing information.
C. Underlay	3. A tunnel endpoint that encapsulates and decapsulates data frames for transfer across a VXLAN network.
D. Overlay	4. Leaf switches connect to end devices and form the edge of the network, while Spine switches act as a central backbone to connect different Leaf switches together.
E. Dynamic VXLAN	5. An identifier used in VXLAN to distinguish different logical networks or segments within the same physical network.
F. Spine/ Leaf	6. A virtual network built on top of an existing physical network, using technologies such as VXLAN to create tunnels between geographically distributed endpoints.
G. Static VXLAN	7. The underlying physical network that supports the overlay network, providing basic IP connectivity between VTEPs in a VXLAN network.
H. Sparse-Mode	8. A multicast routing protocol to efficiently manage the distribution of multicast data streams across different underlying routing protocols in a network.
I. PIM	9. This mode uses one or more central points, called "Rendezvous Points (RP)", to manage and distribute multicast group information only to those network devices that express a need for it through an explicit subscription.

3. The following exercise refers to the network topology presented in this Lab, where PC1 is connected to LEAF1, and PC2 is connected to LEAF2. The communication between them takes place over a VXLAN fabric, with SPINE1 acting as a transit node, and both LEAF1 and LEAF2 functioning as VTEPs (VXLAN Tunnel Endpoints).

   Rearrange the steps that enable **PC1,** connected to **LEAF1**, to communicate with **PC2,** connected to **LEAF2**, via **SPINE1:**

   - **Tunnel creation:** Leaf1 sends the VXLAN frame through an IP/UDP tunnel established between the VTEPs. The tunnel is typically established between Leaf switches (Leaf1 and Leaf2 in this case) by passing through Spine1, which acts as a simple transit device.
   - **Reception by Leaf2:** Leaf2 (VTEP recipient) receives the VXLAN frame and decapsulates it to extract the original packet intended for PC2.
   - **Encapsulation at Leaf1:** When PC1 sends a packet to PC2, the Leaf1 switch (source VTEP) encapsulates the original packet in a VXLAN frame. This frame includes a VXLAN header specifying the VNI that identifies the virtual network to which PC1 and PC2 belong.
   - **Delivery to PC2:** Leaf2 transmits the decapsulated packet to PC2, completing communication between PC1 and PC2 over the VXLAN network.
   - **Transit through Spine1:** The VXLAN frame passes through Spine1. Spine1 routes the frame based on the IP address of the destination VTEP (Leaf2), without having to understand or modify the VXLAN header.

Part B: Establishing Basic Device Configuration

1. Configure PC IP addresses.
2. Enable the "grace-period" license on all switches to enable the desired functions.

```
(config)# license grace-period
```

3. On SPINE1, configure interface IP addresses.

```
SPINE1 (config)#int e2/1
no switchport
ip address 10.1.0.1/30
no shutdown
mac-address 0000.0000.011f
```

Note: If you use the "titanium-final.7.3.0.D1.1" image, you'll notice that all switch interfaces share the same MAC address. It is therefore necessary to add the command "mac-address [0000.0000.011f] (to be modified for each interface)" to correct this anomaly.

```
SPINE1 (config)#int e2/2
no switchport
ip address 10.3.0.1/30
no shutdown
mac-address 0000.0000.013f
```

4. Repeat the previous step on the SPINE2, LEAF1 and LEAF2 switches, referring to the addressing table.
5. Assign an IP address to the "loopback0" interface on each switch.

```
SPINE1 (config)#int loopback0
SPINE1 (config-if)#ip add 1.1.1.1/32
SPINE2 (config)#int loopback0
SPINE2 (config-if)#ip add 2.2.2.2/32
LEAF1 (config)#int loopback0
LEAF1 (config-if)# ip add 3.3.3.3/32
LEAF2 (config)#int loopback0
LEAF2 (config-if)# ip add 4.4.4.4/32
```

6. Configure the **OSPF** (or **IS-IS**) routing protocol on switches.

```
(config)# feature ospf
(config-if)#router ospf 1
(config)#int e2/1
(config-if)# ip router ospf 1 area 0.0.0.0
(config-if)# ip ospf network point-to-point
(config)#int e2/2
(config-if)# ip router ospf 1 area 0.0.0.0
(config-if)# ip ospf network point-to-point
(config)#int loopback0
(config-if)# ip router ospf 1 area 0.0.0.0
```

7. Verify that the routing tables are correctly populated and make sure you can *ping* between routers.

Part C: Setting Up the PIM Protocol for VXLAN

1. Enable **PIM** functionality on all switches.

```
(config)# feature pim
```

2. On SPINE1 and SPINE2, activate the **PIM** protocol on all interfaces.

```
(config)# int e2/1 -2
(config-if)# ip pim sparse-mode
(config)# int loopback0
(config-if)# ip pim sparse-mode
```

3. On LEAF1 and LEAF2, activate the **PIM** protocol on the appropriate interfaces.

```
(config)# interface e1/1- 2
(config-if)# ip pim sparse-mode

(config)# interface Loopback 0
(config-if)# ip pim sparse-mode
```

4. Set SPINE1 as the **collection point** (RP) for multicast traffic for <u>all switches</u>.

```
(config)# ip pim rp-address 1.1.1.1 group-list 224.0.0.0/4
```

Part D: Creating and Configuring VXLANs

On LEAF1 and LEAF2:

1. Activate the **"nv overlay"** and **"vn-segment-vlan-based"** features to use VXLANs.

```
(config)# feature vn-segment-vlan-based
(config-if)# feature nv overlay
```

2. Create and configure a VLAN and VXLAN.

```
(config)# vlan 10
(config-vlan)# vn-segment 50010
(config)# Ethernet interface 2/3
(config-if)# switchport
(config-if)# switchport access vlan 10
```

3. Configure the **nve** interface.

```
(config)# interface nve1
(config-if-nve)# no shutdown
(config-if-nve)# source-interface loopback0
(config-if-nve)# member vni 50010
(config-if-nve-vni)# mcast-group 239.1.1.1
```

Part E: Verification, Testing, and Explanation Results

1. Show the routing table of SPINE1:

```
...
1.1.1.1/32, ubest/mbest: 2/0, attached
    *via 1.1.1.1, Lo0, [0/0], 00:35:36, local
    *via 1.1.1.1, Lo0, [0/0], 00:35:36, direct
2.2.2.2/32, ubest/mbest: 1/0
    *via 10.1.0.2, Eth2/1, [110/81], 00:33:11, ospf-1, intra
3.3.3.3/32, ubest/mbest: 1/0
    *via 10.1.0.2, Eth2/1, [110/41], 00:33:15, ospf-1, intra
4.4.4.4/32, ubest/mbest: 1/0
    *via 10.3.0.2, Eth2/2, [110/41], 00:32:20, ospf-1, intra
              10.1.0.0/24, ubest/mbest: 1/0, attached
...
```

2. Show the multicast routing table of SPINE1:

```
SPINE1# sh ip mroute
IP Multicast Routing Table for VRF "default
(*, 232.0.0.0/8), uptime: 00:37:48, pim ip
  Incoming interface: Null, RPF nbr: 0.0.0.0
  Outgoing interface list: (count: 0)
(*, 239.1.1.1/32), uptime: 00:23:14, pim ip
  Incoming interface: loopback0, RPF nbr: 1.1.1.1
  Outgoing interface list: (count: 2)
    Ethernet2/1, uptime: 00:23:05, pim
    Ethernet2/2, uptime: 00:23:14, pim
(3.3.3.3/32, 239.1.1.1/32), uptime: 00:23:05, pim mrib ip
  Incoming interface: Ethernet2/1, RPF nbr: 10.1.0.2, internal
  Outgoing interface list: (count: 2)
    Ethernet2/1, uptime: 00:08:26, pim, (RPF)
    Ethernet2/2, uptime: 00:23:05, pim
(4.4.4.4/32, 239.1.1.1/32), uptime: 00:23:14, pim ip
  Incoming interface: Ethernet2/2, RPF nbr: 10.3.0.2, internal
  Outgoing interface list: (count: 2)
    Ethernet2/2, uptime: 00:10:38, pim, (RPF)
    Ethernet2/1, uptime: 00:23:05, pim
```

3. Use the "sh run pim" command on all switches to ensure that the **PIM** protocol is configured.

```
....
feature pim
ip pim rp-address 1.1.1.1 group-list 224.0.0.0/4
ip pim ssm range 232.0.0.0/8
interface loopback0
  ip pim sparse-mode
Ethernet2/1 interface
  ip pim sparse-mode
Ethernet2/2 interface
 ip pim sparse-mode
```

4. Verify the configuration of **e2/3** interfaces on **LEAF1** and **LEAF2** switches

```
LEAF2# sh run int e2/3
...
Ethernet2/3 interface
  switchport
  switchport access vlan 10
 no shutdown
```

5. From PC1, verify connectivity with PC2 using a **ping** test.
6. Define **Underlay** and **Overlay** network elements
7. Connect a **Cisco router** to LEAF1's e2/4 port and configure it as a **DHCP** server for VLAN 10 (**172.16.10.0/24**). Then check that PC2 can obtain an IP address dynamically.
8. Outline the steps for PC2 to obtain an IP address from the DHCP server, highlighting the role of **VTEPs**.

Lab 16: Static VXLAN Deployment Over FortiGate with Overlay/ Underlay Integration

Objectives

- Understand an architecture integrating underlay and overlay networks.
- Identify the key components of this architecture.
- Deploy a FortiGate network to implement static VXLANs.

Case Study

This case study examines the integration of underlay and overlay networks into a network architecture, identifying the essential building blocks of this structure. It also guides the configuration of a FortiGate network to implement static VXLANs, providing an advanced network segmentation and management solution for complex environments.

ABC aims to segment groups of servers. However, the segmentation should extend to remote sites connected through WAN (typically Internet) links. The servers must maintain consistent network addressing. The company has therefore opted to use VXLAN technology.

Required Software

- **GNS3 or equivalent**

Network Topology

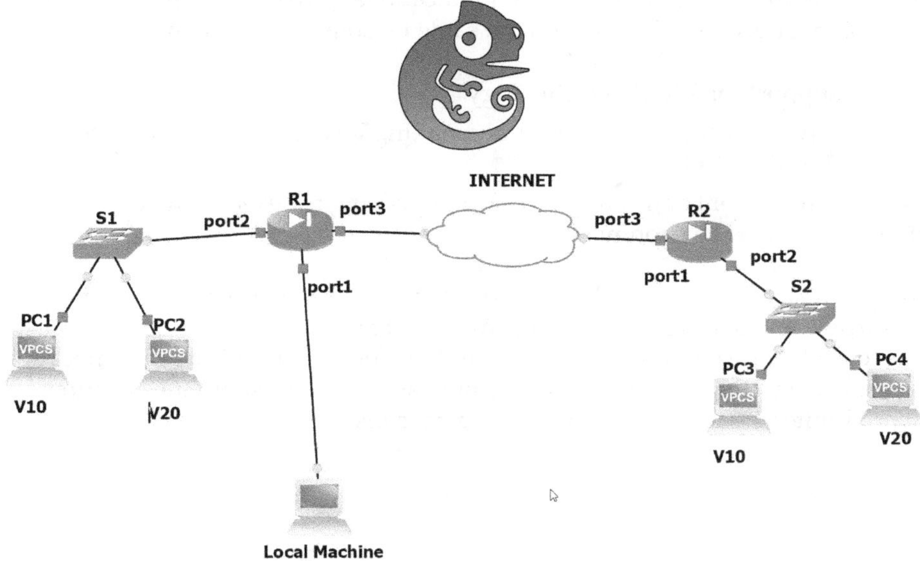

IP Address Table

Emulated Device	Device	Interface	IP Address/Subnet Mask	Default Gateway
FortiGate Virtual Appliance (v7.2.4.2)	R1	port1	172.16.1.10/24	–
FortiGate Virtual Appliance (v7.2.4.2)	R1	port2	V10: 192.168.10.1	–
FortiGate Virtual Appliance (v7.2.4.2)	R1	port2	V20: 192.168.20.1	–
FortiGate Virtual Appliance (v7.2.4.2)	R1	port3	40.0.0.1/30	–
FortiGate Virtual Appliance (v7.2.4.2)	R2	port1	172.16.1.10/24	–
FortiGate Virtual Appliance (v7.2.4.2)	R2	port2	V10: 192.168.10.254	–
FortiGate Virtual Appliance (v7.2.4.2)	R2	port2	V20: 192.168.20. 254	–
FortiGate Virtual Appliance (v7.2.4.2)	R2	port3	40.0.0.2/30	–
VPCS	PC1	eth0	192.168.10.2 (VLAN10)	192.168.10.1
VPCS	PC2	eth0	192.168.20.2 (VLAN20)	192.168.20.1
VPCS	PC3	eth0	192.168.10.3 (VLAN10)	192.168.10.254
VPCS	PC4	eth0	192.168.20.3 (VLAN20)	192.168.20. 254
GNS3 Cloud	Local Machine	VMware Interface	172.16.1.1/24	
Ethernet switch	INTERNET	–	–	–

Note: The use of the FortiGate Virtual Appliance (v7.2.4.2) for the creation and configuration of VXLANs in this lab was chosen for educational purposes, even though it is not an SDN controller. This choice is based on the same reasons already mentioned:

a. Native support for VXLAN technology.
b. Low hardware resource consumption, making it compatible with platforms such as GNS3 or EVE-NG.
c. Ease of deployment and configuration, simplifying the execution of the manipulations in a virtual environment.

This compromise allows us to illustrate key concepts, such as VXLAN tunnels, without unnecessarily complicating the working environment.

It is nevertheless essential that students understand that FortiGate does not replace an SDN controller, and that its use here serves only as a practical substitute within a learning framework limited by technical and pedagogical constraints."

Part A: Establishing Basic Device Configuration

Step 1:

1. Configure PC IP addresses.
2. On switch S1, create VLAN10, VLAN20, and configure truck mode (dot1q).
3. Assign IP addresses to R1 interfaces

a. **Basic configuration:**
   - Access R1 with the username "admin" and leave the password field empty. Set the password to **"123456"**.
   - Use the following commands to assign an IP address to **port1:**

```
config system interface
edit port1
set mode static
set ip 172.16.1.10 255.255.255.0
append allowaccess http
end
```

b. Assign IP address for the port3 interface:
   - From the Local Machine, open a web browser.
   - Type the URL: http://172.16.1.10 and connect to R1.
   - In the "**Network > Interface**" menu, double-click on the port3 interface.
   - Assign the appropriate IP address to the interface.
   - Enable **ping** requests on this interface.

c. Creation of VLAN 10 on interface port2:
   - In the "**Network > Interface**" menu, click on "Create New" to add a new interface.

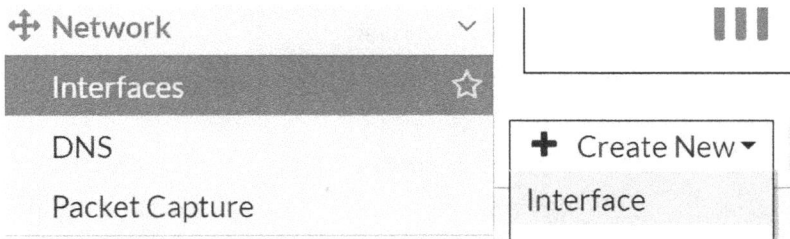

– Configure the parameters of **VLAN 10**, as shown in the following figure:

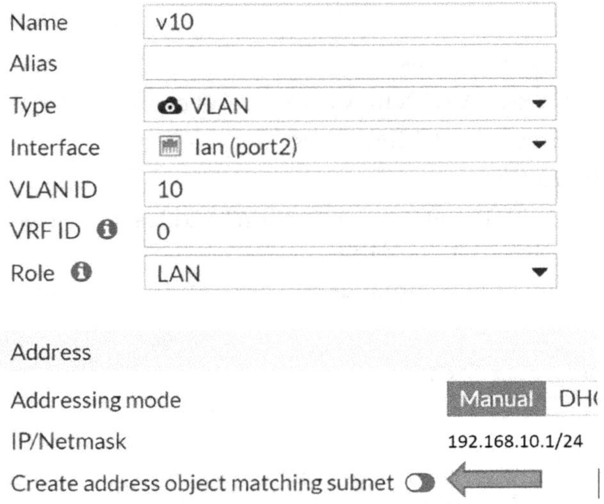

– Do not configure an IP address on this interface.

a. Repeat the previous step to configure VLAN 20.

d. Verify your final configuration.

	admin (port1)	Physical Interface		172.16.1.10/255.255.255.0
−	lan (port2)	Physical Interface		0.0.0.0/0.0.0.0
	v10	VLAN		0.0.0.0/0.0.0.0
	v20	VLAN		0.0.0.0/0.0.0.0
	port4	Physical Interface		0.0.0.0/0.0.0.0
	port5	Physical Interface		0.0.0.0/0.0.0.0
	port6	Physical Interface		0.0.0.0/0.0.0.0
	port7	Physical Interface		0.0.0.0/0.0.0.0
	port8	Physical Interface		0.0.0.0/0.0.0.0
+	wan (port3)	Physical Interface		40.0.0.1/255.255.255.252

4. Create VXLAN 1010 and 1020 on R1.

   Start the console window on R1 and type the following commands:

```
config system vxlan
edit vxlan1010
set vni 1010
set interface port3
set remote-ip 40.0.0.2
end

config system vxlan
edit vxlan1020
set vni 1020
set interface port3
set remote-ip 40.0.0.2
end
```

5. Ensure that VXLANs are correctly configured under port3

Name	Type	IP/Netmask	Access
wan (port3)	Physical Interface	40.0.0.1/255.255.255.252	PING
vxlan1010	VXLAN	0.0.0.0/0.0.0.0	
vxlan1020	VXLAN	0.0.0.0/0.0.0.0	

6. Associate VXLAN 1010 with VLAN 10.
   - In the "**Network > Interface**" menu, click on "Create New" to add a new interface.
   - Configure the parameters of VLAN 10, as shown in the following figure:

Name vxlan-v10
Alias
Type Software Switch
VRF ID 0
Interface members v10 vxlan1010
Role LAN

Address
Addressing mode Manual DHCP Auto-managed by FortiIPAM
IP/Netmask 192.168.10.1/24
Create address object matching subnet
Name vxlan-v10 address
Destination 192.168.10.1/24
Secondary IP address

Administrative Access
IPv4 HTTPS PING FMG-Acce
SSH SNMP FTM
RADIUS Accounting Security Fabric Connection
OK

7. Associate VXLAN 1020 with VLAN 20.

Name vxlan-v20
Alias
Type Software Switch
VRF ID 0
Interface members v20 vxlan1020
Role LAN

Address
Addressing mode Manual DHCP Auto-managed by FortiIPAM
IP/Netmask 192.168.20.1/24
Create address object matching subnet
Name vxlan-v20 address
Destination 192.168.20.1/24
Secondary IP address

Administrative Access
IPv4 HTTPS PING FMG-Acce
SSH SNMP FTM
RADIUS Accounting Security Fabric Connection
OK

8. Ensure the VXLAN-to-VLAN mapping is properly configured.

vxlan-v10	Software Switch	v10 vxlan1010	192.168.10.1/255.255.255.0	PING
vxlan-v20	Software Switch	v20 vxlan1020	192.168.20.1/255.255.255.0	PING

9. On PC1, check that you can **ping** 192.168.10.1 and on PC2, check that you can **ping** 192.168.20.1.

Step 2:

1. Assign IP addresses to R2 interfaces
   b. Basic configuration:
   – Access R2 with the username "admin" and leave the password field empty. Set the password to "123456".
   – Use the same commands as above to assign an IP address to port1.

c. Configure IP address for the port3 interface:
   - Reconnect the Local Machine connection to R2's "port1" interface for configuration.
   - On the Local Machine, open a web browser.
   - Assign the IP address R2's port3 interface, referring to the addressing table.

d. Creation of VLANs 10 and 20 on the port2 interface:
   - Repeat the same procedure on R1 to create VLANs 10 and 20 on R2.

e. Check your final configuration.

Name	Type	Members	IP/Netmask	Administrative Access
admin (port1)	Physical Interface		172.16.1.10/255.255.255.0	PING HTTPS SSH HTTP FMG-Access
port2	Physical Interface		0.0.0.0/0.0.0.0	
v10 (v10)	VLAN		0.0.0.0/0.0.0.0	
v20 (v20)	VLAN		0.0.0.0/0.0.0.0	
port4	Physical Interface		0.0.0.0/0.0.0.0	
port5	Physical Interface		0.0.0.0/0.0.0.0	
port6	Physical Interface		0.0.0.0/0.0.0.0	
port7	Physical Interface		0.0.0.0/0.0.0.0	
port8	Physical Interface		0.0.0.0/0.0.0.0	
wan (port3)	Physical Interface		40.0.0.2/255.255.255.252	PING

2. Create VXLAN 1010 and 1020 on R2.

   Start the console window on **R2** and type the following commands:

```
config system vxlan
edit vxlan1010
set vni 1010
set interface port3
set remote-ip 40.0.0.1
end

config system vxlan
edit vxlan1020
set vni 1020
set interface port3
set remote-ip 40.0.0.1
end
```

3. Verify that VXLANs are correctly configured under port3
4. Connect VXLANs 1010 and 1020 with VLANs 10 and 20.

Note: Assign addresses 192.168.10.254 and 192.168.20.254 to the virtual interfaces of **vxlan-v10** and **vxlan-v20**.

5. Verify that **VXLAN-VLAN** mapping is correctly configured.

vxlan-v10	Software Switch	v10 (v10) vxlan1010	192.168.10.254/255.255.255.0	PING
vxlan-v20	Software Switch	v20 (v20) vxlan1020	192.168.20.254/255.255.255.0	PING

6. On PC3, check that you can **ping** 192.168.10.254 and on PC4, check that you can **ping** 192.168.20.254.

Part B: Testing and Explaining the Result

1. From PC1, verify connectivity with PC3 using a **ping** test.
2. From PC2, verify connectivity with PC4 using a **ping** test
3. Defining underlay and overlay network elements.

8

Orchestration in an SDN Environment with Ansible

This chapter provides a comprehensive examination of orchestration in a software-defined networking (SDN) environment using Ansible. We begin by defining the role of SDN orchestrators and exploring their benefits. We then examine the general architecture of SDN orchestrators and introduce the primary orchestrators currently in use.

The second part of this chapter focuses on leveraging Ansible for SDN network orchestration. We'll introduce Ansible, its key features, its components, and how it integrates network APIs. We'll also describe the steps involved in an automated process with Ansible and introduce AWX, Ansible's user interface. Finally, we'll provide practical examples of using Ansible with Playbook and inventory files.

To conclude, we'll discuss the synergy between Ansible and SDN networks, explaining why Ansible is essential as a complement to the SDN controller and presenting practical cases of combined use of these technologies.

This chapter seeks to deliver a comprehensive and practical understanding of SDN orchestration with Ansible, combining theoretical concepts with practical application examples.

This chapter covers the following topics:

1. Introduction
2. Definition and role of SDN orchestrators
3. Advantages of SDN orchestrators
4. General architecture of an SDN orchestrator
5. Main SDN orchestrators
6. Orchestrating a network with Ansible
7. Conclusion.

8.1 Introduction

In an SDN architecture, orchestrators are vital for simplifying the management and automation of complex networks. While an SDN controller delivers centralized network control, SDN orchestrators enhance this by coordinating interactions among network components and automating large-scale processes.

DOI: 10.1201/9781003679394-8

8.2 Definition and Role of SDN Orchestrators

An SDN orchestrator is a sophisticated software system designed to automate and coordinate large-scale network operations. It functions like an orchestra conductor, ensuring seamless coordination of network components to meet specific operational goals. The orchestrator manages network policies, resource allocation, and network configuration and ensures service compliance with application and end-user requirements (Figure 8.1).

Key features of an SDN orchestrator include:

- **Service provisioning:** Automated creation and deployment of virtual network services (NFV) on SDN infrastructure.
- **NFV lifecycle management:** Start, stop, scale, and remove NFVs as needed.
- **Network configuration:** Automated application of network configuration rules on SDN controllers and network devices.
- **Performance optimization:** Monitoring and optimization of network traffic to ensure optimum performance and availability.
- **Network security:** Implements and enforces security policies to safeguard the network against threats.
- **Incident management:** Automated detection and resolution of network incidents to minimize downtime.

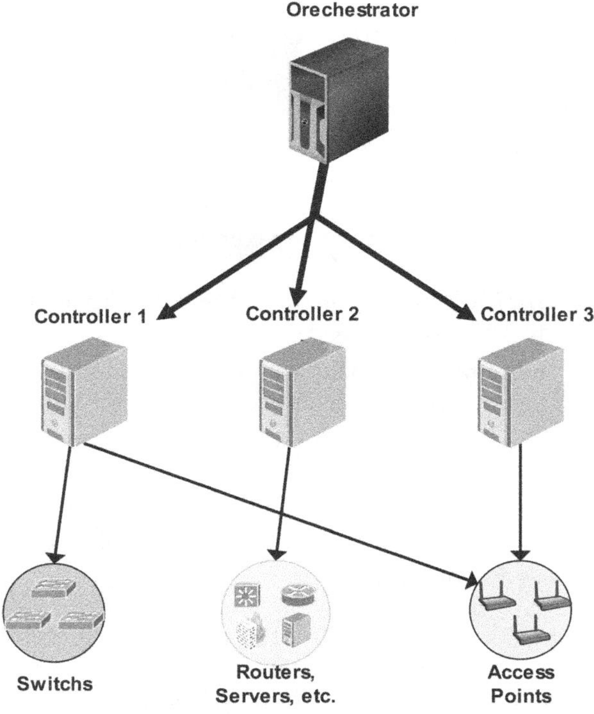

FIGURE 8.1
Hierarchical structure of an SDN network with orchestrator and controllers.

8.3 Advantages of SDN Orchestrators

Implementing an SDN orchestrator offers numerous benefits to organizations, including:

- **Enhanced agility:** Accelerates deployment and configuration of network services, enabling organizations to respond swiftly to market changes and customer demands.
- **Improved efficiency:** Automation of manual tasks, reducing human error and freeing IT teams to concentrate on more strategic tasks.
- **Resource optimization:** More efficient allocation and use of network resources, reducing operating costs.
- **Better visibility and control:** Centralized overview of the network, enabling better decision-making and faster problem resolution.
- **Greater scalability:** Easily handle network growth and increased service demands.

Additionally, SDN orchestrators enable rapid integration of new technologies and services, helping organizations stay competitive in a dynamic technological landscape.

8.4 General Architecture of an SDN Orchestrator

No single, universal standard exists for SDN orchestrator architectures, but organizations like the Open Networking Foundation (ONF) and the International Engineering Task Force (IETF) have proposed several reference models. These organizations are striving to establish standards to facilitate interoperability between different network devices and software.

An SDN orchestrator's architecture operates as a layer above SDN controllers within the network management stack. Here are the main components and their interactions:

- **User/administration interface:** Allows administrators to define policies and configurations to guide orchestration decisions.
- **Orchestration components:** Includes various modules responsible for decision-making, task automation, resource management, and policy enforcement.
- **Integration APIs:** Enable integration with external systems, enterprise applications, and cloud services. These APIs provide the means by which the orchestrator can receive data and send commands to controllers and network devices.
- **Database/storage:** Stores configuration information, policies, and network device status for fast access and handling.

An SDN orchestrator interacts closely with SDN controllers to deploy and manage network policies across various devices and domains. Controllers communicate with network devices via protocols such as OpenFlow, while orchestrators use APIs such as REST or NETCONF to integrate various services and applications on top of this control layer. This distinction between managing flows (controllers) and coordinating policies and services (orchestrators) is essential to understanding the operational efficiency of SDN.

8.5 Leading SDN Orchestrators

Here's a list of the most popular SDN orchestrators, with an overview of their distinctive features. Each orchestrator has its own strengths and may be better suited to certain applications or network environments.

Ansible: A widely adopted automation tool for SDN orchestration, developed by Red Hat. It is distinguished by its user-friendly interface and YAML-based configuration for task definition. Ansible is also recognized for its extensibility, thanks to a wide range of modules adapted to various network devices and services, as well as for its robust configuration automation, deployment management, and application orchestration capabilities.

- **Open Network Automation Platform (ONAP):** Managed by the Linux Foundation, ONAP focuses on managing and orchestrating large-scale network services, including 5G networks and cloud services. ONAP features a modular architecture that favors a high degree of customization and can be integrated with traditional network management systems as well as virtualized environments.
- **Cisco's Network Services Orchestrator:** It stands out for its ability to manage devices from multiple manufacturers, using NETCONF and YANG for device configuration and management. It is particularly well-suited to production environments with high availability and performance requirements.
- **Juniper Contrail, from Juniper Networks:** It supports SDN networks for data centers and is based on open standards, enabling integration with third-party solutions. Juniper Contrail is also designed to support very large-scale network environments, making it particularly scalable.
- **VMware NSX from VMware:** Deeply integrated with the VMware ecosystem, including vSphere and other VMware products. Oriented primarily toward data center virtualization, VMware NSX places particular emphasis on security, offering advanced segmentation and protection features.
- **Puppet:** A creation of Puppet Labs, it is widely used for its declarative approach to configuration management, enabling users to specify the desired state of systems with a high level of automation. Puppet excels at managing multiple servers, facilitating administration and compliance assurance across complex environments.
- **Chef:** Developed by Chef Software, it focuses on infrastructure coding, enabling developers and system administrators to manage and configure their servers through recipes and cookbooks that define how applications and systems should be configured. Chef is renowned for its robustness and adaptability, helping companies to manage both cloud and traditional infrastructures.
- **OpenStack:** An open source cloud computing platform for creating and managing public or private cloud infrastructures. Its modular architecture enables users to deploy only the components they need for their infrastructure. Each OpenStack module or project works in an integrated way to provide a complete cloud management solution. This modularity makes OpenStack a highly flexible solution, adapted to the needs of various types of enterprises and capable of supporting large-scale workloads.

8.6 Orchestrating a Network with Ansible

8.6.1 Introducing Ansible

Ansible is an open-source automation tool that manages IT configurations, software deployments, and task orchestration. Using YAML, it remotely configures and executes commands via SSH, making it ideal for frequent, large-scale software deployments and centralized configuration management across multiple servers. In the IT sector, particularly in cloud and virtualization environments, it is widely used for its robust automation features.

Ansible is deeply integrated into DevOps practices, not only because of the speed and efficiency it brings, but also because of its ability to facilitate collaboration between development and operations teams. It supports continuous delivery processes, enabling frequent and reliable updates of applications and infrastructures alike. This tight integration with DevOps enables organizations to minimize the risks associated with regular deployments, while ensuring greater compliance and reinforcing security.

Additionally, Ansible is well-suited for supporting the Infrastructure as Code (IaC) approach. IaC is a model for managing IT infrastructure through configuration files, rather than through a graphical user interface or manual command-line scripting sequences. This approach enables infrastructure to be created, modified, and managed in a secure, consistent, traceable, and reproducible way.

As an orchestration and configuration management tool, Ansible is widely used in fields such as telecommunications, data centers (orchestration of virtualization and networking), and many others.

8.6.2 Key Ansible Features and Use Cases

Key features of Ansible include the following:

- **Agentless architecture:** Ansible requires no agents on the devices to be managed, using SSH for communication, which reduces the load on network resources.
- **Simple language (YAML):** Configurations are defined in YAML, a data serialization language that's easy to understand and write.
- **Scalable modules:** Ansible has an extensive library of modules that can interact with a wide range of equipment and network interfaces, making it highly adaptable to different environments.
- **Idempotence:** Ansible's ability not to modify the state of a system if it is already in the desired state, thus guaranteeing configuration consistency without unnecessary intervention.

Ansible provides an open-source automation solution that minimizes complexity and adapts to nearly any task. Here are some common examples of how Ansible is used:

- **Automated network configuration:** Ansible can automatically configure routers, switches, and other network devices, ensuring consistent, policy-compliant configuration.

- **Change and update management:** Ansible enables teams to track, revise, and deploy configuration changes in a controlled, automated way, minimizing interruptions and downtime.
- **Multi-cloud integration:** With support for numerous cloud service providers, Ansible makes it easy to orchestrate resources across hybrid and multi-cloud environments.

8.6.3 Ansible Orchestrator Components

Ansible is a powerful configuration management and automation tool that simplifies complex, repetitive tasks for IT systems. Here's an overview of the key components that make up Ansible (Figure 8.2).

- **Inventories:** The inventory is a file containing information about the hosts and host groups on which Ansible can operate. The inventory can be static (text file) or dynamic (script generating an inventory from external sources such as cloud services). It defines the host structure, the variables associated with each host, and the server groups for orchestration.
- **Playbooks:** Playbooks are YAML files that define automation policies, tasks, and configurations to be applied to target systems. They enable users to program complex sequences of actions, such as application deployment or system updates, in a format that is easy to read and maintain.
- **Modules:** Modules are the basic units of Ansible that are run directly on remote hosts. Each module is designed to handle a specific task in the management system, such as managing services, working with files, or managing users. Ansible includes hundreds of ready-to-use modules, and it is also possible to create custom modules as required.

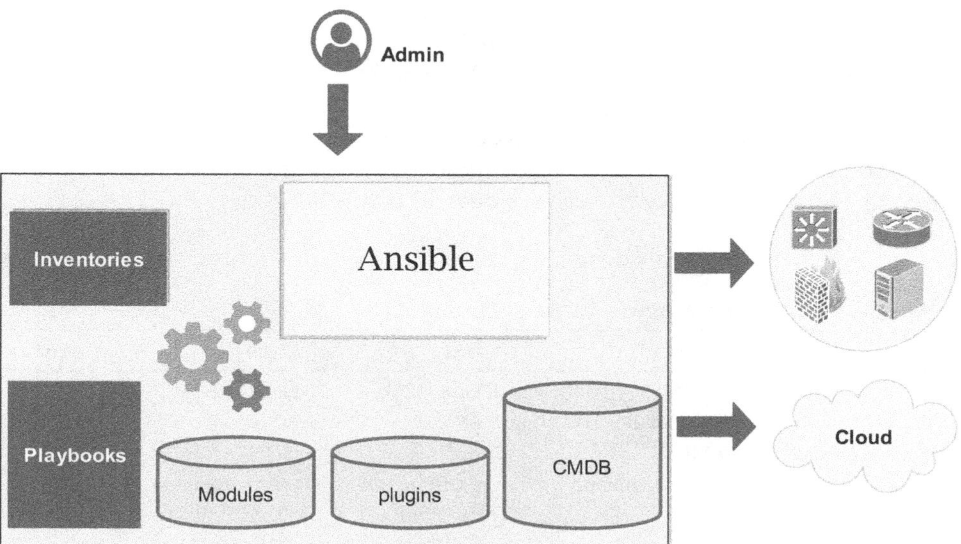

FIGURE 8.2
Ansible orchestrator components.

- **Plugins:** Ansible uses plugins to extend its basic functionality. Plugins can be used to add custom functionality or to integrate Ansible with other tools and services. There are many different types of plugins, such as connection plugins, search plugins, callback plugins, and so on.
- **Configuration management database (CMDB):** A CMDB is a repository that contains all relevant information about important IT infrastructure elements and their configurations. Although Ansible does not directly provide a CMDB, it can integrate with the existing CMDBs to retrieve or update information when running Playbooks. This integration enables Ansible to operate in complex environments, using the most up-to-date configuration data to manage systems accurately and efficiently.
- **Hosts and networking:** Ansible manages not only individual hosts, but also complex network configurations. It can be used to automate network configuration tasks, managing firewalls, switches, routers, and other network devices across multiple vendors and platforms.
- **Cloud:** Ansible supports the automation of cloud environments, enabling users to manage infrastructure as a service. Thanks to specialized modules, Ansible can interact with cloud platforms such as AWS, Microsoft Azure, Google Cloud Platform, and others to create, configure, and manage cloud resources in an automated way.

These Ansible components work together to provide a robust and flexible platform for automating administrative tasks across a wide range of systems and environments. Whether for application deployment, configuration management, or ongoing maintenance, Ansible offers a scalable solution that helps IT teams improve efficiency and reduce manual errors.

8.6.4 Network API Integration with Ansible

As network vendors began to support APIs for their network operating systems (such as NETCONF for JunOS, NXAPI for NX-OS, or eAPI for Arista), Ansible integrated support for these APIs to communicate with network devices in order to return structured data to Ansible. In this way, Ansible translated the XML or JSON data returned as the result of executed commands into valid data structures that could then be used by Ansible as tasks or variables to control playbook execution. The topology below illustrates Ansible's approach to communicating with network devices (Table 8.1).

TABLE 8.1

Using Ansible Modules to Manage Network Platforms

Manufacturer	Juniper	Cisco	Cisco	Arista
Platform	JunOS	IOS/IOS-XR	Nexus-OS	EOS
API	NETCONF	SSH	NX-API	eAPI
Data exchange format	XML	String	JSON	JSON
Ansible modules	junos_command junos_config junos_facts	ios_command ios_config ios_facts	nxos_command nxos_config nxos_facts	eos_command eos_config eos_facts

8.6.5 Stages of an Ansible Automated Process

The steps in an automated Ansible process are implemented in the form of tasks, defined in YAML format in what is known as a Playbook. Playbooks also associate variable definitions and a list of hosts, called inventory, on which the tasks will be performed (Figure 8.3).

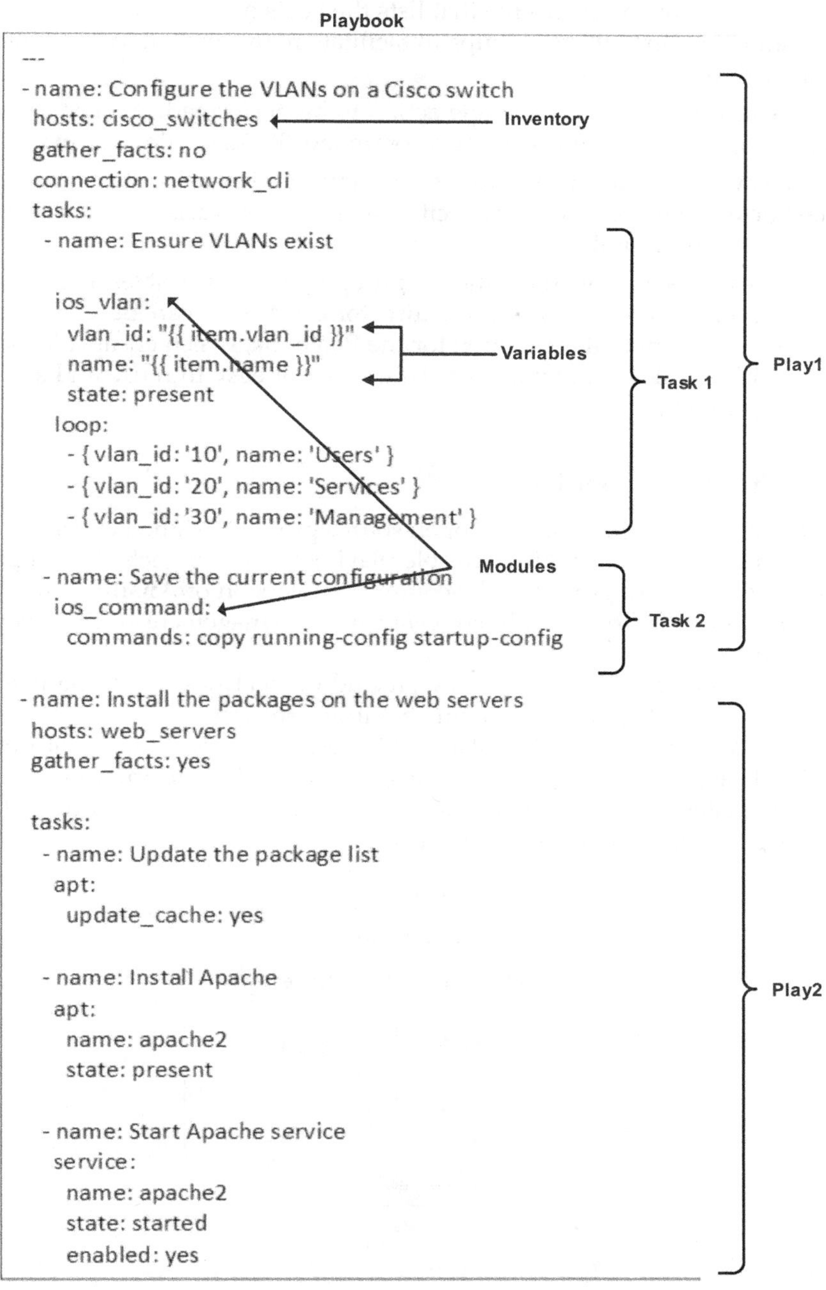

FIGURE 8.3
Steps in an Ansible automated process.

Here is a clarification of these elements:

- **Playbook:** A playbook is a YAML file that defines the set of tasks to be executed on one or more hosts. It can contain one or more playbooks, with each playbook specifying a set of tasks to be executed on a group of hosts.
- **Inventory:** The inventory is a file that lists the hosts on which tasks are to be run. Hosts can be organized into groups to facilitate management. The inventory can be a static or dynamic file.
- **Tasks:** A task in Ansible is a single action to be performed, such as installing a package, copying a file, or executing a command. Tasks are defined in playbooks.
- **Variables:** Variables in Ansible are used to parameterize tasks. They can be defined in playbooks, inventory files, or specific variable files. Variables make playbooks more flexible and reusable.
- **Roles:** Roles are a way of automatically grouping tasks, variables, files, templates, and managers into well-structured directories. A role can be compared to a sub-procedure or modular function for the Playbook, which encapsulates a set of tasks, variables, files, and templates. This makes it easy to reuse and share complex configurations.

8.6.6 AWX: The Ansible User Interface

AWX is a web-based user interface and open source project designed to provide a graphical interface and APIs for managing Ansible playbooks and projects. Developed by Red Hat, AWX is the upstream project of the commercial version of **Ansible Tower**, enabling Ansible users to benefit from simplified, centralized management of their deployments and configurations.

AWX can be deployed in a variety of ways, including via Docker or Kubernetes containers, making it easy to integrate into existing environments.

In AWX, you can define a Job Template, which associates playbooks with inventories, variables (local or global), credentials, configuration, and so forth, and execute them. Several Job Templates can be used to create a Workflow that defines the order of execution (sequential or parallel) of these tasks (Figure 8.4).

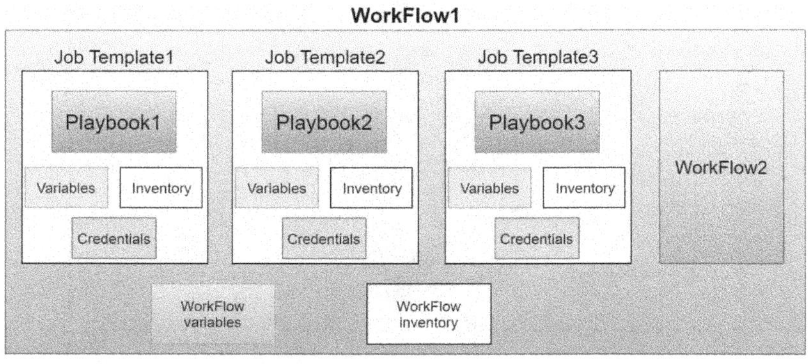

FIGURE 8.4
Structuring workflows and job templates in Ansible.

8.6.7 Practical Examples of Using Ansible: Playbook and Inventory

8.6.7.1 Examples of inventory files on Ansible

8.6.7.1.1 Example 1

This inventory file is used to define routers and switches with their IP addresses and authentication methods. Here's an example of a "**hosts**" file:

```
[cisco_routers]
R1 ansible_host=192.168.1.1

   ansible_password=
   ansible_network_os=ios
   ansible_connection=network_cli
   ansible_become=yes
   ansible_become_method=enable
   ansible_become_password=xxxx
R2 ansible_host=192.168.1.
   ansible_password= passe2

 ansible_connection=network_cli

 ansible_become_password=xxxx
[cisco_switches]
S1 ansible_host=192.168.2.1

 ansible_connection=network_cli

 ansible_become_password=xxxx

...
[lan:children]
cisco_routers
cisco_switches

[lan:vars]
ansible_ssh_common_args='-o StrictHostKeyChecking=no'
```

Explanations of the Inventory File

- **Parameter list:**
  - **R1:** Host name in an Ansible inventory.
  - **ansible_host=192.168.1.1:** IP address of the target host.
  - **ansible_user=admin:** User name for SSH connection.
  - **ansible_password=xxxx:** Password for SSH connection.
  - **ansible_network_os=ios:** Device operating system (Cisco IOS).
  - **ansible_connection=network_cli:** Use the network CLI interface for connection.
  - **ansible_become=yes:** Enable privilege elevation.

- **ansible_become_method=enable:** Use the "enable" method to elevate privileges.
- **ansible_become_password=xxxx:** Password to access privileged mode (enable) on Cisco equipment.

- **Host groups:**
  - **[cisco_routers]:** This group contains Cisco routers R1 and R2.
  - **[cisco_switches]:** This group contains Cisco S1, S2, and S3 switches.
- **Host definitions:**
  - **R1 ansible_host=192.168.1.1...** Defines the R1 router with its IP address, user, password, network operating system (IOS), connection method (network_cli), and privilege settings (enable).
  - Definitions for other equipment follow the same pattern.
- **Children's group:**
  - **[lan:children]:** The "lan" group contains the two previous groups (cisco_routers and cisco_switches).
- **Group variables:**
  - **[lan:vars]:** This group of variables applies to all Cisco equipment. Here, the **ansible_ssh_common_args** variable is used to disable strict SSH host key checking.

This inventory is ready for use with Ansible playbooks to manage Cisco router and switch configurations.

8.6.7.1.2 Example 2

Here's an example of an inventory file for two Ubuntu Linux servers named Server1 and Server2:

```
[ubuntu_servers]
Server1
    ansible_host=192.168.3.1
    ansible_user=admin
    ansible_password=xxxx
    ansible_become=yes
    ansible_connection=ssh // Optional
Server2
    ansible_host=192.168.3.2
    ansible_user=admin
    ansible_password=xxxx
    ansible_become=yes
[all:vars]
ansible_ssh_common_args='-o StrictHostKeyChecking=no'
```

Explanations of the Inventory File

- **Host groups defined:**
  - **[ubuntu_servers]** contains the Server1 and Server2 servers.

- **Host definitions:**
  - **Server1 ansible_host=192.168.3.1 ansible_user=admin ansible_password=xxxx ansible_become=yes:** Defines Server1 with its IP address, user, password, and elevation of privileges permission.
  - **Server2 ansible_host=192.168.3.2 ansible_user=admin ansible_password=xxxx ansible_become=yes:** Sets Server2 with the same parameters as Server1.
- **Group variables:**
  - **[all:vars]:** Apply the **ansible_ssh_common_args** variable to disable strict SSH key checking on all hosts.

8.6.7.2 Example of a Playbook File on Ansible

8.6.7.2.1 Example 1

What follows is a simple example of an Ansible playbook that illustrates how this can be done. This example uses Ansible's **ios_vlan** module, designed to manage VLANs on Cisco IOS devices.

```
---
- name: Configuring VLANs on a Cisco switch
  hosts: cisco_switches
  gather_facts: no
  connection: network_cli

  tasks:
   - name: make sure VLANs exist
       ios_vlan:
         vlan_id: "{{ item.vlan_id }}"
         name: "{{ item.name }}"
         state: present
       loop:
         - { vlan_id: '10', name: 'Users' }
         - { vlan_id: '20', name: 'Services' }
         - { vlan_id: '30', name: 'Management' }

   - name: Save current configuration
       ios_command:
         commands: copy running-config startup-config
```

Playbook Explanation

- **Playbook begins:**
  - **---:** Start of a YAML file
  - **- name: Configuring VLANs on a Cisco switch:** Playbook description
  - **hosts: cisco_switches:** Targets the Cisco switch group defined in the Ansible inventory
  - **gather_facts: no:** Disables data collection to speed up execution
  - **connection: network_cli:** Uses the network CLI connection to communicate with devices

- **Tasks:**
  - **name: check existence of VLANs:** Task description
  - **ios_vlan:** Uses Ansible's **ios_vlan** module
  - **vlan_id** and **name:** Specifies VLAN ID and name
  - **state: present:** Ensures that the specified VLAN is present on the switch.
  - **loop:** Repeats the task for each VLAN listed (VLAN 10, 20, 30 in this example)
- **Configuration backup:**
  - **name: Backup current configuration:** Backup task description
  - **ios_command:** Uses the **ios_command** module to execute commands on IOS devices
  - **commands: copy running-config startup-config:** Copies the running configuration to the startup configuration to make it persistent.
- **Prerequisites:**
  - Cisco devices must be accessible via SSH and configured to accept CLI commands.
  - Cisco switch credentials and IP addresses must be correctly configured in the Ansible inventory.

8.6.7.2.2 Example 2

Here is an example of an Ansible Playbook file for:

- Ping every 10 seconds from Server1 to Server2.
- Install the bind package on Server2.

```
---
- name: Managing Ubuntu servers
  hosts: ubuntu_servers
  become: yes
  tasks:

 - name: Ping Server2 every 10 seconds from Server1
     ansible.builtin.command:
       cmd: "ping -i 10 192.168.3.2"
     when: inventory_hostname == 'Server1'
     async: 60
     poll: 0
     ignore_errors: yes

 - name: Install bind package on Server2
     ansible.builtin.apt:
       name: bind9
       state: present
     when: inventory_hostname == 'Server2'
```

Playbook Explanations

- **Playbook header:**
  - **name: Managing Ubuntu servers:** Playbook description.
  - **hosts: ubuntu_servers:** Targets the **ubuntu_servers** host group defined in the inventory.
  - **become: yes:** Use privilege elevation for tasks.
- **Tasks:**
  - **name: Ping Server1 every 10 seconds:**
    - **ansible.builtin.command:** Uses the **command** module to execute the **ping** command.
    - **cmd: "ping -i 10 192.168.3.2":**
      - **ping:** Command to send ICMP requests.
      - **-i 10:** Option to send pings every 10 seconds.
      - **192.168.3.2:** Server2's IP address. This means that Server1 will send pings to Server2 every 10 seconds.
    - **when: inventory_hostname == "Server1":** Requirement to run this task only on Server1.
    - **async: 60** and **poll: 0:** Allows the task to be executed asynchronously with a maximum duration of 60 seconds.
    - **ignore_errors: yes:** Ignores any errors in this task.
  - **name: Install bind package on Server2:**
    - **ansible.builtin.apt:** Uses the **apt** module to manage packages on Debian-based systems.
    - **name: bind9:** Name of the package to be installed.
    - **state: present:** Ensures that the packet is present.
    - **when: inventory_hostname == "Server2":** Requirement to run this task only on Server2.

8.7 Synergy between Ansible and SDN Networks

8.7.1 Why Ansible is Essential as a Complement to the SDN Controller

Using Ansible in an SDN environment might appear redundant, as SDN relies on a centralized controller for network task automation. However, there are several reasons for using Ansible in addition to an SDN controller:

- **Multi-vendor management:** In heterogeneous network environments, where devices are sourced from different vendors, SDN controllers may not support all device types or APIs in a uniform way. Ansible enables the creation of automation scripts that support diverse devices and APIs, ensuring consistent and standardized management.
- **Automation of complete configurations:** The SDN controller is primarily focused on managing data flows and enforcing network policies. Ansible can automate not

only network configurations, but also system configurations, software management, updates, and other infrastructure tasks, offering a more complete automation solution.

- **Orchestration beyond the network:** Ansible can orchestrate tasks beyond the network, including servers, applications, cloud services, and storage systems. This makes it possible to automate complex workflows that require interaction between different IT infrastructure components.
- **Flexibility and adaptability:** Ansible is highly flexible and can be used for specific scenarios where the SDN controller may not offer the necessary capabilities, for example, for very detailed configuration tasks or customized integrations with other systems.
- **Ease of use and development:** Ansible uses simple YAML-based syntax, making it easy to create and maintain playbooks. Teams can quickly develop and deploy automations without requiring in-depth programming skills.

In summary, Ansible enhances automation in SDN environments by providing advanced management, flexibility, and integration capabilities, complementing the SDN controller's functions.

8.7.2 Case Studies in Using Ansible in Conjunction with SDN

The following scenarios demonstrate how Ansible can be used alongside SDN controllers to enhance network automation and management.

8.7.2.1 Use Case 1: From User to Device via SDN then Ansible

In this first type of scheme, the user interacts with the SDN controller, which in turn uses Ansible to apply specific configurations or perform firmware updates on network devices (Figure 8.5).

- **Scenario 1: Deploying specific network configurations**
  Description: A user wishes to apply specific configurations to a set of network devices that are not fully supported by the SDN controller.

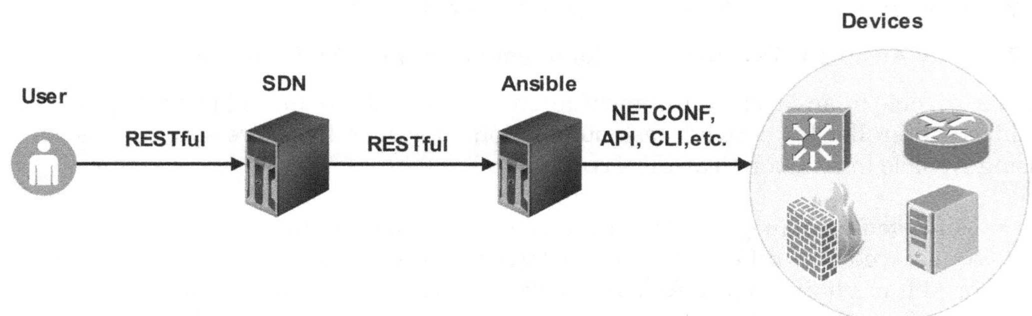

FIGURE 8.5
Use case 1: User → SDN → Ansible → Equipment.

Steps:

Communication flows in this scenario use APIs at each key stage of the process:

1. **From the User to the SDN Controller:** The user's configuration request is sent to the SDN controller, usually via a RESTful API. This API allows the user to specify the required configurations in a standardized and secure way.
2. **From the SDN Controller to Ansible:** Once the SDN Controller has analyzed the request and determined the specific configurations required, it uses a Playbook to pass on these instructions to Ansible. This Playbook defines the tasks to be performed by Ansible to apply the specific configurations to the devices.
3. **From Ansible to equipment:** Ansible uses specific modules for each type of equipment to deploy configurations. These modules communicate directly with the devices via their respective APIs (such as NETCONF, eAPI, or CLI) to apply the requested configurations.

- **Scenario 2: Coordinated Firmware Update**

  Description:

  A user wants to update the firmware of network equipment in a coordinated way.

  Steps:

1. **User:** Initiates firmware update request via an SDN controller.
2. **SDN controller:** Schedules updates and triggers the execution of Ansible scripts for each device.
3. **Ansible:** Runs firmware update playbooks on network devices.
4. **Equipment:** Receive and install new firmware versions.

8.7.2.2 Use Case 2: From the User to the Device via Ansible and then SDN

The second type of topology shows how Ansible can orchestrate network services and security configurations in coordination with the SDN controller, enabling seamless system integration and complete automation of network infrastructures (Figure 8.6).

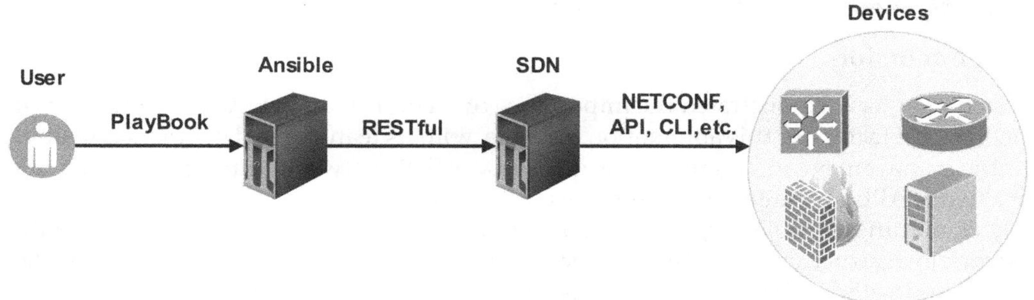

FIGURE 8.6
Use Case 2: User → Ansible → SDN → Equipment.

- **Scenario 1: Orchestration of Network and System Services**
  Description:
  A user wants to orchestrate a series of services involving both network configurations and system deployments.
  Steps:

1. **From the User to Ansible:** The user initiates the deployment of a complete service by launching an Ansible Playbook. This Playbook contains all the instructions needed to orchestrate the various configurations and deployments. Communication between the user and Ansible takes place via a command-line interface (CLI/SSH) or a RESTful API, enabling standardized, secure command submission.
2. **From Ansible to the SDN Controller:** Ansible runs the Playbook and orchestrates network configurations by sending commands to the SDN controller via an API. This API enables Ansible to communicate the specific configurations required to the SDN controller.
3. **From the SDN controller to Devices:** The SDN controller applies the necessary network configurations by sending the appropriate instructions to the devices via their respective APIs (such as OpenFlow, NETCONF, etc.). The devices receive and implement the configurations provided by the SDN controller.

- **Scenario 2: Integration of Network Security and Policies**
  Description: A user wishes to apply network security policies in coordination with other security systems.
  Steps:

4. **User:** Triggers an Ansible Playbook to apply security policies.
5. **Ansible:** Runs the Playbook, configuring security policies via the SDN controller.
6. **SDN Controller:** Applies security policies to network devices.
7. **Equipment:** Configured with new security policies.

8.8 Conclusion

This chapter has demonstrated the importance of orchestration in SDN environments and how Ansible facilitates this automation. Ansible, with its features and components, simplifies the management and improves the efficiency of SDN networks through the integration of network APIs and automated processes.

By combining Ansible and SDN, organizations can optimize the management of their network infrastructures, offering greater flexibility and responsiveness. Using Ansible in conjunction with SDN controllers enables efficient orchestration, meeting modern network requirements with improved performance and management.

Lab 17: Automating Network Configuration with Ansible Orchestrator

Objectives

- Understand the foundational principles of an SDN Orchestrator.
- Deploy and operate the Ansible orchestrator.

Case Study

This case study aims to understand the fundamentals of an SDN orchestrator and explore the configuration and use of the Ansible orchestrator. It examines how Ansible can automate and simplify the management of SDN networks, enabling efficient orchestration of large-scale configurations and operations.

Company ABC owns multiple switches and routers. It intends to automate VLAN creation, port assignment, and inter-VLAN routing configuration, all using the Ansible orchestrator.

Software to Use

- GNS3 or equivalent

Network Topology

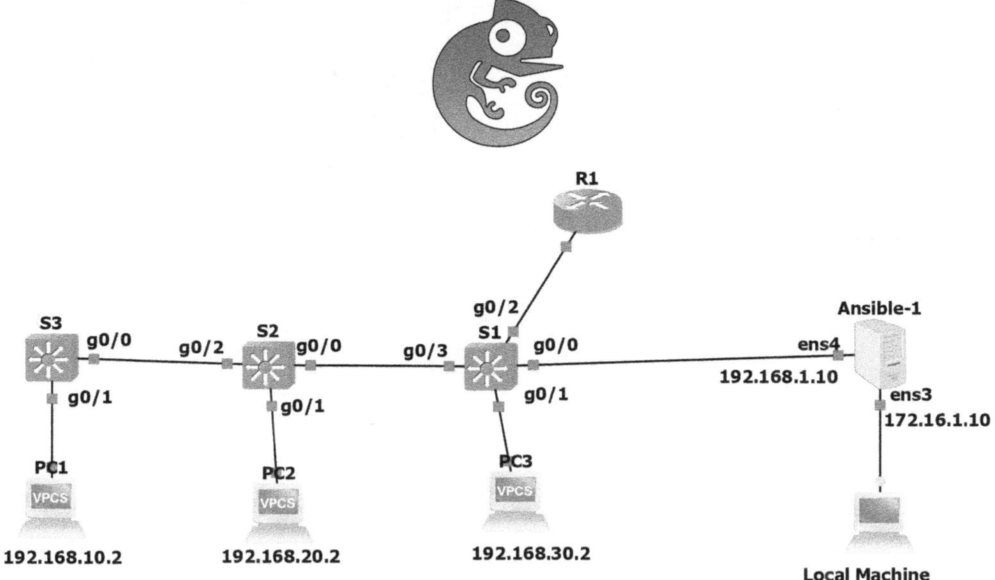

IP Address Table

Emulated Device	Device	Interface	IP Address/ Subnet Mask	Default Gateway
Ubuntu Linux with Ansible Control Node	Ansible-1	ens3	172.16.1.10/24	–
Ubuntu Linux with Ansible Control Node	Ansible-1	ens4	192.168.1.10	–
Docker Ipterm	PC1	eth0	192.168.10.2	192.168.10.1
Docker Ipterm	PC2	eth0	192.168.20.2	192.168.20.1
Docker Ipterm	PC3	eth0	192.168.30.2	192.168.30.1
GNS3 Cloud	Local Machine	VMware Interface	172.16.1.1/24	–
Cisco Router – C7200 (Dynamips, v15.2)	R1	G0/0	192.168.1.1	–
Cisco IOSvL2 Switch (v15.2(6))	S1	Vlan1	192.168.1.20	–
Cisco IOSvL2 Switch (v15.2(6))	S2	Vlan1	192.168.1.21	–
Cisco IOSvL2 Switch (v15.2(6))	S3	Vlan1	192.168.1.22	–

Part A: Establishing Basic Device Configuration

1. Create the network topology.
2. Assign IP addresses to device interfaces according to the addressing table.
3. Test network connectivity by pinging all network elements.
4. On each network element:
   a. Add a user named "**cisco**" with the password "**123456**".
   b. Set up the domain name "**cisco.com**".
   c. Generate an RSA public key of 1024 bits.
   d. Create an ssh connection.
   e. Enable SSH protocol version 2.
   f. Define the "enable" mode password as **"123456"**.
5. On Ansible-1, create SSH entries for each network element. To do this, follow these steps:
   a. Edit the **"~/.ssh/config"** file using the nano editor.

b. Append the following lines:

```
Host 192.168.1.20
    KexAlgorithms +diffie-hellman-group1-sha1
    HostKeyAlgorithms +ssh-rsa
                PubkeyAcceptedKeyTypes +ssh-rsa
Host 192.168.1.21
    KexAlgorithms +diffie-hellman-group1-sha1
    HostKeyAlgorithms +ssh-rsa
                PubkeyAcceptedKeyTypes +ssh-rsa
Host 192.168.1.22
    KexAlgorithms +diffie-hellman-group1-sha1
    HostKeyAlgorithms +ssh-rsa
                PubkeyAcceptedKeyTypes +ssh-rsa
Host 192.168.1.1
    KexAlgorithms +diffie-hellman-group1-sha1
    HostKeyAlgorithms +ssh-rsa
                PubkeyAcceptedKeyTypes +ssh-rsa
```

c. Save the file.

d. Ensure SSH connectivity to all network elements. Use the command:

```
#ssh user1@{element IP address}
```

Note: The IP addresses of the elements are listed in the provided **IP Address Table.**

e. Confirm the connection when prompted.

6. On Ansible-1, create a folder for your project's Playbook scripts, and give it the appropriate permissions:

```
#sudo mkdir /var/lib/awx/projects/projet1
#sudo chown awx project1/
```

Part B: Reminder of the Basic Principles of an Orchestrator

1. Recall the definition of an Orchestrator.
2. Recall Ansible orchestrator components
3. Recall the steps of an Ansible Automated Process

Part C: Application of Group-Based Policy Techniques for Traffic Filtering

Task 1: Create VLANs on the Three Switches

Task Objective

- Discover how to use Ansible variables such as **ansible_host** and **ansible_ssh_user**, among others.

- The use of specific modules for managing network elements, such as **ios_vlan**, **ios_command**, and others,
- Using global variables to manage groups of elements

1. Create an "**Inventory**" object for company ABC
   - On the Local Machine, open a web browser.
   - Type the URL: http://172.16.1.10, and connect to Ansible-1 using the "**admin**" login and "**admin**" password.
   - In the "**Inventories**" menu, click on "**Add > Add Inventorie**".
   - Create an Inventory object named **ABC**.
   - In the same window, click on "**Groups**", Add a Groups object for switches named **Switches**.
     Note: You can delete all other inventories if these items bother you.
2. Create a "**Host**" object and a "**Group**" object.
   - Using the Ansible-1 GUI, click on the "**Hosts**" menu.
   - Add a host object for switch S1 based on the parameters in the following table:

Name	**S1**
Inventory	ABC
variables	ansible_host: 192.168.1.20 ansible_port: 22 ansible_ssh_user: user1 ansible_ssh_pass: 123456 ansible_network_os: ios ansible_become: true ansible_become_method: enable ansible_become_pass: 123456

   - Confirm changes.
   - Explain the meaning of each variable listed in your configuration:

Ansible Variable	**Explanation**
ansible_host: 192.168.1.20	
ansible_port: 22	
ansible_ssh_user: user1	
ansible_ssh_pass: 123456	
ansible_network_os: ios	
ansible_become: true	
ansible_become_method: enable	
ansible_become_pass: 123456	

   - In the same window, navigate to "**Groups**" and associate S1 with the **Switches** group.

3. Create a new Ansible project:
   - Using the Ansible-1 graphical interface, click on the "**Projetcs**" menu.
   - Add a project based on the parameters in the following table:

Name	**Project1**
Description	Configuring network elements
Source Control Credential Type	Manual
Playbook Directory	project1

4. Create a **Playbook** in the "**project1**" folder named **create_vlans.yaml:**

```
# cd /var/lib/awx/projects/projet1
# sudo nano create_vlans.yaml
```

5. Copy the following script into the *Playbook* and explain the required elements:

```
---
- name: Configuring VLANs on a Cisco switch
  hosts: Switches        ⬅ 1
  gather_facts: no
  connection: network_cli

  tasks:
    - name: create VLANs
      ios_vlan:          ⬅ 2
        vlan_id: "{{ item.vlan_id }}"
        name: "{{ item.name }}"
        state: present
      loop:
        - { vlan_id: '10', name: 'Users' }
        - { vlan_id: '20', name: 'Services' }
        - { vlan_id: '30', name: 'Management' }

    - name: Save current configuration
      ios_command:       ⬅ 3
        commands:
          - command: 'copy running-config startup-config'
            prompt: 'Destination filename \[startup-config\]?
            answer: "\r"
```

6. Create a "**Job Templates**" object:
   - Using the Ansible-1 graphical interface, click on the "**Templates**" menu.

- Add a "**Job Template**" object based on the parameters in the following table:

Name	Create_vlans
Description	Creating vlans
Inventory	ABC
Project	project1
Playbook	create_vlans.yaml

7. Save and execute the Ansible task. Validate VLAN creation on S1.
8. Define common **Ansible** variables for all switches:
   - Using the Ansible-1 graphical interface, click on the "**Inventories**" menu.
   - Click on "**ABC**", then on "Groups/Switches".
   - Click on "**Edit**" to define common variables between switches.
   - Enter the following lines:

```
ansible_port: 22
ansible_ssh_user: user1
ansible_ssh_pass: 123456
ansible_network_os: ios
ansible_become: true
ansible_become_method: enable
ansible_become_pass: 123456
```

   - Confirm changes.
9. Create two "**Host**" objects for switches S2 and S3
   - Using the Ansible-1 GUI, click on the "**Hosts**" menu.
   - Add two host objects for switches S2 and S3 based on the parameters in the following table:

Name	S2
Inventory	ABC
variables	ansible_host: 192.168.1.21

Name	S3
Inventory	ABC
variables	ansible_host: 192.168.1.22

10. Add the two hosts S1 and S2 to the **Switches** group.

11. Modify the configuration of S1 variables as follows:

Name	**S1**
Inventory	ABC
variables	ansible_host: 192.168.1.20

12. Re-run the **Create_vlans** task. Verify on S2 and S3 that the VLANs have been created.

Task 2: Configure Switch Interfaces

Task Objective

- The use of custom variables to fine-tune applied configurations.

1. Modify the Host S1, S2, and S3 variables as follows:

Host	**S1**
variables	--- ansible_host: 192.168.1.20 interface: - GigabitEthernet0/0 - GigabitEthernet0/1 - GigabitEthernet0/2 - GigabitEthernet0/3 mode: - access - access - trunk - trunk wham: - 1 - 10

Host	**S2**
variables	ansible_host: 192.168.1.21 interface: - GigabitEthernet0/2 - GigabitEthernet0/0 - GigabitEthernet0/1 mode: - access - trunk - trunk wham: - 20

Host	S3
variables	--- ansible_host: 192.168.1.22 interface: - GigabitEthernet0/1 - GigabitEthernet0/0 mode: - access - trunk wham: - 30

Note: It is crucial to ensure that the names of the interfaces to be configured in **trunk** or **access** mode are correct to guarantee proper operation of the **Playbook.**

2. Explain the use of **interface, mode,** and **vlan** custom variables in hosts S1, S2, and S3.
3. Create a Playbook in the **project1** folder named **config_interfaces.yaml.**
4. Copy the following script into the **Playbook:**

```
---
 - name: Configuring switch interfaces with specific configurations
   hosts: Switches
   gather_facts: no
   connection: network_cli

   tasks:

     - name: Configuring access mode interfaces
       ios_l2_interfaces:
         configuring:
           - name: "{{ item.0 }}"
             access:
               vlan: "{{ item.2 if item.1 == 'access' else omit }}"

    with_together:
         - "{{ interface }}"
         - "{{ mode }}"
         - "{{ vlan }}"
       when: item.1 == 'access'
     - name: Configuring interfaces in Trunk mode step1
       ios_l2_interfaces:
         configuring:
           - name: "{{ item.0 }}"
             trunk:
               encapsulation: dot1q
       when: item.1 == 'trunk'
       with_together:
         - "{{ interface }}"
         - "{{ mode }}"
```

```
- name: Configuring interfaces in Trunk mode step2
  ios_l2_interface:
    name: "{{ item.0 }}"
    mode: trunk
  when: item.1 == 'trunk'
  with_together:
    - "{{ interface }}"
    - "{{ mode }}"
```

5. Add a "**Job Template**" object based on the parameters in the following table:

Name	**config_interfaces**
Description	Interface configuration
Inventory	ABC
Project	project1
Playbook	config_interfaces.yaml

6. Save the Ansible task and run it. Verify the result on the switches.

   Note: If the Ansible task returns a "...timeout value 30 seconds reached..." error message, please run it again.

Task 3: Configure Router Sub-Interfaces

Task Objective

- The use of custom variables to fine-tune applied configurations.

1. Create a "**Host**" object for R1 and a "**Group**" object named **Routers**.
2. Modify the R1 variables as follows:

Host	**R1**
variables	--- ansible_host: 192.168.1.1 interface: - GigabitEthernet0/0 subinterface: - GigabitEthernet0/0.10 - GigabitEthernet0/0.20 - GigabitEthernet0/0.30 wham: - 10 - 20 - 30 ipaddress: - "192.168.10.1 255.255.255.0" - "192.168.20.1 255.255.255.0" - "192.168.30.1 255.255.255.0"

3. Modify the variables in the **Routers** group as follows:

Group	Routers
variables	--- ansible_port: 22 ansible_ssh_user: user1 ansible_ssh_pass: 123456 ansible_network_os: ios ansible_become: true ansible_become_method: enable ansible_become_pass: 123456

4. Create a **Playbook** in the **project1** folder named **config_router.yaml.**
5. Copy the following script into the **Playbook:**

```
---
 - name: Configuring switch interfaces with specific configurations
   hosts: Routers
   gather_facts: no
   connection: network_cli

   tasks:
     - name: Configuring IPv4 addresses for subinterfaces
       ios_config:
         lines:
           - "interface {{ item[0] }}"
           - "encapsulation dot1q {{ item[1] }}"
           - "ip address {{ item[2] }}"
       with_together:
         - "{{ subinterface }}"
         - "{{ vlan }}"
         - "{{ ipaddress }}"
```

6. Add a **"Job Template"** object based on the parameters in the following table:

Name	config_router
Description	Router configuration
Inventory	ABC
Project	project1
Playbook	config_router.yaml

7. Save the Ansible task and run it. Verify the result on the router.
8. Ensure successful **ping** connectivity between the three PCs.

Task 4: Extraction of Configuration Files from Elements

Task Objective

- Use personalized authentication to connect to network elements.
  1. Create a **Credentials** object:
- Using the Ansible-1 graphical interface, click on the "**Credentials**" menu.
- Add a "**Credentials**" object based on the parameters in the following table:

Name	**user1**
Description	Equipment administrator
Credential Type	Machine
User name	User1
Password	123456

- Confirm changes.
  2. Modify the variables of the **Switches** and **Routers** groups as follows:

Group	**Routers | Switches**
variables	--- ansible_network_os: ios ansible_become: true ansible_become_method: enable ansible_become_pass: 123456

  3. Create a **Playbook** in the **project1** folder named **afficher_confguration.yaml**.
  4. Copy the following script into the *Playbook* and explain the requested elements:

```
---
- name: Display information about Cisco devices
  hosts: Switches:Routers  ⬅ 1
  gather_facts: no
  connection: network_cli
  tasks:
    - name: Display basic information about a Cisco device
      ios_command:
        commands
          - command: 'show version'
      register: show_version_output

    - name: Write result to file
      local_action:
        module: copy
        content: "{{ show_version_output.stdout[0] }}"
        dest: "/var/lib/awx/projects/projet1/result.txt"  ⬅ 2
```

5. Add a "**Job Template**" object based on the parameters in the following table:

Name	**display_configuration**
Description	Router configuration
Inventory	ABC
Project	project1
Playbook	afficher_confguration.yaml
Credentials	user1

6. Save the Ansible task and run it. Verify the result of the file "**/var/lib/awx/projects/projet1/result.txt**"

9

Reinventing Enterprise Networks with Cisco SD-Access

This chapter provides an in-depth exploration of Cisco SD-Access, an innovative solution designed to revolutionize enterprise network management. Cisco SD-Access delivers advanced automation, integrated security policies, and robust network segmentation, simplifying the deployment, management, and security of campus networks. Through detailed sections, we explore the comprehensive architecture of SD-Access, its core components, and the management and data planes that define this technology.

We also examine the integrated tools and platforms supporting SD-Access operation and administration, including Cisco DNA Center and Cisco Identity Services Engine (ISE), and their roles in policy orchestration and access security. In addition, the integration of SD-Access with other network technologies, such as SD-WAN and existing protocols, will be discussed to illustrate its flexibility and breadth of application.

Finally, a comparison with Cisco ACI will enable us to distinguish between these two Cisco solutions, highlighting their applicability to different network environments. Note that, for pedagogical and simplification purposes, certain SD-Access features and details are not covered in this chapter. Readers wishing to explore certain aspects in greater depth can refer to the additional documentation available.

This chapter covers the following topics:

1. Introducing the SD-Access solution
2. Cisco SD-ACCESS architecture
3. Platforms and management tools integrated into Cisco SD-Access
4. Integrating Cisco SD-Access into external networks
5. Comparative analysis: Cisco ACI Vs. Cisco SD-Access
6. Conclusion

9.1 Introducing the SD-Access Solution

Cisco Software-Defined Access (SD-Access) is an advanced solution that streamlines enterprise network management through software-defined networking (SDN) principles. Designed to meet growing needs for flexibility and security, SD-Access enables centralized management of network policies, while offering greater visibility and control.

As enterprise networks grow increasingly complex due to the proliferation of connected devices and heightened security demands, SD-Access provides an effective solution.

DOI: 10.1201/9781003679394-9

It is based on a multi-layer architecture that enables network segmentation and automation of operations, improving the responsiveness and efficiency of IT teams.

The evolution of enterprise networks, driven by the shift to hybrid and multi-cloud environments, has underscored the significance of SD-Access. By integrating features such as micro-segmentation and dynamic threat management, this approach offers greater security for data flows and simplified network management.

9.2 Cisco SD-ACCESS Architecture

The Cisco SD-Access architecture leverages the core components of a standard SD-LAN framework, which collaborate to deliver advanced automation and centralized orchestration.

9.2.1 Main Components

The SD-Access architecture is based on several elements described below (Figure 9.1):

- **Fabric nodes:** These are the fundamental elements of the Cisco SD-Access structure. They are divided into three types:
  - **Edge nodes:** These devices, often switches, represent the entry and exit points for users and devices within the network. They are responsible for enforcing security policies and routing data to the border nodes.
  - **Border nodes:** These provide the connection between the internal network (the Fabric) and external networks, such as the Internet or other private networks. They manage incoming and outgoing traffic, ensuring a secure interface with the outside world.
  - **Control plane nodes:** These devices manage routing within the network, utilizing the Locator/ID Separation Protocol (LISP) for efficient data packet routing.
- **Cisco DNA Center:** It serves as both the SDN controller and orchestrator for the SD-Access solution. It provides a unified graphical interface for supervising and automating network configuration, performance monitoring, and policy management.
- **ISE:** This is the AAA server of the SD-Access architecture. It provides centralized identity and access management, enabling security policies to be applied based on the identity of users, devices, and roles. ISE plays a key role in micro-segmentation, ensuring that only authorized users and devices can access network resources and isolating potential threats to limit their propagation.
- **Intermediate nodes:** These routers or Layer 3 switches connect edge nodes and border nodes. Their main role is to transport traffic between these different points of the Fabric, ensuring that packets reach their final destination without interruption. Unlike the other types of nodes in the SD-Access Fabric, intermediate nodes

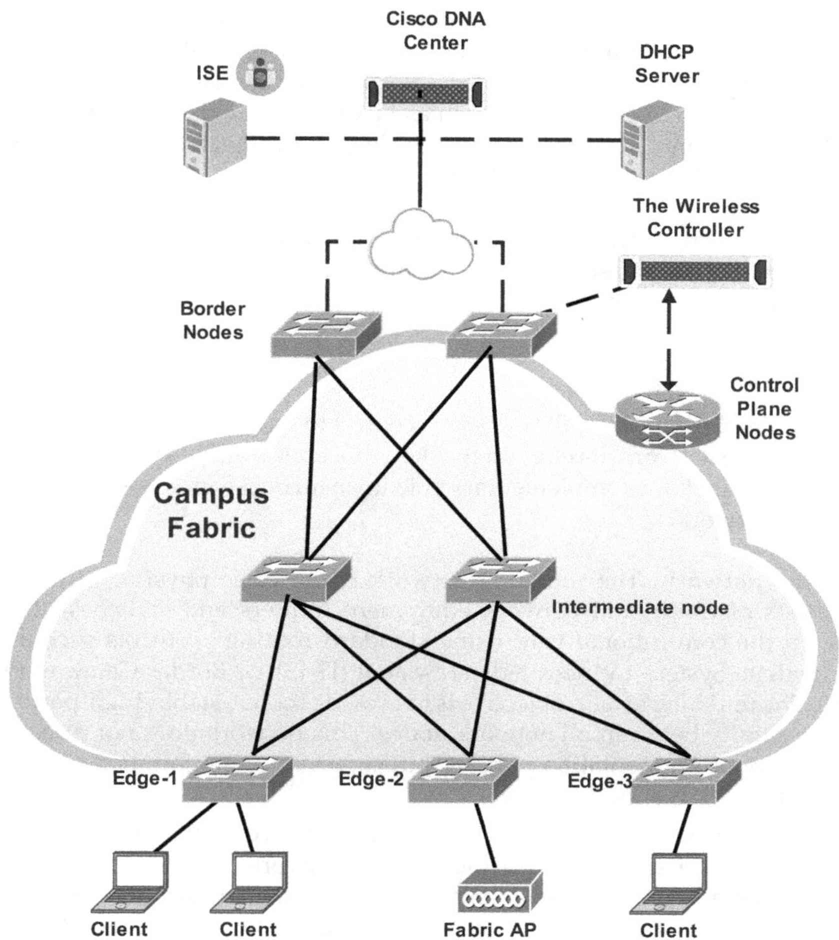

FIGURE 9.1
Main components of an SD-Access architecture.

are not directly responsible for managing security policies or enforcing segmentation policies and are not configured via the Cisco DNA Center. Their function is purely to provide basic IP connectivity, making them essential for keeping traffic flowing smoothly through the Fabric, but without the advanced policy management functions.

- **The wireless controller:** This is a crucial element in the SD-Access structure, guaranteeing efficient, centralized management of wireless networks. Thanks to its integration with Cisco DNA Center, it enables wireless access points to be deployed, configured, and managed in an automated way that is consistent with the rest of the SD-Access Fabric. Its role extends from simple access point management to security policy enforcement, mobility management, and wireless performance optimization, ensuring a high-quality user experience and reliable connectivity throughout the SD-Access network.

- **The fusion router:** The fusion router plays an essential role in the Cisco SD-Access architecture, although it is not explicitly mentioned as a native component of the SD-Access solution. The fusion router is used to interconnect the SD-Access Fabric with other networks or domains, such as WAN services, data center networks, or cloud environments. In the topology, the element designated as "IP/SDA transit" is where the fusion router is positioned.

Collectively, these components create a cohesive, robust architecture that empowers organizations with a more agile, secure, and manageable network, while reducing operating costs and enhancing efficiency.

9.2.2 Fabric Architecture

The Fabric architecture in Cisco SD-Access is central to its ability to deliver a flexible, segmented, and secure network. It relies on two key concepts, overlay and underlay networks, each playing a distinct but complementary role in ensuring seamless, secure communication across the network.

- **Underlay network:** The underlay network is the basic physical infrastructure. It consists of traditional network equipment (routers and switches) that route traffic in the conventional way, using standard routing protocols such as OSPF, Intermediate System to Intermediate System (IS-IS), or Border Gateway Protocol (BGP). The underlay's main objective is to provide robust, stable, high-performance IP connectivity between all network nodes. This network does not directly manage security or segmentation policies, but serves as the foundation on which the overlay network is superimposed.
- **Overlay network:** The overlay network is a virtual layer that relies on the underlay to establish secure tunnels across the physical network. These tunnels are dynamically created and managed to enable network segmentation, policy management, and service enforcement. The overlay is responsible for routing user traffic flows and securing data. The overlay enables rapid deployment of new functionalities without requiring modifications to the underlay's physical configuration, providing significant flexibility to the network infrastructure.

9.2.3 Different Planes in SD-Access

In Cisco SD-Access architecture, as with SDN networks, network management is organized into several functional planes, each fulfilling a specific role in data processing, policy management, and network oversight. These planes separate the various network functions, facilitating automation, security, and centralized management.

Here are the main planes used in SD-Access:

9.2.3.1 Management Plane

The Management Plane focuses on the configuration, monitoring, and administration of the SD-Access network. It is primarily embodied by the Cisco DNA Center, which provides a unified interface for network management. This plane enables administrators to define policies, monitor network performance, and automate routine operations, simplifying management and enhancing operational efficiency.

Key functions of the Management Plane:

- **Task automation:** Simplifies network configuration and deployment.
- **Real-time monitoring:** Provides tools for observing network health and performance.
- **Centralized management:** Allows you to monitor and control the entire Fabric from a single platform.

9.2.3.2 Policy Strategy Plane

The Policy Plane is responsible for managing and enforcing security and access policies within the network. In the SD-Access architecture, this plane is based on the Cisco ISE element. The Policy Strategy Plane lets you define rules based on user identities, device types, or user groups. These rules are then applied consistently across the network, regardless of users' physical location.

The key functions of the Policy Plane can be summarized as follows:

- **Definition of security rules:** Based on identity, context, or user groups.
- **Policy enforcement:** Ensures that rules are applied consistently throughout the Fabric.
- **Micro-segmentation:** Creates secure network segments to limit the spread of threats.

9.2.3.3 Control Plane

The Control Plane manages the routing and location of users and devices in the SD-Access network. The Control Plane is essential to the creation of the Fabric, as it enables packets to be located and routed efficiently without depending on the underlying physical subnet. In SD-Access, the Control Plane uses the LISP protocol to separate the user's identifier (ID) from its physical location (Locator), enabling great flexibility and mobility within the network. In this architecture, the Control Plane is embodied by Control Plane Nodes.

Key functions of the Control Plane:

- **Dynamic routing:** Manages routes within the Fabric using protocols such as LISP.
- **Identity and location management:** Facilitates user mobility and service continuity.
- **Address resolution:** Translates user IDs into network locations for optimal routing.

9.2.3.4 Data Plane

The Data Plane is responsible for the actual routing of data packets across the network. In SD-Access, this plane relies primarily on the use of the Virtual Extensible LAN (VXLAN) protocol, which enables Layer 2 packets to be encapsulated in Layer 3 tunnels, facilitating network segmentation and secure data transport. What's more, in SD-Access, the VXLAN frame is extended to include a TAG (Security Group Tag or SGT), which links each frame directly to the defined security policies, ensuring consistent application of security rules throughout the network. The Data Plane ensures that packets are transmitted according to the rules defined by the Policy Plane, while guaranteeing high performance and low latency.

The key functions of the Data Plane:

- **Data encapsulation:** Uses VXLAN to transport packets securely.
- **Efficient transmission:** Fast, reliable routing of data through the Fabric.
- **Network services support:** Enables the integration and transport of essential services such as quality of service or security policies.

9.2.4 Protocols and Technologies Used in SD-Access

Several protocols and technologies are essential to the operation of the SD-Access Fabric, each playing a specific role in the management of overlay and underlay networks:

- **BGP:** This is commonly used in the underlay to manage the exchange of routes between different administrative domains. In the context of Cisco SD-Access, BGP can also be used to interconnect overlay segments on different parts of the network or to integrate the SD-Access network with external environments, such as the cloud or other corporate networks.
- **IS-IS:** This protocol enables efficient transmission of routing information between network nodes, ensuring that traffic is optimally routed through the underlay, regardless of network complexity or size.
- **LISP:** It is used to manage addressing and routing within the Fabric. This protocol separates node identifiers (IDs) from their locations (locators), enabling seamless mobility of users and devices without the need for network reconfiguration. LISP improves routing efficiency and enables dynamic localization of resources, contributing to network flexibility and responsiveness.
- **VXLAN:** It is the key protocol used to create the overlay network. It allows Layer 2 packets to be encapsulated in Layer 3 packets, enabling virtual LANs (VLANs) to be extended beyond traditional physical boundaries. VXLAN thus facilitates the creation of virtual tunnels that carry data across the overlay network, while maintaining the segmentation and isolation required for each subnet.
- **Virtual Routing and Forwarding (VRF):** This **is** a technology that enables the creation of a virtual routing instance, which can contain its own routing table, separate from other instances on the same device. In Cisco SD-Access, VRFs are essential for creating secure, isolated network segments. They are used to manage communications between different segments of the enterprise, ensuring that sensitive data remains confined to specific segments without interference or visibility from other segments.
- Security Group Access Control Lists (**SGACLs**)**:** SGACLs are access control lists applied on the basis of Security Group Tags (SGTs) assigned to users, devices, or resources in the network. They enable the application of specific access control policies based on these tags, facilitating precise micro-segmentation.

Please note that all the above-mentioned technologies have been discussed in detail in this document. Readers can refer to the dedicated sections for further information.

9.3 Platforms and Management Tools Integrated into Cisco SD-Access

Cisco SD-Access provides a suite of advanced features that streamline enterprise network management while bolstering security and agility. These features are designed to meet modern network management challenges, offering powerful tools for automation, segmentation, and compliance.

9.3.1 Cisco DNA Center

9.3.1.1 Presentation

The Cisco DNA Center controller is a centralized platform for automating and managing networks, especially SD-Access networks in the enterprise. It succeeds the Application Policy Infrastructure Controller–Enterprise Module (APIC-EM), a prior Cisco product that provided network automation functions with a more limited scope. Cisco DNA Center stands out for its more integrated approach, covering not only automation, but also service assurance, security, and network policy management in a unified environment. It offers advanced features such as automated device configuration, network visibility via interactive dashboards, and network assurance to detect and resolve performance issues faster. Cisco DNA Center represents a significant evolution from APIC-EM, enabling more holistic and proactive management of modern networks.

DNA Center is central to the intent-based networking approach. This approach allows administrators to define desired outcomes (e.g., quality of service and security) and let DNA Center orchestrate the infrastructure to achieve these goals without the need to manually configure each network element (Figure 9.2).

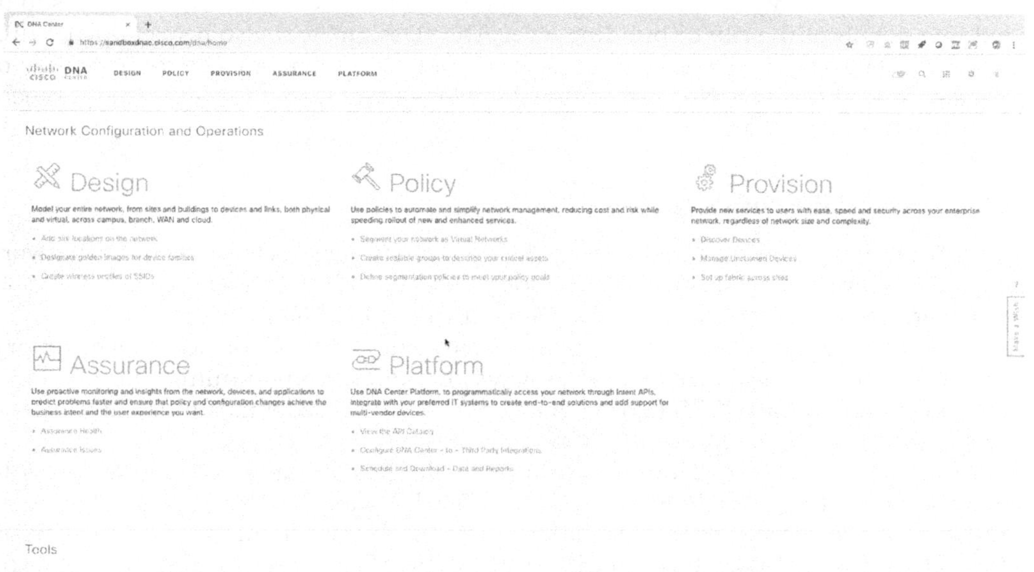

FIGURE 9.2
DNA Center server home page.[1]

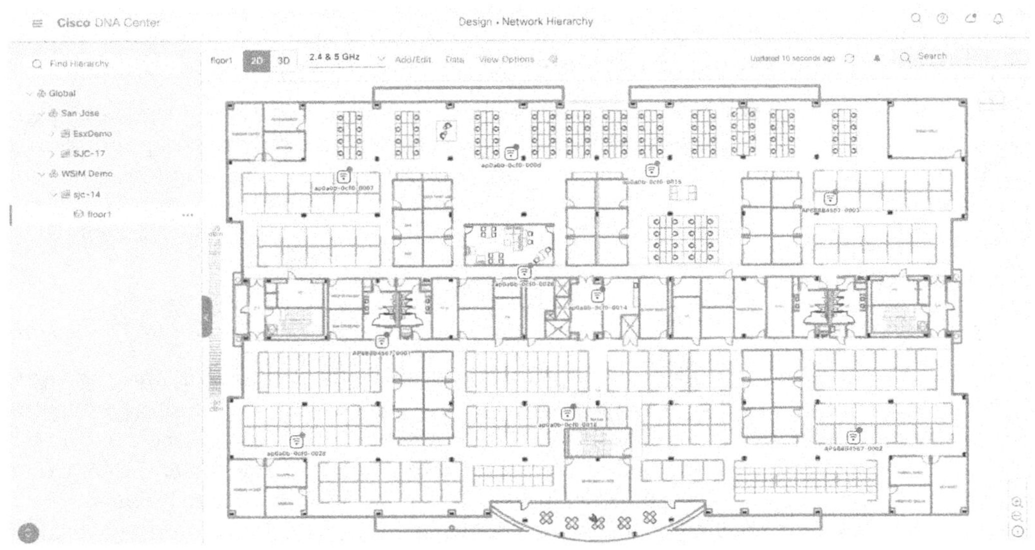

FIGURE 9.3
Setting up a location-based network hierarchy in the DNA Center.[1]

9.3.1.2 Network Design

Cisco DNA Center facilitates network design with its intuitive "Design" tool, enabling administrators to visualize and define the geographical layout of the network. This tool supports the definition of a network hierarchy based on a company's geographical locations, such as regions, buildings, and floors. This task, performed from the outset, ensures that the network is correctly modeled for efficient management. For example, companies can define segments at the global, continental, or national level, which are then subdivided into details at the city or building level. The "Design" tool also helps to plan wireless deployments in collaboration with the Wi-Fi controller, enabling the configuration of options such as SSIDs and Wi-Fi security parameters, which can be applied to equipment during deployment (Figure 9.3).

9.3.1.3 Discovering Network Equipment

Cisco DNA Center offers an automated method of discovering devices within the network using its "Discovery" tool. It supports various protocols such as Cisco Discovery Protocol, Link Layer Discovery Protocol, and IP address ranges to identify devices.

In order for Cisco DNA Center to correctly discover and add each device to its inventory, it must have the necessary credentials to access the devices. As a minimum, read-only Command Line Interface (CLI) (SSH/Telnet) and SNMPv2 credentials must be provided to enable the discovery process to be carried out.

During discovery in a traditional architecture, devices are automatically assigned to roles such as "CORE", "ACCESS", or "DISTRIBUTION". This classification is particularly useful in migration scenarios from traditional network infrastructure to SD-Access architecture. Discovery and inventory via Cisco DNA Center facilitates this transition, offering complete visibility of equipment and enabling efficient management of the migration to Fabric (Figure 9.4).

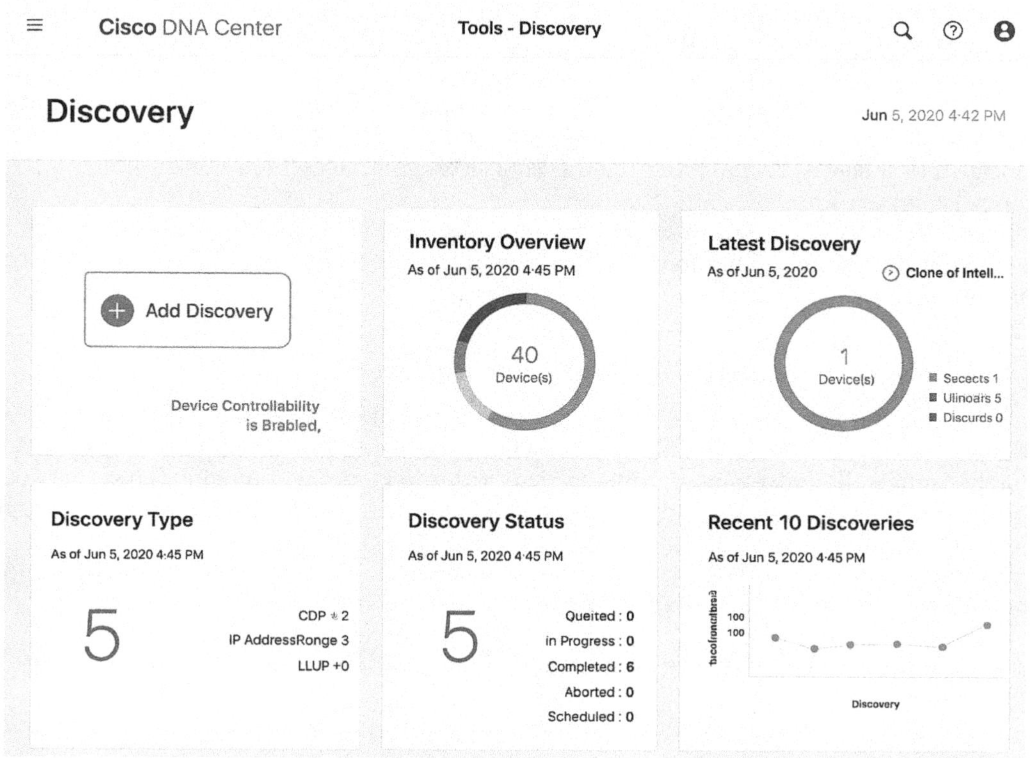

FIGURE 9.4
Graphical interface for network device discovery in the DNA Center.[1]

Once equipment has been discovered, it is added to the inventory, where it can be managed and monitored.

9.3.1.4 Equipment Configuration and Provisioning

Device configuration in Cisco DNA Center is managed via the "Provision" tool, which automates the application of configuration changes to multiple devices simultaneously. This tool uses predefined templates from the design phase to apply network parameters across the entire hierarchy, saving time and reducing errors associated with manual configuration. Provisioning can be scheduled during maintenance windows or applied immediately, offering flexibility in network operations. What's more, management of software and firmware updates is simplified thanks to the software image management functionality.

9.3.1.5 Automatic Underlay Creation

Cisco DNA Center offers a feature called LAN Automation, which automates the configuration of the underlay. This feature is designed to eliminate the need to manually configure every link and route in the core network, which can be complex and error-prone in traditional deployments.

With LAN Automation, Cisco DNA Center discovers the devices in the network, automatically assigns IP addresses, and configures the necessary routing protocols (typically IS-IS or OSPF) to establish connectivity between the various network components. This creates an efficient and resilient underlay, ensuring equipment connectivity without the need for manual intervention at every stage. Once the underlay has been configured, it serves as the basis for the SD-Access overlay, where network virtualization services are applied.

This automation process not only reduces deployment time but also reduces the risk of configuration errors by guaranteeing a uniform, standardized setup of the core network for the Fabric.

9.3.1.6 Creating the Fabric and Assigning Equipment Roles

Fabric creation begins with the definition of the control plane, data plane, and network edges. Cisco DNA Center facilitates this task by providing preconfigured templates that enable subnets, IP address pools, and security rules to be defined quickly. Then, network equipment such as switches and routers can be integrated into the Fabric using the provisioning tool.

In a second step, Cisco DNA Center lets you manually define which devices will occupy specific roles in the Fabric. The three main roles assigned are as follows:

- **Edge nodes:** These devices act as entry points for end-users and devices in the Fabric.
- **Border nodes:** They are responsible for connecting the Fabric to external networks.
- **Control plane nodes:** These nodes manage device location information and serve as a database for routing and mobility in the network.

These roles are not assigned automatically when devices are discovered, but must be specifically assigned by the network administrator according to requirements and the desired topology. Cisco DNA Center provides an intuitive graphical interface for configuring and managing these roles, simplifying the process of assigning and adjusting devices in the Fabric.

9.3.1.7 Anycast Gateway Concept

An "anycast gateway" is an IP gateway that is simultaneously available on several devices in the network. This allows multiple access points, such as Edge switches in the Fabric, to share the same gateway IP address.

Each Edge switch in the SD-Access Fabric is configured with the same gateway IP address, enabling users and devices to connect to the network regardless of their physical location. This greatly enhances mobility, as users can move around the network environment without changing IP gateways, eliminating the disruption associated with changing IP addresses or subnets.

The anycast gateway simplifies IP address management and improves network efficiency by enabling rapid convergence when hosts are mobile. It also ensures continuity of service for network-sensitive applications such as voice calls or video streams, which do not tolerate interruptions in connectivity.

9.3.1.8 Automating Tasks with DNA Center

Automation in Cisco DNA Center is designed to simplify and streamline network management using a variety of technologies and methods:

- **CLI:** Cisco DNA Center automates network configuration via CLI, enabling the execution of standardized commands to reduce errors and save time.
- **Network configuration:** Standard configuration templates in Cisco DNA Center facilitate rapid, consistent deployment of network policies throughout the organization.
- **NETCONF/YANG models:** Cisco DNA Center uses NETCONF and YANG for efficient configuration management, enabling structured and precise communications between network devices and the controller.
- **RESTful Application Programming Interface (API):** RESTful APIs in Cisco DNA Center enable integration with third-party applications, providing customized, responsive solutions to specific network needs.

9.3.2 Cisco ISE in SD-Access

Cisco ISE is a key component in Cisco's SD-Access architecture. It plays an essential role in managing identity-based access, enforcing security policies, and dynamically segmenting users and devices.

The ISE server, in addition to the standard AAA functions, performs additional checks on several key aspects. It analyzes the type of device seeking access to the network, such as a computer, printer, smartphone, and so forth, to determine whether it is authorized. It also assesses the time of connection to ensure that it takes place within authorized time slots, and checks the device's location to ensure secure access. Finally, it examines the connection mode, whether wired, wireless, or via a virtual private network (VPN), to ensure that it complies with corporate security policies.

In addition to the tasks already explained, ISE offers the following functions:

9.3.2.1 Device Profiling

With the increasing number and diversity of devices in modern networks (e.g., smartphones, tablets, printers, cameras, etc.), it becomes crucial to understand what type of device is connecting to the network in order to apply appropriate policies to it. Profiling helps companies to identify and classify these devices, which is essential for effective segmentation and security policy management.

Cisco ISE uses "probes" to collect the attributes needed to classify terminals. These probes can include SNMP requests, DHCP traffic captures, DNS queries, HTTP protocol information, and so forth.

Once a device has been correctly profiled, it can be automatically placed in a specific network, such as a voice VLAN for IP phones or a camera VLAN for surveillance cameras. This dynamic classification helps reduce the attack surface by ensuring that devices receive only the necessary privileges and aids detection and response to suspicious behavior.

9.3.2.2 Device Compliance

When a device attempts to connect to the network, Cisco ISE checks its compliance status against defined security policies (Posture Assessment). This can include checks on the status of software updates, the presence of antivirus software, encryption status, and other security parameters.

Non-compliant devices can be isolated in specific segments of the network, where they will have limited access to resources until they are deemed compliant. This ensures that insecure devices do not compromise the integrity of the rest of the network.

9.3.2.3 Network Device Admission Control (NDAC) Functionality

NDAC is an ISE feature that enhances network security by controlling access to network devices themselves, not just end users. NDAC uses 802.1X principles to authenticate network devices such as switches and routers, ensuring that only authorized devices can connect to the network.

Here are some key facts about NDAC:

- **Certificate-based authentication:** NDAC often uses certificates to authenticate network devices, guaranteeing that each device is legitimate and authorized to participate in the network.
- **Integration with 802.1X:** As mentioned, it leverages the 802.1X protocol framework to provide a robust authentication method. This includes the use of RADIUS as a mechanism for transmitting authentication information between the network device and Cisco ISE.
- **Enhanced network security:** By verifying the identity of network devices before allowing them access to the network, NDAC helps prevent potential attacks via unauthorized or compromised devices.
- **Policy management:** Once network devices have been authenticated, Cisco ISE can apply specific policies that regulate their behavior on the network, including access levels and authorizations.

9.3.2.4 Change of Authorization (CoA)

CoA is a mechanism used by Cisco ISE to dynamically modify the access privileges of a user or device once it has already been authenticated and connected to the network. This process is particularly important in environments where guest access needs to be managed flexibly and securely.

The advantages of CoA for access can be summarized as follows:

- **Real-time adaptability:** CoA enables access policies to be readjusted without interrupting the connection, guaranteeing a smooth user experience while maintaining security.
- **Enhanced security:** With Cisco ISE and CoA, administrators can ensure that users receive only the appropriate level of access, and that this access can be changed if the behavior or compliance status of the device changes.

9.3.2.5 Guest management in Cisco ISE

One of Cisco ISE's key features for guest management is authentication via customizable captive portals. Guests can register themselves or be sponsored by an employee, with a variety of authentication options, such as PIN codes or temporary credentials. Once authenticated, Cisco ISE applies specific security policies to guests, often more restrictive than for internal users, placing them in dedicated, isolated network segments. ISE continuously monitors guest sessions, with options for real-time re-evaluation of access rights (CoA), session duration limits, and quarantine measures if security standards are not met. Administrators can manage these accesses via a centralized interface, enabling guest account supervision and compliance monitoring.

9.3.2.6 Dynamic Segmentation and Group-based Access Control

Within the Cisco SD-Access architecture, Cisco ISE enables segmentation at two levels: macro-segmentation using VRF and micro-segmentation using SGTs. Cisco ISE applies group-based policies based on Cisco TrustSec technology.

9.3.2.6.1 SD-Access Macro-Segmentation

Macro-segmentation isolates different user groups or departments within virtual networks (VNs). Each VN has its own independent routing table, providing complete isolation of traffic flows between different groups or departments. This separation ensures that no undesirable interaction can take place between critical segments (e.g., between a guest network and a secure internal network), enhancing overall network security.

9.3.2.6.2 SD-Access Micro-Segmentation

Micro-segmentation is achieved using SGTs. These tags are associated with data packets, dynamically identifying the source (user, device, or application) within VNs. SGTs enable Cisco ISE and Cisco TrustSec to apply precise security policies based on the identity and role of the user or device. This ensures that communication is restricted only to interactions between authorized groups, while enabling granular security controls within VNs themselves (Figure 9.5).

9.3.2.6.3 Cisco TrustSec

Cisco TrustSec is a security technology essential to the dynamic segmentation approach in Cisco SD-Access. It enables security policies to be applied based on the roles and identities of users or devices, rather than relying solely on traditional IP addresses. This simplifies security management in increasingly complex and dynamic network environments. With TrustSec, policies can be adjusted and implemented more quickly and consistently, improving network flexibility while enhancing security. Management is centralized and made more efficient, as it is based on user identity and role, reducing the complexity of IP-based ACLs.

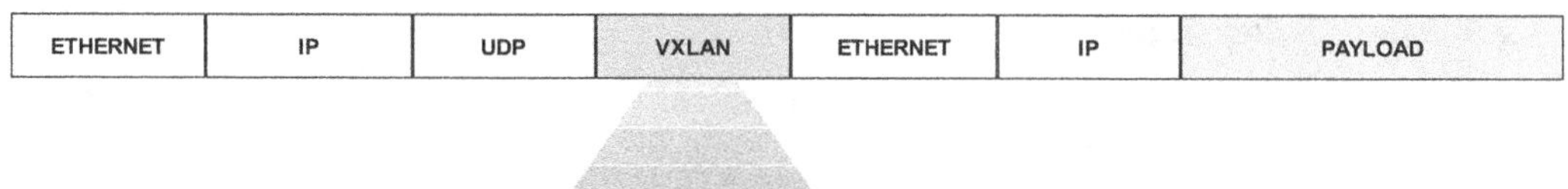

FIGURE 9.5
Frame structure for applying security policies based on SGT and VRF.

9.3.2.7 GTS Allocation Methods

Cisco ISE offers two main methods for assigning SGT: dynamic assignment and static assignment.

- **Dynamic assignment:** Dynamic SGT assignment occurs automatically during user or device authentication processes. When authentication is performed via protocols such as 802.1x, MAB, or WebAuth, Cisco ISE assigns the corresponding SGT to the connected device or user. This process enables flexible, centralized management of SGTs, where access rights and security policies are dynamically applied according to user roles or profiles.
- **Static assignment:** In environments where port authentication is not required, SGTs can be statically defined on compatible network devices. This includes assigning SGTs to different network elements, such as IP addresses, subnets, VLANs, or to Layer 2 and Layer 3 interfaces. This mode of assignment is useful in scenarios where security requirements do not call for continuous authentication, but where SGT tagging remains essential for controlling and segmenting network traffic.

Cisco ISE also allows you to manage a database of IP addresses for static mapping to SGTs, facilitating the implementation of security policies throughout the network.

These two assignment methods, dynamic and static, give SD-Access administrators the flexibility they need to implement granular security policies, while guaranteeing simplified management of identities and access rights within the network.

9.3.2.8 Securing Ports in SD-Access

In the SD-Access architecture, Cisco ISE offers several connection modes to secure access to network ports. These modes allow you to control and manage how hosts connect, ensuring secure access in line with security policies.

- **Single-host mode** is designed to restrict each port to a single connected device. This mode is used to ensure that only one device, be it a computer or another device, can authenticate to a specific port, thus reinforcing network security.
- **Multi-host mode** allows multiple devices to connect simultaneously to the same port. Although it allows multiple connections, this mode ensures that all devices are properly authenticated, thus ensuring security while offering flexible access.
- Finally, **Multi-Domain** Mode allows simultaneous authentication of two different types of devices on the same port, such as a user device and a network device like an IP phone. This mode is particularly useful in corporate environments where it is common to see network devices connected with user terminals on the same port.

9.3.2.9 Safety Policy Matrix

The Security Policy Matrix is an essential graphical tool for defining access relationships between different groups in a group-based security architecture. It relies on the use of SGTs and SGACLs to manage segmentation and network access policies.

The Security Policy Matrix takes the form of a grid, with the headers corresponding to the origin and destination groups. Each cell at the intersection of these groups indicates

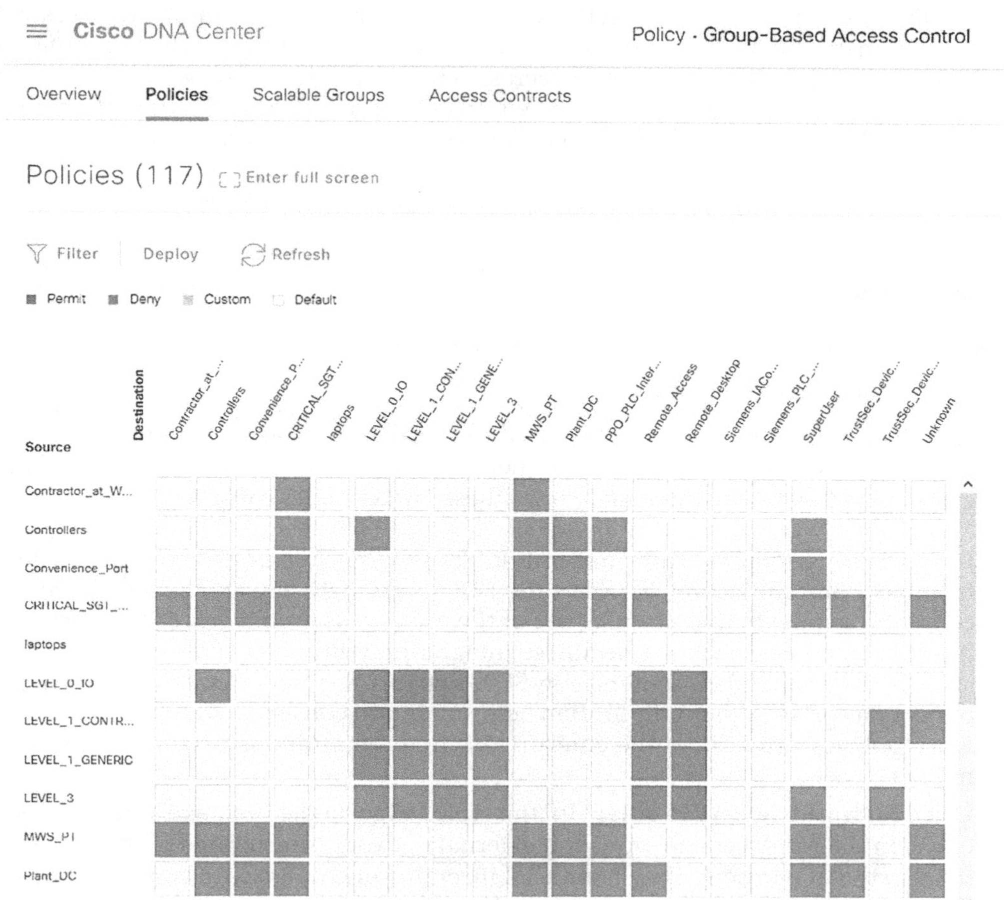

FIGURE 9.6
DNA center security policy matrix.

whether communication is authorized or prohibited, with colors such as green (authorized) and red (not authorized). This makes it easy to quickly visualize access policies for each group of users and devices.

These policies are applied at switch, router, or access point level within the SD-Access infrastructure (Figure 9.6).

9.3.3 Wireless Controller

The Wi-Fi controller, using the WAPCAP protocol to manage access points, is responsible for applying network policies to them. It handles tasks such as user authentication, in collaboration with the ISE server, bandwidth management, radio channel control, and load balancing between access points. The controller also ensures seamless mobility for users, enabling them to move from one access point to another without loss of connectivity.

In SD-Access environments, the Wi-Fi controller also supports security services such as micro-segmentation, enabling users or devices to be isolated according to administrator-defined policies. In large SD-Access networks, multiple Wi-Fi controllers can be integrated to ensure high availability and fault tolerance, guaranteeing optimum network resilience.

Cisco DNA Center integrates directly with Wi-Fi controllers to simplify wireless network management and orchestration. This integration enables administrators to configure and deploy network policies consistently across wired and wireless networks from a single interface. DNA Center offers complete visibility over wireless network performance, providing analysis and assurance tools to quickly identify and resolve connectivity or performance issues.

9.4 Cisco SD-Access Integration in External Networks

9.4.1 Edge Node Terminologies

In a Cisco SD-Access network, border nodes are critical, serving as interconnection points between the SD-Access network and other networks, whether internal, external, or both. Here's an explanation of the three main roles these border nodes can play:

- **Rest of the company (internal-only):** These edge nodes are configured to facilitate communication between the SD-Access network and other internal company segments that are not part of the SD-Access architecture. They act as internal gateways, enabling seamless integration with other internal networks such as traditional data centers, non-SDN network segments, or other branches of the enterprise. This configuration helps maintain consistent security and network policies throughout the enterprise, while remaining isolated from external networks.
- **Outside world (external-only):** In this role, edge nodes manage interactions between the SD-Access network and external networks, including the Internet or other external partners. They handle all incoming and outgoing communications that cross company boundaries. This includes VPN management, address translation (NAT), and the application of security policies to protect the network against external threats. These nodes ensure that all data entering or leaving the company is inspected and complies with established security policies.
- **Anywhere (internal and external):** Edge nodes that are configured for the "Anywhere" role manage both internal and external communications. They are versatile, serving as a bridge between the internal SD-Access network and the outside world, while also managing interactions with other internal parts of the company. This configuration is ideal for environments where nodes need to be flexible and capable of handling a wide range of communication and security tasks without compromising efficiency or security.

9.4.2 Fusion Router

The Fusion Router interconnects the SD-Access Fabric with other networks or domains, including traditional services like DHCP, DNS, NTP, WAN services, data centers, or cloud environments. It functions as a transition point, where Fabric policies, based on identities and network segmentation, are translated and adapted to external networks, which may use different routing and security schemes.

Main functions of the Fusion router:

- **Mapping VLANs and VRFs:** The Fusion router enables segments and VRFs in the SD-Access Fabric to be mapped to VLANs and VRFs in external networks. This ensures seamless integration between different routing and segmentation instances, without compromising traffic flow isolation or security.
- **Policy interconnection:** Policies defined within the SD-Access Fabric, which are often based on user identities or security groups, can be translated and applied in other domains via the Fusion router. This ensures consistent application of security and access control rules across the entire network infrastructure, including non-SD-Access networks.
- **Inter-domain communication:** The Fusion router facilitates communication between the SD-Access Fabric and other routing domains, ensuring that the protocols and routing mechanisms used in the Fabric are correctly translated for the underlay or external networks. This is essential for maintaining seamless connectivity, even when interconnected domains use different technologies or protocols.

9.4.3 The DHCP Server in SD-Access

In an SD-Access architecture, a particular challenge arises in the communication between Fabric clients and the DHCP server due to the use of an anycast gateway. This gateway, with an identical IP address duplicated on all Edge nodes in the network, introduces ambiguity for the DHCP server when assigning IP addresses to clients. This is because, as clients move around the network, their DHCP requests appear to originate from the same anycast gateway IP address, irrespective of the point of entry into the network. This makes it difficult for the DHCP server to determine the precise origin of the request, and thus to provide adequate configuration information.

To address this ambiguity, DHCP option 82, known as the "DHCP Relay Agent Information Option," must be enabled. This option enables the Edge Nodes of the SD-Access Fabric, which relay DHCP requests, to add additional information to each request. This information includes a unique identifier for the Edge switch, as well as the specific port where the client is connected.

By enabling option 82, each DHCP request relayed to the server contains details of the specific Edge switch that relayed the request, enabling the DHCP server to differentiate between clients and assign them correct IP addresses and precise network configurations.

9.4.4 SD-Access Interoperability with Other Networks

9.4.4.1 The SGT Exchange Protocol (SXP) Protocol

In a Cisco SD-Access environment, the SXP facilitates the exchange of security information and extends the visibility and enforcement of security policies across the network infrastructure, even in traditional networks where hardware functionality is limited. This Cisco-specific protocol is not a standard supported by all manufacturers of network equipment such as routers, switches, or firewalls. It is mainly used to extend Security Group Tagging functionality to devices that do not natively support this technology.

The role of SXP can be summarized as follows:

- **Extending SGTs:** SXP enables SGTs to be extended to parts of the network that do not natively support SGT functionality, such as legacy devices. This ensures consistent application of security policies throughout the network.
- **Interoperability:** By enabling interoperability between devices capable and incapable of understanding and applying SGTs, SXP plays an essential role in heterogeneous environments. This enables a gradual transition to a fully SD-Access-compatible infrastructure without the need for an immediate hardware upgrade.
- **Simplified security policy management:** By centralizing security information and distributing it to the necessary devices, SXP helps simplify security policy management, making the network easier to manage and more secure.

SXP works using a peer-to-peer relationship between the SXP "Speaker" and "Listener" devices. Here are the key steps in its operation:

- **Establishing the relationship:** An SXP relationship is established between a Speaker device, which holds information about SGTs, and a Listener device, which needs this information but cannot generate it itself.
- **Information exchange:** Once the relationship has been established, the Speaker transmits the SGT-IP mappings to the Listener. This process ensures that SGT-based security policies can be applied even on devices that are not directly aware of these tags.
- **Dynamic updating:** SXP enables dynamic updating of SGT-IP mappings. When a change occurs, the Speaker sends an update to the Listener to ensure that the information is always up-to-date, enabling a rapid response to policy changes or network evolution.
- **Scalability and reliability:** SXP has been designed to be both scalable and reliable, enabling it to be deployed in large enterprise networks without performance degradation.

9.4.4.2 The In-Line Tagging Technique

In-line tagging is a method used in SD-Access networks to extend visibility and enforcement of security policies across the network infrastructure. This approach involves incorporating SGTs directly into packet headers as they transit across the network. The main tunnel types that can be used in this technique include GRE, IPsec, DMVPN (Dynamic Multipoint VPN), and GETVPN (Group-Encrypted Transport VPN) tunnels.

This technique works as follows:

- **Encapsulation of SGTs:** In an SD-Access environment, SGTs are encapsulated within packets as they pass through secure tunnels. This is typically done using encapsulation protocols such as VXLAN, which can transport data with embedded SGTs across wide-area networks.

- **Secure transmission:** SGT encapsulation enables security information to be transmitted securely between different devices across the network, including remote sites. This ensures that security policies are applied uniformly, regardless of the physical location of resources or users in the network.
- **Policy extraction and enforcement:** On receipt of packets, network devices capable of reading SGTs (such as Cisco switches and routers) extract security tags and enforce the corresponding policies. This can include access rules, traffic control rules, or other security measures based on the identity associated with the SGT.

9.4.5 Unified Integration of Cisco SD-Access and SD-WAN

The Cisco SD-Access solution integrates seamlessly with Cisco SD-WAN to ensure centralized management of network policies on campuses, data centers, and branches via SD-WAN. Cisco DNA Center orchestrates this integration, playing a key role in coordinating network controllers, including for SD-WAN. By creating an overlay network for segmentation, DNA assigns users and devices according to their access privileges. This enables uniform policy enforcement, avoids complex VPN connections, and improves enterprise-wide data collection and analysis.

9.4.6 Cisco pxGrid in SD-Access

Cisco pxGrid is an integration platform that enables Cisco ISE to share contextual security data with other systems in an SD-Access environment. One of pxGrid's strengths lies in its ability to enable various systems, even from different vendors, to work together to better protect the network. These systems can include security automation platforms, intrusion detection systems, firewalls, vulnerability management systems, behavioral analysis solutions, and so forth. pxGrid ensures that all these platforms interact seamlessly, ensuring centralized management and coordinated action in an SD-Access environment. pxGrid also enables the automation of real-time responses to threats, thus strengthening network protection. Thanks to this integration, security policies can be dynamically applied and threats quickly contained.

9.5 Comparative Analysis: Cisco ACI vs Cisco SD-Access

The following table compares two of Cisco's automated networking solutions: Cisco ACI and Cisco SD-Access. Each of these technologies brings specific benefits and is optimized for different network environments, Cisco ACI being geared toward data centers and Cisco SD-Access toward campus networks. This comparison is presented for illustrative purposes, to highlight the main differences and similarities between the products. Note that Cisco ACI offers a broader range of features, which are not fully detailed here for simplicity. For a more in-depth understanding of each solution, the reader is encouraged to consult the additional documentation available (Table 9.1).

The previous presentation highlights the points of convergence and divergence between SD-Access and ACI, helping to understand when and why to choose one over the other.

TABLE 9.1

Points of Convergence and Divergence Between SD-Access and ACI

Technology Parameter	CISCO ACI	CISCO SD-Access
Definition	Centers network management around applications, automating and optimizing network policies in data centers.	Simplifies network access management, automates user and device policies, and secures network access.
SDN controller	Cisco APIC (Application Policy Infrastructure Controller)	Cisco DNA Center
Architecture	Leaf-spine architecture. Centralized configuration via APIC GUI.	Customizable leaf/edge device configuration via Cisco DNA Center.
Constraints	• Uniformity required: All switches/controllers must be on the same version. • Uniform configuration on all leaf/spine. • IS-IS is automatically propagated to all equipment via APIC.	• Flexible version compatibility between switches/controllers as long as they are supported by Cisco DNA. • Customizable configuration of border nodes. • IS-IS is configured manually on each piece of equipment, unless automation is enabled. • The underlay architecture can use OSPF or LISP.
Control Plan Protocol	BGP and IS-IS	LISP
Segmentation name	VRF	VN
TAG name for micro-segmentation	Endpoint Group	SGT
Data Plane	VXLAN	VXLAN
Safety policies	Contracts	SGACLs
Uses/Applications	Application optimization, high performance, and deep integration with data centers and cloud environments.	Simplified identity and access management for campus environments.

9.6 Conclusion

In conclusion, this chapter has elucidated Cisco SD-Access, emphasizing its robust architecture, advanced components, and integrated management mechanisms that are transforming enterprise network design, deployment, and management. Through exploration of its different architectural layers and platforms such as Cisco DNA Center and Cisco ISE, we saw how SD-Access facilitates more agile, secure, and automated network management.

SD-Access integration with other technologies, including SD-WAN, and interoperability with various Cisco protocols and solutions were also discussed to illustrate the versatility and scalability of this solution in complex network environments. By comparing SD-Access with Cisco ACI, we highlighted their complementary roles in the panorama of Cisco networking solutions, each effectively targeting specific areas.

Although certain SD-Access details and features are not comprehensively covered here for pedagogical purposes, this chapter aims to provide a solid foundation for understanding the fundamentals of this transformative technology. For those wishing to explore this solution in depth, Cisco's additional documentation and training resources remain invaluable references for furthering your knowledge and skills.

Recommendation for SD-Access Technology Practical Workshops in the Classroom:

Due to the very high resource requirements of the equipment used in an SD-Access solution, in particular the Cisco DNA controller, as well as licensing constraints, it is impossible to carry out the practical work in the classroom under current conditions.

Consequently, there are two options available to the trainer to overcome this limitation and enable students to discover this technology:

Use the Cisco Labs site: The trainer could direct students to the online labs available on the Cisco Labs site. This option would allow the practical work to be carried out in a virtual environment, while using available Cisco resources, guaranteeing a hands-on experience close to reality.

Show videos of completed labs: An alternative would be to show videos of completed SD-Access labs. This approach would demonstrate the concepts and operation of the technology in a visual and explanatory way, while circumventing hardware constraints.

These two options offer viable and appropriate solutions for ensuring quality training, despite the technical and material limitations encountered.

Lab 18: Cisco SD-LAN Deployment with TrustSec-Based Micro-Segmentation

Objectives

- Understand SD-LAN architecture leveraging Cisco equipment.
- Understand the principles of micro-segmentation in a Cisco environment.
- Configure a Cisco network to deploy group-based access management using Cisco TrustSec technology.

Case Study

This case study explores SD-LAN architecture using Cisco equipment, with particular emphasis on the principles of micro-segmentation in a Cisco environment. It identifies the building blocks of this architecture and guides the configuration of a Cisco network to implement group-based access management via Cisco TrustSec technology, offering a solution for secure and optimized network access management.

ABC intends to implement an SD-LAN solution using Cisco equipment.

Required Software

- **GNS3 or equivalent**

Network Topology

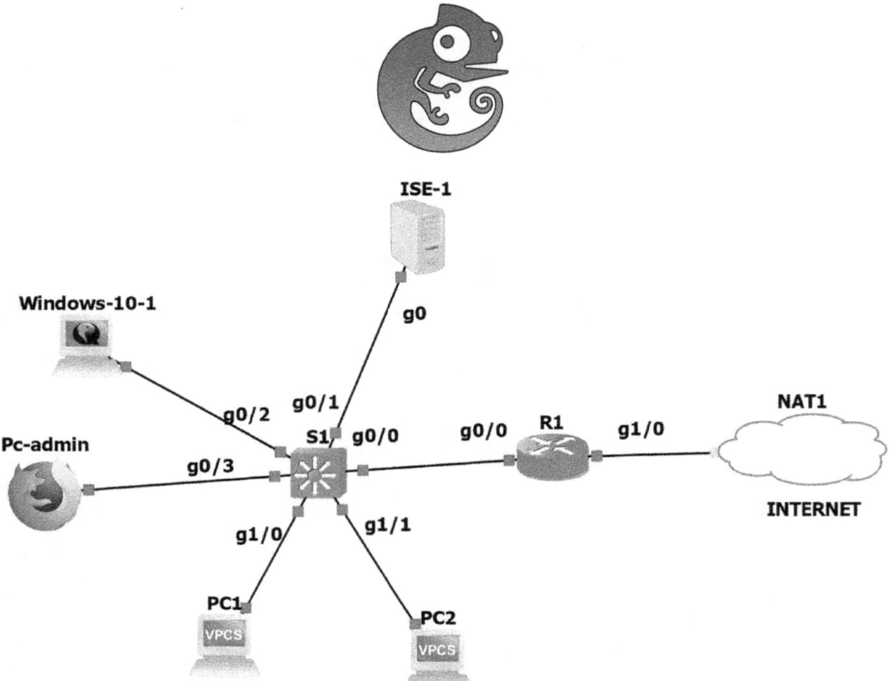

IP Address Table

Emulated Device	Device	Interface	IP Address/ Subnet Mask	Default Gateway	Default Gateway
Cisco IOSvL2 Switch (v15.2(6))	S1	Vlan1	192.168.1.2/24	–	–
Cisco Router—C7200 (Dynamips, v15.2)	R1	G0/0	192.168.1.1/24	–	–
Cisco Router—C7200 (Dynamips, v15.2)	R1	G1/0	DHCP	–	–
Cisco ISE VM (v2.7.0.356)	ISE	G0	192.168.1.10/24	192.168.1.1	192.168.1.1
Docker Container—Webterm	PC-admin	eth0	DHCP	DHCP	DHCP
VPCS	PC1	eth0	DHCP	DHCP	DHCP
VPCS	PC2	eth0	192.1681.4	192.1681.4	192.168.1.1
Windows 10 VM (32-bit, 2 GB RAM)	Wind10-1	etho	DHCP	DHCP	DHCP
GNS3 Cloud NAT	NAT1	–	–	–	–

Part A: Reminder of Some Theoretical Notions About SD-Access Architecture

Link each item in the table with its corresponding definition.

1. Group-based policy management (GBP)	A. A security label assigned to data packets to dynamically identify the security groups to which users or devices belong, facilitating the management of security policies.
2. AAA server	B. A technique for dividing the network into smaller secure segments, down to the application or user level, to improve security and limit lateral movement in the event of compromise.
3. Micro-segmentation	C. An authentication, authorization, and accounting server that manages access to network resources by verifying users' identities, controlling their permissions, and tracking their activities.
4. SGT	D. A network authentication protocol based on the IEEE 802.1X standard, which controls network access by verifying the identity of users before they can access the network.
5. MAB	E. A feature that dynamically modifies the access rights of a user or device on the network without requiring a reconnection, following an update of authorizations.
6. Dot1x	F. An authentication mechanism that allows devices without 802.1X capability to connect to the network using the MAC address for authentication.
7. CoA	G. Allows you to define network access and security rules based on user or device groups, rather than IP addresses, simplifying access management.

Part B: Establish Basic Device Configuration

1. Configure R1's interfaces by referring to the addressing table.
2. Ensure Internet connectivity using **ping** tests.

3. Configure **PAT** (Port Address Translation) on router R1.

```
(config)#ip nat inside source list 10 interface GigabitEthernet1/0
  overload
(config)# access-list 10 permit 192.168.1.0 0.0.0.255
(config)# interface GigabitEthernet0/0
ip nat outside
(config)# interface GigabitEthernet1/0
ip nat inside
```

4. Deploy R1 as a DHCP server for the LAN.

```
(config)#ip dhcp excluded-address 192.168.1.1 192.168.1.20
(config)#ip dhcp pool lan
 network 192.168.1.0 255.255.255.0
 default-router 192.168.1.1
 dns-server 8.8.8.8
```

5. Set up PC-admin's IP interface and validate Internet connectivity.
6. Set up PC1's IP interface and verify connectivity with 8.8.8.8. Note its **MAC** address using the "**show ip**" command.
7. Install and configure the **Cisco ISE** server. Ensure all critical services are up and running by using the "**sh application status ise**" command.

```
ise/admin# sh application status ise

ISE PROCESS NAME                        STATE             PROCESS I
-------------------------------------------------------------------
Database Listener                       running           23922
Database Server                         running           65 PROCES
Application Server                      running           31984
Profiler Database                       running           29984
ISE Indexing Engine                     running           34808
AD Connector                            running           36645
M&T Session Database                    running           29792
M&T Log Processor                       running           32163
Certificate Authority Service           running           36402
EST Service                             running           68748
SXP Engine Service                      disabled
Docker Daemon                           running           25624
TC-NAC Service                          disabled

Wifi Setup Helper Container             disabled
pxGrid Infrastructure Service           disabled
```

Note: You can use the **"application start ise safe"** command if startup fails.

Part C: Configuring Cisco ISE Equipment

Step 1:

1. Connect to the ISE server
   - On PC-admin, open a web browser.
   - Type the URL: http://192.168.1.10, and connect to R1.
   - Enter your login and password.

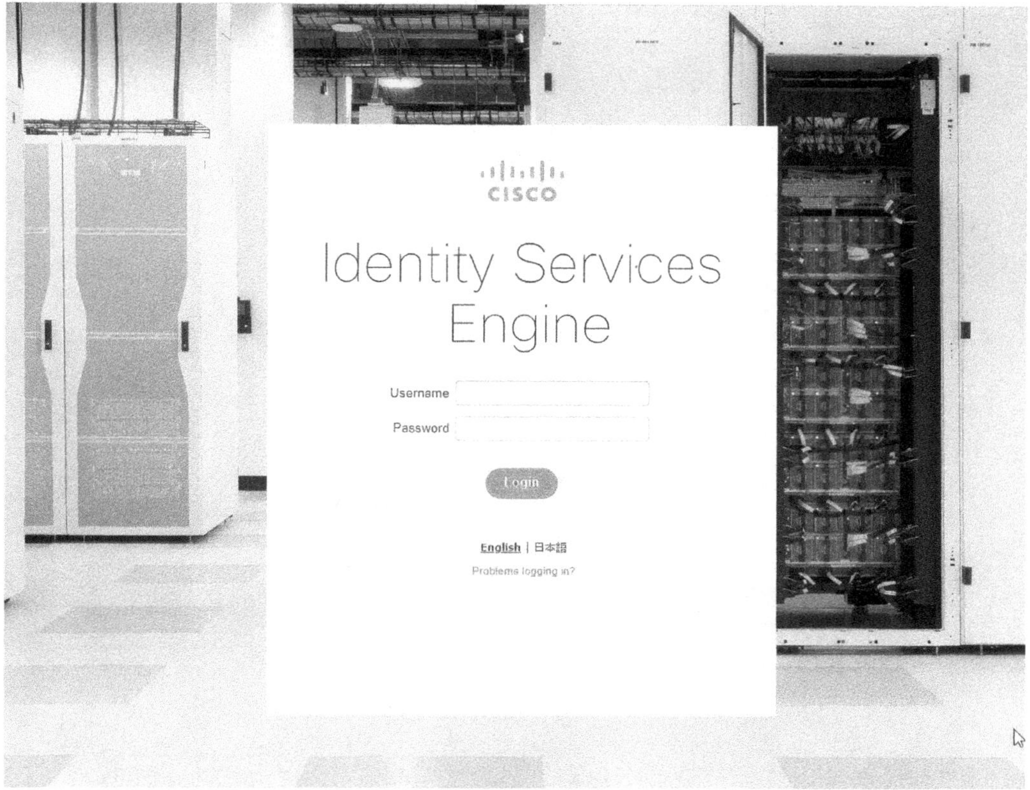

2. Register S1 within the list of managed devices in ISE.
   - Using the graphical interface, click on the menu: "**Administration > Network Devices**".

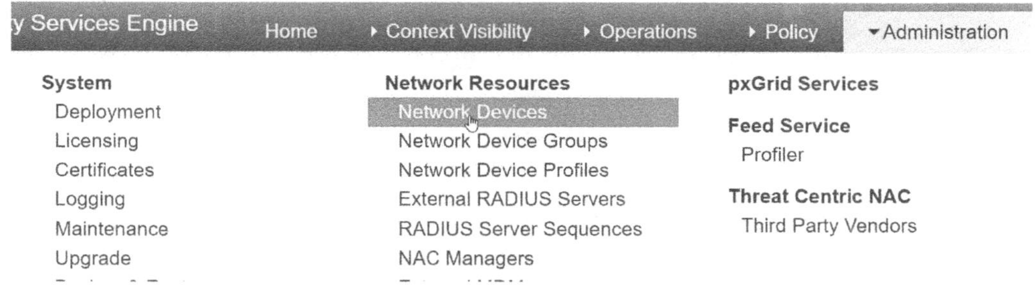

   - Click on the "**add**" button.

– Add the S1 switch parameters as shown below:

1- Network settings

Network Devices List > **New Network Device**

Network Devices

* Name S1

Description Switch 1

IP Address * IP : 192.168.1.10 / 32

2- RADUIS server parameters

RADIUS Authentication Settings

RADIUS UDP Settings

Protocol **RADIUS**

* Shared Secret cisco Hide

Use Second Shared Secret

3- TrustSec settings

Advanced TrustSec Settings

Device Authentication Settings

Use Device ID for TrustSec Identification

Device Id S1

* Password cisco Hide

TrustSec Notifications and Updates

* Download environment data every 15 Minutes

* Download peer authorization policy every 15 Minutes

* Reauthentication every 1 Days

* Download SGACL lists every 15 Minutes

Other TrustSec devices to trust this device

Send configuration changes to device Using CoA CLI (SSH)

Send from ise Test connection

Ssh Key

Device Configuration Deployment

Include this device when deploying Security Group Tag Mapping Updates ☑

Device Interface Credentials

* EXEC Mode Username: user1

* EXEC Mode Password: cisco [Hide]

Enable Mode Password: cisco [Hide]

3. Set up an access policy for S1.
   - Using the graphical interface, click on the menu: "**Work Centers > TrustSec Policy**".
   - Click on the "**Network Device Authorization**" menu.
   - Create a policy named **"Ndac Policy1"** and add the group **"ALL Device"** to the predefined group **"TrustSec_Devices":**

Network Device Authorization

Define the Network Device Authorization Policy by assigning SGTs to network devices. Drag and drop rules to change the order.

	Rule Name		Conditions		Security Group
☑	Ndac Policy 1	If	DEVICE:Device Type equals to All Device Types	then	TrustSec_Devices
☑	Default Rule	If	no rules defined or no match	then	Unknown

4. Configure **EAP FAST** parameters.
   - Using the graphical interface, click on the menu: "**Administration > System > Setting**".
   - Click on the "**Protocols > EAP FAST**" menu.
   - Configure EAP FAST as described below:

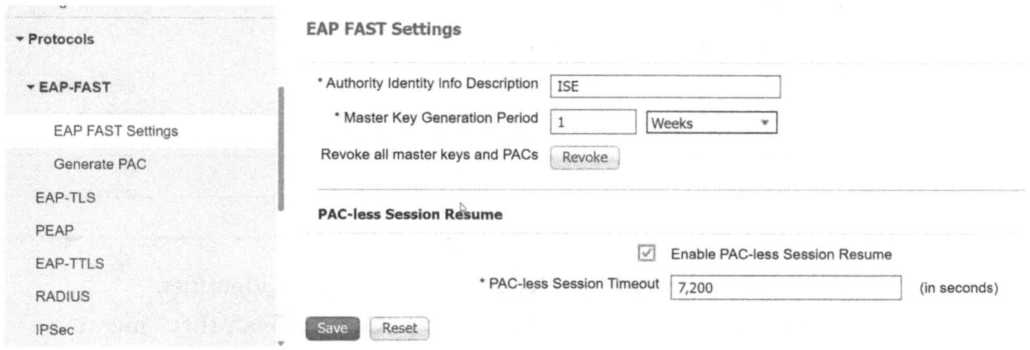

Step 2:

1. Define a user group for network authentication using login credentials.
   - Using the graphical interface, click on the menu: "**Administration > Identity Mangement**".

- Click on the "**Groups**" menu and then on " **Endpoint Identity Groups**".
- Register the **"grp1"** group according to the specifications below:

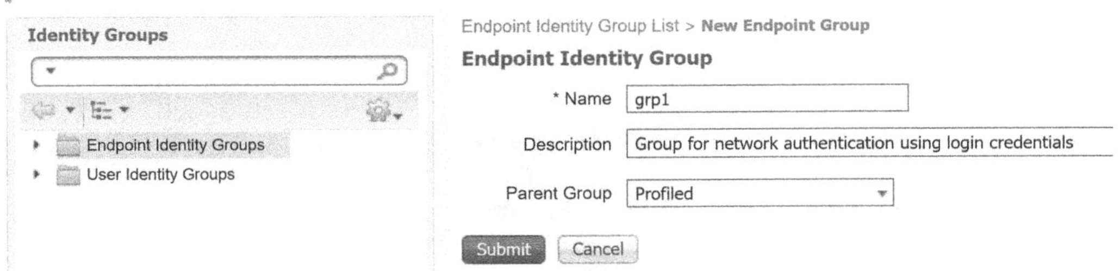

2. Define a machine group for MAC-based authentication.
   - Using the graphical interface, click on the menu: "**Administration > Identity Management**".
   - Click on the "**Groups**" menu and then on "**Endpoint Identity Groups**".
   - Add the **"MyMABGroup1"** group as described below:

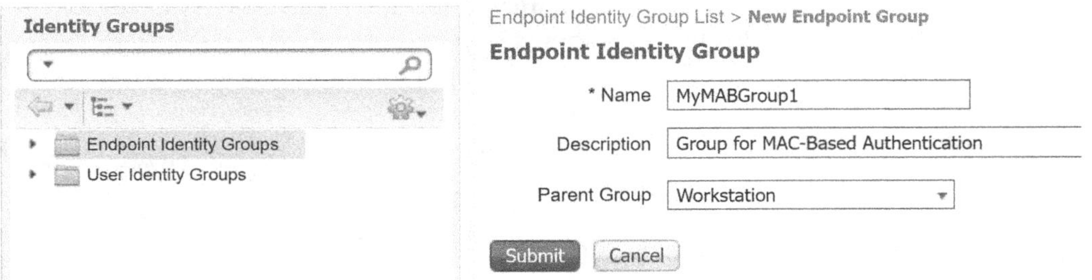

   - In the same way, add a machine group **"MyMABGroup2"**.
3. Define a network user with a login and password.
   - Using the graphical interface, click on the menu: "**Administration > Identity Management**".
   - Click on the "**Identities**" menu.
   - Add user **"grp1"** as shown below:

Name	user1
Password	Ise123-
Group	Grp1

4. Create a network user (MAB) with a MAC address as an identifier.
   - Using the graphical interface, click on the "**Context Visibility**" menu.
   - Click on the "+" button to add an item.

- Add the **"PC1"** machine based on its MAC address and the indications below:

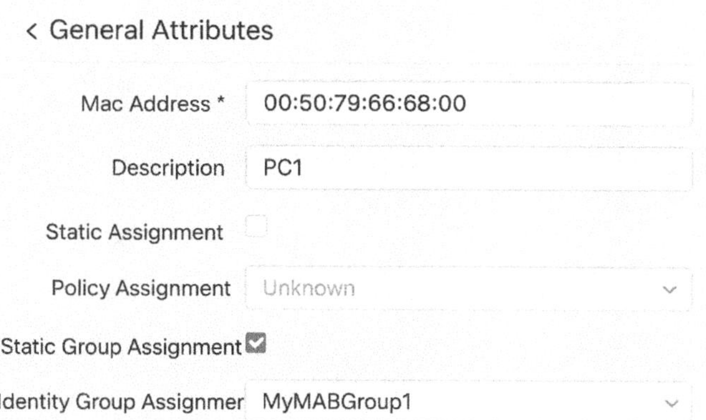

- In the same way, add the **"PC2"** machine and assign it to the **"MyMABGroup2"** machine group.

5. Create network security groups.
   - Using the graphical interface, click on the menu: "**Work Centers > TrusecPolicy**".
   - Click on the "**Components**" menu.
   - Add a security group **"SGT_1"**, based on the indications below:

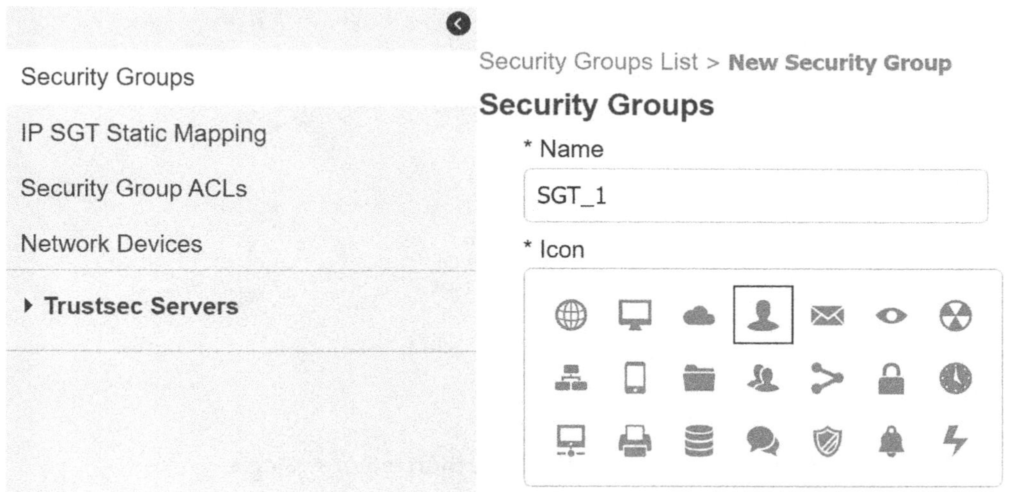

   - In the same way, add the **"SGT_2"**, **"SGT_3"**, **"ISE"**, and **"DNS-Server"** security groups.
6. Create a static mapping between network security groups and their IP addresses.
   - Using the graphical interface, click on the menu: "**Work Centers > TrusecPolicy**".
   - Click on the "**Components > IP SGT Static Mapping**" menu.

– Add a static mapping based on the indications below:

IP SGT static mapping > New

IP address(es) * × 192.168.1.4

○ Add to a mapping group

◉ Map to SGT individually

SGT * SGT_3 (18/0012)

Send to SXP Domain × default

Deploy to devices All TrustSec Devices

Cancel Save

– Similarly, add a static mapping between IP address **"1.1.1.1"** and **"DNS-Server"** and between IP address **192.168.1.10** and **"ISE"**.

7. To streamline configuration, remove non-essential security groups and preserve only the following:

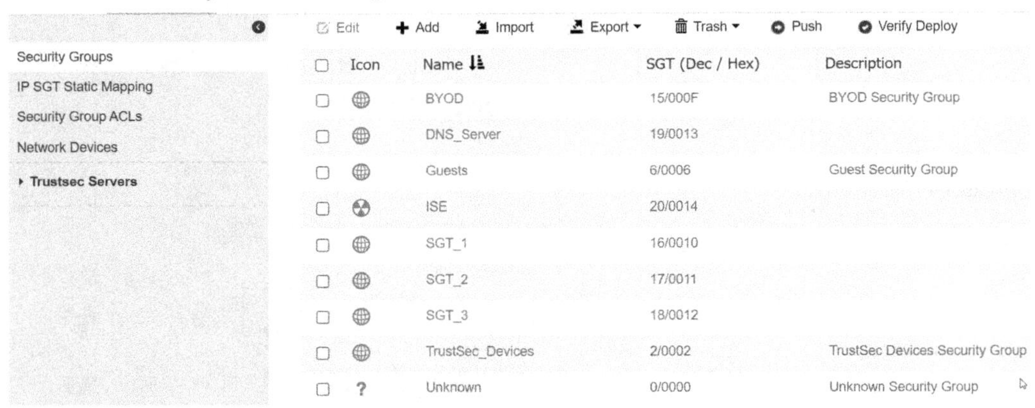

Icon	Name	SGT (Dec / Hex)	Description
	BYOD	15/000F	BYOD Security Group
	DNS_Server	19/0013	
	Guests	6/0006	Guest Security Group
	ISE	20/0014	
	SGT_1	16/0010	
	SGT_2	17/0011	
	SGT_3	18/0012	
	TrustSec_Devices	2/0002	TrustSec Devices Security Group
?	Unknown	0/0000	Unknown Security Group

Step 3:

Define connection, authentication, and authorization strategies.

- Using the graphical user interface, click on the "**Policy > Policy Sets**" menu.
- Add the "**Connection Type**" connection strategy.
- Add authentication parameters as shown below:

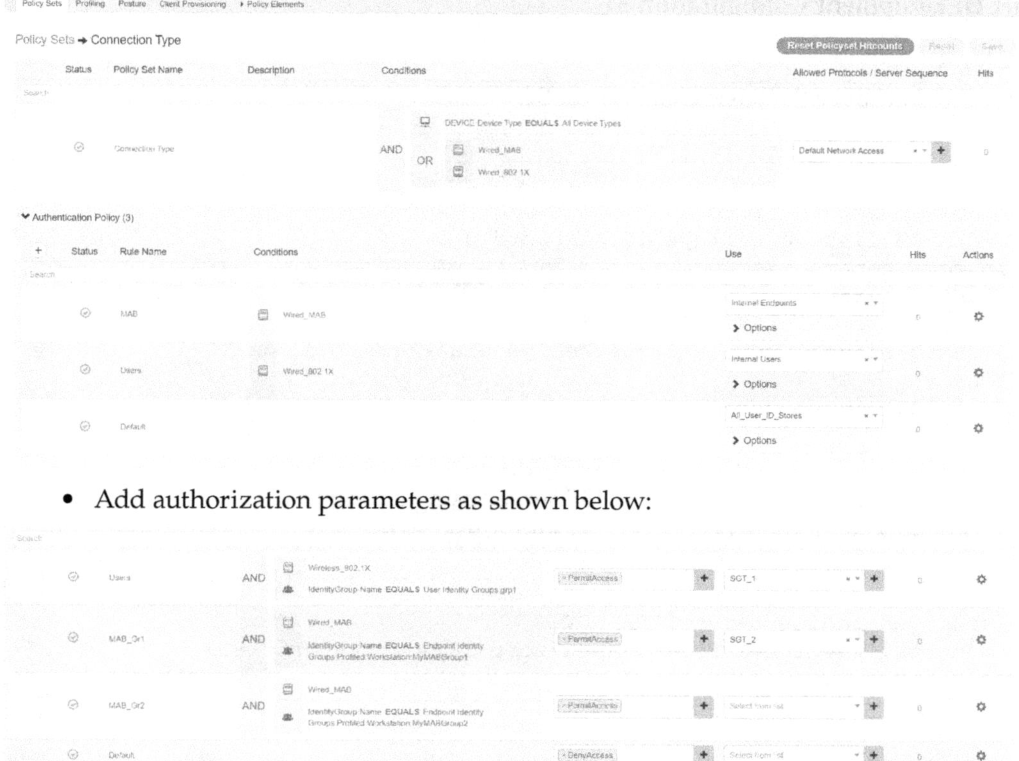

- Add authorization parameters as shown below:

Here's a detailed explanation of access rules:

Users rule
Condition: Wired 802.1X AND IdentityGroup-Name EQUALS User Identity Groups
Action: PermitAccess
SGT: SGT_1
Description: This rule is applied to users connecting via 802.1X who are members of the "grp1" identity group. If these conditions are met, access is authorized and the SGT_1 security tag is applied. This tag is used to control access to specific resources in the network based on the user's identity.
MAB_Gr1 rule
Condition: Wired MAB AND IdentityGroup-Name EQUALS Endpoint Identity Groups:Profiled:Workstation
Action: PermitAccess
SGT: SGT_2
Description: This rule is intended for devices that connect by MAC address and are profiled as belonging to "MyMABGroup1". Access is permitted under these conditions, and the SGT_2 security tag is assigned.
MAB_Gr2 rule
Condition: Wired MAB AND IdentityGroup-Name EQUALS Endpoint Identity Groups:Profiled:Workstation
Action: PermitAccess
SGT: Not specified
Description: Similar to rule "MAB_Gr1", this rule applies to devices identified as being part of "MyMABGroup2". Access is allowed, but the SGT to be applied must be assigned manually. In our case, the static mapping between PC2's IP address and its security group has already been configured.
Default rule
Description: This rule denies access to all other unrecognized users and devices.

Part D: Equipment Configuration S1

Step 1:

1. Configure the basic elements on **S1**.

```
(config)# hostname S1
enable password cisco
username cisco privilege 15 password 0 cisco
ip domain-name cisco
Vlan1 interface
 ip address 192.168.1.2 255.255.255.0
(config)#crypto key generate rsa general-keys modulus 1024
line vty 0 15
transport input ssh
```

2. Validate connectivity to the ISE server using a **ping** test.
3. Deploy a RADIUS server named ISE-SRV.

```
(config)# radius server ISE-SRV
 address ipv4 192.168.1.10 auth-port 1812 acct-port 1813
 pac key cisco
```

4. Enable the **"CoA"** feature to permit the specified client to send requests to the server.

```
(config)# aaa server radius dynamic-author
 client 192.168.1.10 server-key cisco
 auth-type any
```

5. Enable the AAA model, create a RADIUS server group named ISE, and associate the ISE-SRV server with this group.

```
(config)# aaa new-model
aaa group server radius ISE
 server name ISE-SRV
 ip radius source-interface Vlan1
```

6. Set AAA parameters.

```
(config)# aaa authentication dot1x default group ISE
aaa authorization network default group ISE
aaa authorization network cts_list group ISE
aaa accounting dot1x default start-stop group ISE
aaa session-id common
```

Step 2:

1. Configure basic parameters on user network interfaces.

```
S1 (config)#int G0/2
switchport mode access
 spanning-tree portfast edge
S1 (config)#int G1/0
switchport mode access
 spanning-tree portfast edge
S1 (config)#int G1/1
switchport mode access
 spanning-tree portfast edge
```

2. Enable **802.1X** authentication globally.

```
S1 (config)# dot1x system-auth-control
  dot1x logging verbose
```

3. Configure **802.1x** authentication options on the G0/2 interface.

```
S1 (config)#int G0/2
authentication port-control auto
authentication periodic
 dot1x pae authenticator
```

4. Configure **802.1x** authentication options on interface G1/0–1.

```
S1 (config)#int range G1/0 - 1
authentication port-control auto
authentication open
authentication periodic
 mab
```

Step 3:

1. Set **Cisco TrustSec** parameters to S1.

```
S1 # cts credentials id S1 password cisco
S1 (config)# cts authorization list cts_list
S1 (config)# cts role-based enforcement
```

2. Validate the **Cisco TrustSec** security configuration on S1.

```
#sh cts pacs
  AID: B4D0BA9FE24E40F621F8CCB9CFBA87EE
  PAC-Info:
    PAC-type = Cisco Trustsec
    AID: B4D0BA9FE24E40F621F8CCB9CFBA87EE
    I-ID: S1
    A-ID-Info: ISE
    Credential Lifetime: 17:16:44 UTC Dec 13 2024
....
```

Part E: Client Workstation Configuration

Step 1: Wind 10–1 Workstation Configuration

1. On the "**search**" bar, type "**run**" and then type "**services.msc**".

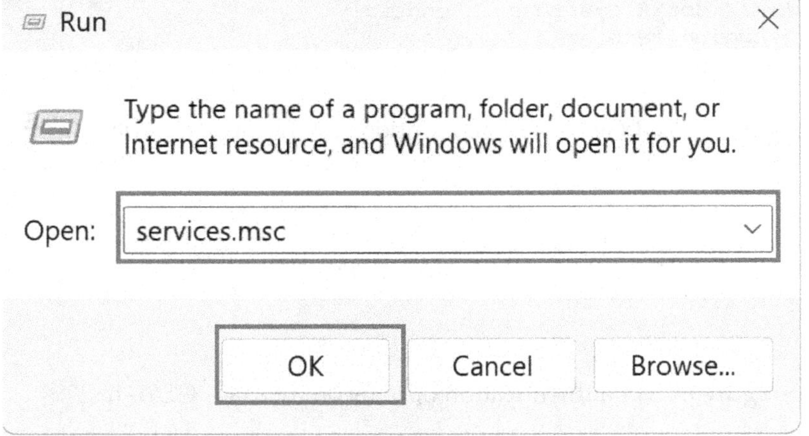

2. Right-click on "**Wired AutoConfig**" and select "**Properties**".

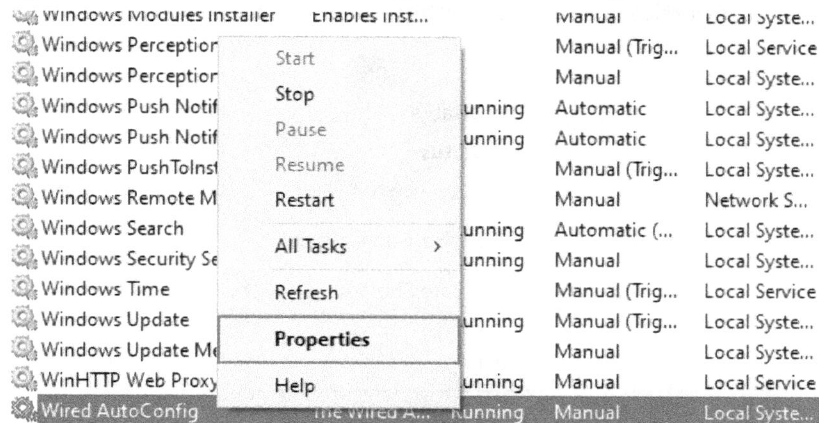

3. Click on the "**General**" tab and select the following settings:

a. Set "Startup type" to "Automatic".

b. Click on "Start" to start the service.

c. Click on "Apply".

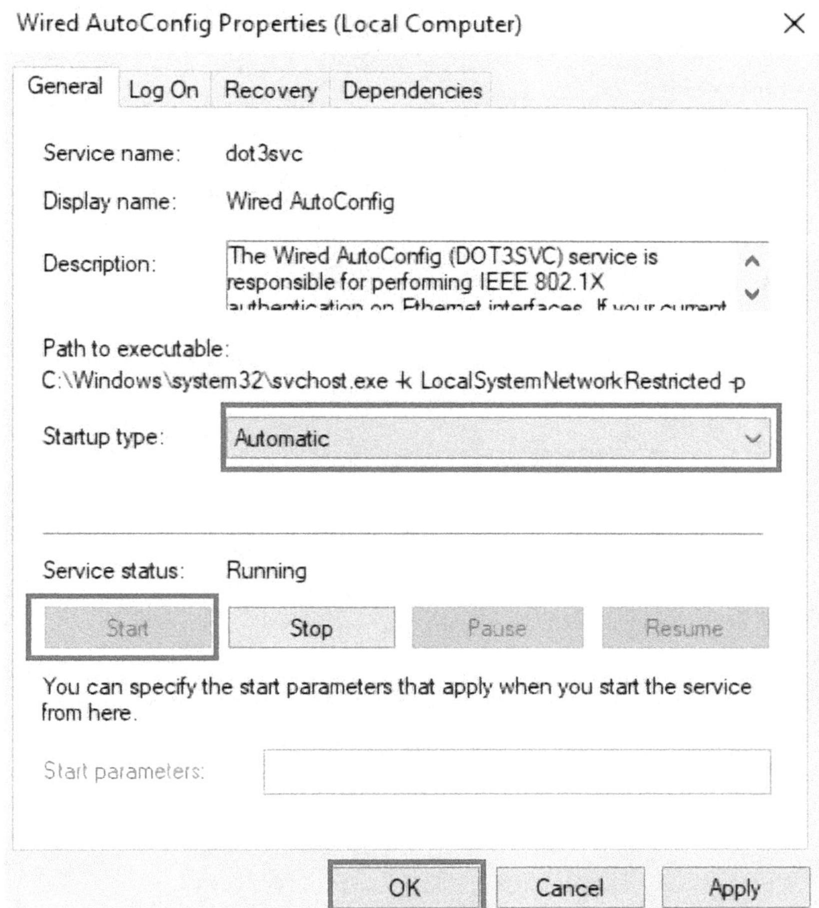

4. Navigate to the network connection manager, right-click on "**Ethernet**" and select "**Properties**" for further configuration.

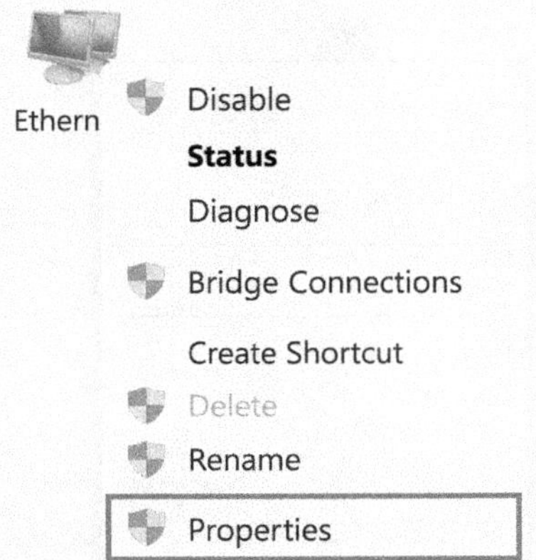

5. Configure options as shown in the images.

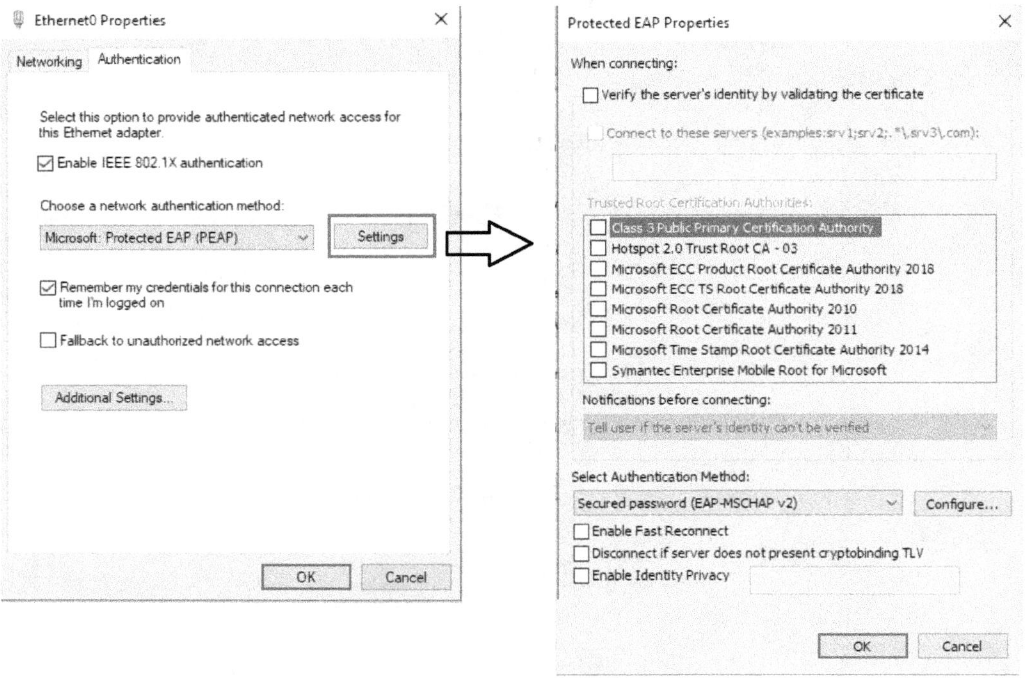

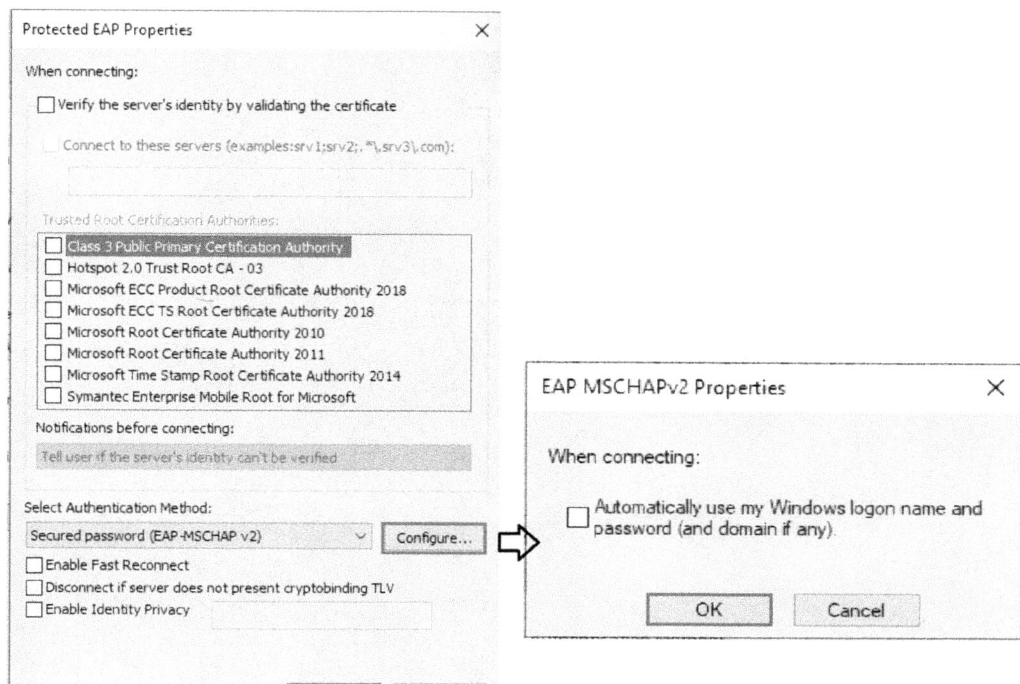

6. Return to the "**Authentication**" tab and configure the following parameters as shown in the images:

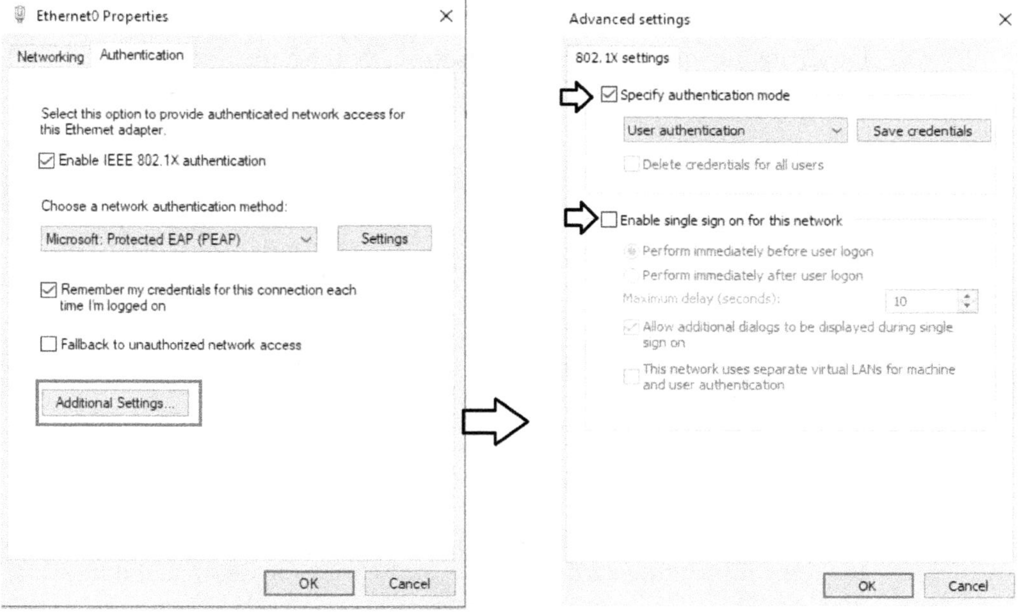

7. Click on the "**Save credentials**" button and enter your username and password.

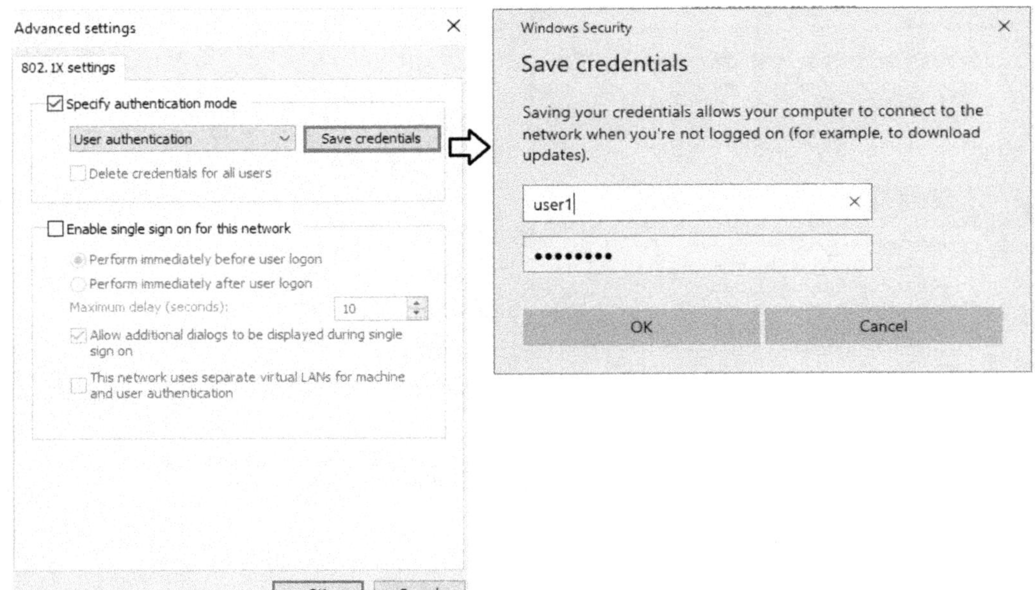

8. Click "**OK**" and save your changes.

Step 2: PC1 and PC2 Configuration

1. Configure PC1 and PC2 by referring to the addressing table.
2. Validate connectivity to the IP address 1.1.1.1.
3. On S1, execute the following commands to verify the authentication status:

```
S1#show dot1x all summary
PAE Client Interface Status
--------------------------------------------------------
Gi0/2 AUTH 0c56.8e7a.0000 AUTHORIZED
```

```
S1#sh mab all summary
Client Interface MAC Authen Status
------------------------------------------------------
Gi0/2 None N/A
Gi1/0 0050.7966.6800 SUCCESS
Gi1/1 0050.7966.6801 SUCCESS
```

Note: You can use the error messages on **S1** to resolve any authentication problems.

```
*Sep 16 09:13:39.162: %RADIUS-4-RADIUS_ALIVE: RADIUS server
   192.168.1.10:1812,18 13 is being marked alive.
*Sep 16 09:15:42.841: %MAB-5- SUCCESS: Authentication successful for
   client (0050.7966.6800) on Interface Gi1/0 AuditSessionID
   C0A80102000001000504BBE
*Sep 16 09:17:46.554: %DOT1X-5-SUCCESS: Authentication successful
   for client (0c 56.8e7a.0000) on Interface Gi0/2 AuditSessionID
   C0A801020000000E00112026
*Sep 16 10:17:48.460: %DOT1X-5-SUCCESS: Authentication successful
   for client (0c 56.8e7a.0000) on Interface Gi0/2 AuditSessionID
   C0A801020000000E00112026
```

4. Verify in the **ISE "Endpoints"** list that both **PCs** and **user1** are displayed:
   - Using the graphical interface, click on the menu: "**Context Visibility> Authentication**".

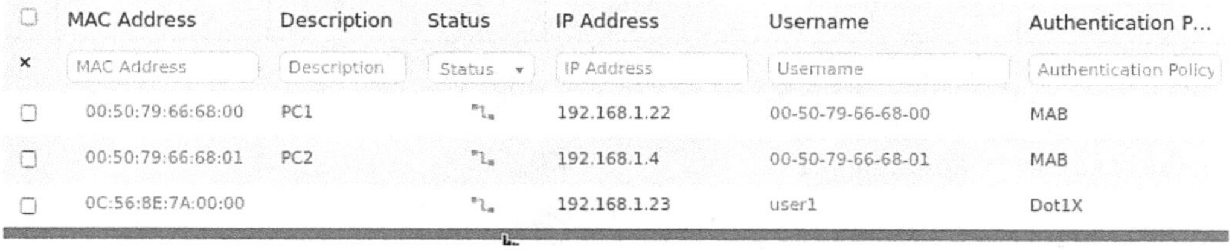

MAC Address	Description	Status	IP Address	Username	Authentication P...
MAC Address	Description	Status	IP Address	Username	Authentication Policy
00:50:79:66:68:00	PC1		192.168.1.22	00-50-79-66-68-00	MAB
00:50:79:66:68:01	PC2		192.168.1.4	00-50-79-66-68-01	MAB
0C:56:8E:7A:00:00			192.168.1.23	user1	Dot1X

   - Using the graphical interface, click on the menu: "**Operations > Live Sessions**".

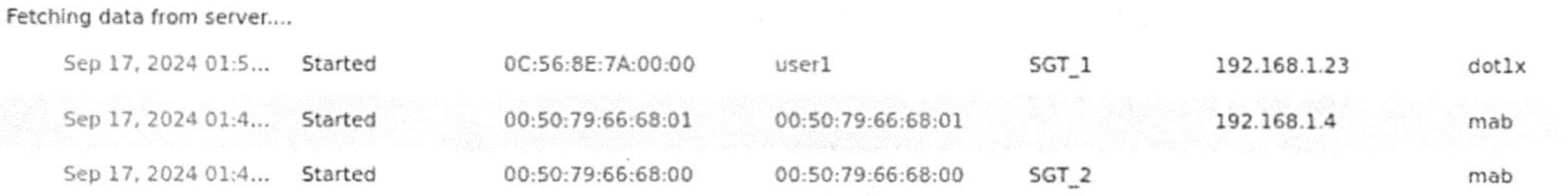

Fetching data from server....

Sep 17, 2024 01:5...	Started	0C:56:8E:7A:00:00	user1	SGT_1	192.168.1.23	dot1x
Sep 17, 2024 01:4...	Started	00:50:79:66:68:01	00:50:79:66:68:01		192.168.1.4	mab
Sep 17, 2024 01:4...	Started	00:50:79:66:68:00	00:50:79:66:68:00	SGT_2		mab

   - Note the mapping between the equipment and its safety group.

Part F: Creating SGACLs

1. Create ACL security groups.
   - Using the graphical interface, click on the menu: "**Work Centers > TrustSec/ Component**".
   - Click on the "**Security Groups ACLs**" menu.
   - Add two **SGACLs**, IPV4-based on the indications below:

ACL	Contents
PermitIP	Permit ip
DenyIP	Deny ip

2. Assign SAGLs to security groups using the "**Security Policy Matrix**" menu, based on the following table:

	DNS-Server	**TrustSec_Devices**	**ISE**
SGT_1	Deny ip	Permit ip	Permit ip
SGT_2	Deny ip	Permit ip	Permit ip
SGT_3	Permit ip	Permit ip	Permit ip
TrustSec_Devices'	Permit ip	Permit ip	Permit ip

Part G: Verification of Results

1. Show the Cisco TrustSec configuration on S1

```
S1#sh cts environment-data
...
CTS Environment Data
====================
Current state = COMPLETE
Last status = Successful
Local Device SGT:
  SGT tag = 2-11:TrustSec_Devices
Server List Info:
Installed list: CTSServerList1-0001, 1 server(s):
 *Server: 192.168.1.10, port 1812, A-ID
  B4D0BA9FE24E40F621F8CCB9CFBA87EE

          Status = ALIVE
          auto-test = TRUE, keywrap-enable = FALSE,
  idle-time = 60 mins, deadtime = 20 secs
Multicast Group SGT Table:
Security Group Name Table:
    0-00:Unknown
    2-00:TrustSec_Devices
    3-00:DNS_Server
    6-00:Guests
    15-00:BYOD
    17-00:SGT_1
    18-00:SGT_2
    19-00:SGT_3
Environment Data Lifetime = 86400 secs
...
```

2. Show the SGACLs configuration on S1

```
...
S1#sh cts role-based permissions
IPv4 Role-based permissions default:
        Permit IP-00
IPv4 Role-based permissions from group 2:TrustSec_Devices to
  group 2:TrustSec_Devices:
        PermitIP-60
IPv4 Role-based permissions from group 3:DNS_Server to
  group 2:TrustSec_Devices:
        PermitIP-60
IPv4 Role-based permissions from group 17:SGT_1 to
  group 2:TrustSec_Devices:
        PermitIP-60
IPv4 Role-based permissions from group 18:SGT_2 to
  group 2:TrustSec_Devices:
        PermitIP-60
IPv4 Role-based permissions from group 19:SGT_3 to
  group 2:TrustSec_Devices:
        PermitIP-60
IPv4 Role-based permissions from group 17:SGT_1 to
  group 3:DNS_Server:
        DenyIP-20
IPv4 Role-based permissions from group 18:SGT_2 to
  group 3:DNS_Server:
        DenyIP-20
IPv4 Role-based permissions from group 19:SGT_3 to
  group 3:DNS_Server:
        DenyIP-20
IPv4 Role-based permissions from group 3:DNS_Server to
  group 17:SGT_1:
        PermitIP-60
RBACL Monitor All for Dynamic Policies: FALSE
```

3. Show the static mapping between IP **"1.1.1.1"** security groups

```
S1#sh cts role-based sgt-map all
Active IPv4-SGT Bindings Information

IP Address SGT Source
========================================
1.1.1.1 3 CLI
192.168.1.2 2 INTERNAL
192.168.1.4 19 CLI
192.168.1.10 2 CLI
```

Note: If you are unable to display the static mapping, perform the operation manually using the "Deploy" button.

Part H (Optional): Verification of Results

If you have sufficient RAM resources, replace router R1 with a "Cisco CSR1000v 17_3_1a" router.

As the IOS system license for this equipment is limited to connecting it to the ISE server, we'll proceed with a manual configuration of TrustSec elements, since the result will be the same in both cases.

Note: You can refer to **Lab 9** to help you complete the required tasks.

1. Create security groups:
   - 3:DNS_Server
   - 17:SGT_1
   - 18:SGT_2
   - 19:SGT_3
2. Create the static mapping between IP addresses and security groups by referring to the relevant section.
3. Create SAGCL access rules between different security groups.
4. Validate the configuration results.

Note

1 Courtesy of Cisco Systems, Inc. Unauthorized use not permitted.

Bibliography

1. Casado, M., Shenker, S., & McKeown, N. (2009). The Origins and Evolution of OpenFlow. *ACM SIGCOMM Computer Communication Review*, 38(2), 69–74. https://doi.org/10.1145/1355734.1355746
2. Cisco Systems (n.d.). *Cisco Software-Defined Access (SD-Access) Solution*. Cisco Press, San Jose, CA. https://www.cisco.com/c/en/us/solutions/enterprise-networks/software-defined-access/index.html
3. Feamster, N., Rexford, J., & Zegura, E. (2014). The Road to SDN: An Intellectual History of Programmable Networks. *ACM SIGCOMM Computer Communication Review*, 44(2), 87–98. https://doi.org/10.1145/2602204.2602219
4. Göransson, P., Black, C., & Culver, T. (2016). *Software Defined Networks: A Comprehensive Approach* (2nd ed.). Morgan Kaufmann, Burlington, MA.
5. Gooley, J., Hasan, R., & Vemula, S. (2020). *Cisco Software-Defined Access: Cisco Secure Enterprise*. Cisco Press, San Jose, CA.
6. Kreutz, D., Ramos, F. M. V., Verissimo, P. E., Rothenberg, C. E., Azodolmolky, S., & Uhlig, S. (2015). Software-Defined Networking: A Comprehensive Survey. *Proceedings of the IEEE*, 103(1), 14–76. https://doi.org/10.1109/JPROC.2014.2371999
7. MMDD Multimedia LLC (2013). *SDN and OpenFlow for Beginners with Hands-On Labs*. MMDD Multimedia LLC, Queensland, Australia.
8. Network Functions Virtualisation (NFV) Architectural Framework. Available online: https://www.etsi.org/deliver/etsi_gs/NFV/001_099/002/01.02.01_60/gs_NFV002v010201p.pdf. (Accessed on 10 November 2019).
9. Open vSwitch (n.d.). *Open vSwitch Documentation*. https://docs.openvswitch.org/en/latest/
10. Red Hat (n.d.). *Ansible Documentation*. https://docs.ansible.com/ansible/latest/index.html
11. Shakil, T., Jain, V., & Louis, Y. (2021). *LISP Network Deployment and Troubleshooting: The Complete Guide to LISP Implementation on IOS-XE, IOS-XR, and NX-OS*. Cisco Press, San Jose, CA.

Index

For Product Safety Concerns and Information please contact our EU representative GPSR@taylorandfrancis.com
Taylor & Francis Verlag GmbH, Kaufingerstraße 24, 80331 München, Germany

www.ingramcontent.com/pod-product-compliance
Lightning Source LLC
Chambersburg PA
CBHW061347210326
41598CB00035B/5909
9781041154280